D0213353

ISO 14001

Y-STO

ISO 14001
A Missed Opportunity for Sustainable Global Industrial Development

Riva Krut and Harris Gleckman

BIBLIOTHÈQUES
u Ottawa
LIBRARIES

Earthscan Publications Ltd, London

First published in the UK in 1998 by
Earthscan Publications Limited

Copyright © Nigel Dudley, 1998

All rights reserved

A catalogue record for this book is available from the British Library

ISBN: 1 85383 507 2 paperback
ISBN: 1 85383 506 4 hardback

Typesetting and page design by PCS Mapping & DTP, Newcastle upon Tyne
Printed and bound by Biddles Ltd, Guildford and Kings Lynn
Cover design by Andrew Corbett

For a full list of publications please contact:

Earthscan Publications Limited
120 Pentonville Road
London N1 9JN
Tel. (0171) 278 0433
Fax: (0171) 278 1142
Email: earthinfo@earthscan.co.uk
http://www.earthscan.co.uk

Earthscan is an editorially independent subsidiary of Kogan Page Limited and publishes in
association with WWF-UK and the International Institute for Environment and Development.

Contents

List of Tables and Boxes

TABLES

BOXES

List of Acronyms and Abbreviations

ABNT	Associação Brasileira de Normas Técnicas, Brazil
AFNOR	Association Française de Normalisation
ANSI	American National Standards Institute
APELL	Awareness and Preparedness for Emergencies at the Local Level
ATI	Alliance Internationale de Tourism
BAPEDAL	Indonesian Environmental Impact agency
BOI	Philippine Bureau of Investments
BPS	Philippine Bureau of Product Standards
BS	British Standard 7750 (on Environmental Management Systems)
BSI	British Standards Institution
CASCO	ISO Committee on Conformity Assessment
CCPA	Canadian Chemical Manufacturers' Association
CD	Committee Draft
CEEM	Centre for Energy and Environmental Management
CEN	Comité Européen de Normalisation
CERES	Coalition for Environmentally Responsible Economies and Societies
CIQC	Computer Industry Quality Conference
CO_2	carbon dioxide
CSD	United Nations Commission on Sustainable Developement
DENR	Philippine Deparment of Environment and Natural Resources
DEVCO	Developing Country Committee (DEVCO)
DGN	Mexican Direccion General de Normas
DIN	Deutsches Institut für Normung
DIS	Draft International Standard (ISO)
DOJ	Department of Justice, US
DSN	Dewan Standardisasi Nasional (the Standardization Council of Indonesia)
DSU	Understanding on Rules and Procedures Governing the Settlement of Disputes
EA	environmental audit
EAC	European Accreditation of Certification
EC	European Community
ECOSOC	United Nations Economic and Social Council
ED	Enquiry Draft
EEB	European Environment Bureau
EIA	Electronics Industry Association
EIA	environmental impact assessment
ELD	environmental labels and declarations
EMAS	Eco-Management and Audit Scheme

EMS	environmental management system
EPA	Environmental Protection Agency, US
EPE	environmental performance evaluation
EU	European Union
EVBAT	economically viable best available technology
FAO	Food and Agriculture Organization
FIDC	International Federation of Consulting Engineers
FTA	Federation Internationale de l'Automobile
FTZ	free trade zone
GANA	Environmental Standardization Supporting Group, Brazil
GATT	General Agreement on Trade and Tariffs
GEMI	Global Environment Management Initiative
GETF	Global Environment and Technology Foundation
IBAMA	Brazilian Institute of the Environment
ICC	International Chamber of Commerce
ICME	International Council on Metals and the Environment
IEC	International Electrotechnical Commission
ILO	International Labour Organization
IMO	International Maritime Organization
INEM	International Network for Environmental Management
ISO	International Organisation for Standardization
ISONET	ISO information network
ITC	International Trade Centre
ITU	International Telecommunications Union
KBS	Kenyan Bureau of Standards
LCA	life cycle analysis
MIT	Massachusetts Institute of Technology
MITI	Ministry of International Trade and Industry, Japan
MOSTE	Malaysian Ministry of Science, Technology and Environment
MSWG	Multi-State Working Group, US
NGO	non-governmental organization
NNI	Netherlands Normalisatie Instituut
NP	new proposal
O-Member	Observing Member
ODC	ozone depleting compound
OECD	Organization for Economic Cooperation and Development
P-Member	Participating Member
PIBA	Pacific Industry Business Association
PPM	Production and Process Method (GATT)
PQPM	Philippine Quality and Productivity Movement
RAB	Registrar Accreditation Board
SABS	South African Bureau of Standards
SAGE	Strategic Advisory Group on Environment (ISO)
SC	Sub-committee of a Technical Committee (ISO)
SEBRAE	Small and Medium Companies Supporting Service, Brazil

SIRIM	Standards and Industrial Research Institute of Malaysia
SISIR	Singapore Institute of Standards and Industrial Research
SMAS	sustainability management audit scheme
SME	small and medium-sized enterprise
SPS	Sanitary and Phytosanitary (Annex, GATT)
TBT	Technical Barriers to Trade (Agreement on, GATT)
TC	Technical Committee (ISO)
TMB	Technical Management Board (ISO)
TNC	transnational corporation
TRI	US Toxic Release Inventory
TSI	Turkish Standards Institute
UNCED	United Nations Conference on Environment and Development
UNCTAD	United Nations Conference on Trade and Development
UNDP	United Nations Development Programme
UNECE	United Nations Economic Commission for Europe
UNEP	United Nations Environment Programme
UNESCO	United Nations Educational, Scientific and Cultural Organization
UNIDO	United Nations Industrial Development Organization
UNIT	Uruguayan Instituto Uraguayo de Normas Tecnicas
USAEP	US–Asian Environmental Partnership
WBCSD	World Business Council for Sustainable Development
WD	Working Draft (ISO)
WG	Working Group
WHO	World Health Organization
WTO	World Trade Organization
WTTC	World Travel and Tourism Council
WWF	Worldwide Fund for Nature

Preface

One of the central paradoxes of our time is the simultaneous increase, on the one hand, of knowledge and technology, and on the other of human and environmental degradation. Globalization and industrialization have been accompanied by widening gaps between rich and poor, and by the depletion of many of our natural resources. Approximately 1 billion people in 110 countries are at risk of losing (or have lost) fertile land on which to grow food to support growing populations. Water related problems are the largest single cause of death and human disease worldwide, but more than 1.5 billion people depend on groundwater for their drinking water and some 1.7 billion people, more than a third of the world's population, are without a safe water supply. 25,000 people die each day as a result of water related problems. About a quarter of the world will suffer from chronic water shortages in the beginning of the next century. This is not only a developing country phenomenon; in some of the richest cities in the world, municipal water treatment plants are functioning at their maximum capacities. Additional demand cannot be absorbed without massive new infrastructure investments.

What is true for the water we drink is true for the air we breathe and the food we eat. 60 per cent of the Earth's population lives within 100 kilometers of the coastline and 3 billion people rely on ocean resources either for food or sustenance. But pollution of the ocean and overharvesting of marine life are major concerns in many countries of the world, from Canada to the Philippines. These issues are raising new debates about environmental management in all spheres of life, from the classroom to the halls of national and international political debate. In almost every area of life, our natural resource limits, previously taken for granted, are becoming pressing considerations. Moreover, it is increasingly recognized that the problems of global environmental management are inextricable from the problems of global development and equity. It is only through a joint approach that sustainable development can be achieved.

This situation has become a source of concern to an ever-broadening group of people. The Gallup Health of the Planet Survey conducted prior to the UN Earth Summit in 1992 found that there is widespread concern for the environment among citizens of all types of countries and that, in the majority of the 22 countries they polled, citizens believe that business and industry are the major causes of environmental problems.[1] Tens of thousands of people have in this decade become galvanized to political activity on environmental issues. Governments everywhere have been putting in place environmental protection regulations. The intergovernmental process has given environment and development issues a central focus, working increasingly with other interested and affected parties, including environmental groups, scientists and business. Industry has responded to these new concerns and demands too – nearly all international and national industry associations now have environmental codes of practice, and several hundred of the largest international firms publish reports on their environmental record and impact.

But progress towards sustainable development is still too slow. Internationally and nationally, the funds or the political will seem absent, and a sense of urgency is lacking in the principal organizations of global governance and the more powerful actors within them. The result is that the gap between what has been done and what needs to happen is widening. Not only has global governance ground to a halt; national-level environmental management faces a myriad of difficulties. Regulators everywhere face difficulties of enforcement both practical and political. Deregulation threatens the very life of regulatory agencies and they therefore seek, cap in hand, partnerships with industry initiatives that will breathe life back into their bodies.[2]

Into this context has stepped a new player, the International Organization for Standardization (ISO), with its new international environmental-management systems standard ISO 14001.[3] The product of just three years of development, this new international standard is being heralded by its creators as industry's answer to the question of global sustainable development. Its advocates argue that ISO 14001 is the product of international consensus, that it will provide the structure for a new paradigm of collaboration between industry and the public sector, that it will become crucial for access to the global marketplace – particularly for doing business with large firms and with important government agencies – and that it will bring sustainable industrial development. Although the voluntary nature of the new standard is stressed, ISO 14001 advocates predict that market forces will make ISO 14001 a condition of doing business globally.[4]

This is a heady mix. In the context of a real presenting problem and more obstacles than solutions, these voices, their energy and their message gain ready ears. This book sounds a strong cautionary note. It argues that the problems of global environmental management and sustainable industrial development are real and need urgent attention. It argues that environmental management systems are an excellent tool among many that will deal effectively with the problem. But it shows that ISO 14001 is one of many kinds of environmental management systems, not *the* environmental management system. This book demonstrates that ISO 14001 is not a leading edge tool that will improve corporate environmental impact but rather an internal management system tool to manage environmental aspects of the firm's operations. It shows that industry, too, has not responded with enthusiasm to the new standard on its own, nor is there evidence of the standard becoming a market condition. It documents that firms, regulators and the public are far from sure that ISO 14001 on its own will bring environmental performance improvement or sustainable industrial development. And it argues that the ISO 'consensus' standard-making system fails to pass an acceptable democratic test by its exclusion of key governments and constituencies. In short, it argues that none of the inferences about ISO 14001 are accurate, and some are incorrect and misleading.

This book will be of interest to all those involved in progressing the debate on global corporate environmental management, from business executives in international firms to small firm suppliers; and from environmental officials lobbied to give special rights to ISO14001-certified firms to government ministers participating in the international environment and trade debates. It will also be of relevance to environmental groups, trade unions and consumers interested in the impacts of corporate environmental management on their local and global environments.[5] The book is based on research contracted to Benchmark Environmental Consulting by the European Environment Bureau (EEB) in Brussels and to Riva Krut from the UN Conference on Trade and Development (UNCTAD) in Geneva. Raymond von Ermen and Dr John Cuddy respectively were the project officers for their organizations. UNCTAD support was from a fund from the Italian Government to support environment and trade negotiations by officials from developing countries. Benchmark Environmental Consulting was founded by the authors in Portland, Maine in 1994, and is currently directed by Riva Krut out of White Plains, New York. Benchmark is a provider of state-of-the-art policy work on sustainable industrial development issues, for environmental agencies, the intergovernmental community, firms and environmental groups. The views expressed are those of the authors in their personal, professional capacity and not those of UNCTAD or other sponsors.

In the first phase of the research, the book drew heavily on the initial reactions of European ministries of the environment who were sent a short analytic study for comment. The second phase of the research benefitted from a telephone and fax survey of officers and senior staff from developing country standard-setting organizations and government agencies who participated in the ISO process (respondents of this survey in the book are called, in shorthand, 'officers'; see Annex A, p 124). 28 officials from 19 countries were interviewed by telephone in English, French, Spanish and Portuguese. Some sent additional material. All had participated at the Oslo meeting to vote on the Draft International Standard in June 1995 or were otherwise active before May 1996.

Significant contributions have been made to the research and writing by a number of people. The authors would like to thank, in particular, various staff at Benchmark Environmental Consulting. Eric Howard contributed to the research and writing of the earlier UNCTAD draft, as did Benchmark interns Peter Thimme and Manuela Palomares-Soler, who surveyed developing country standard-setting officials around the world. Stefanie Gitter, Danielle Pattison and Heather Storlazzi helped with the editing and typing and endless revisions.

Early versions of sections of this study were presented at various industry and environmental agency briefings and conferences and benefitted from feedback. These included: the conference of the European Environmental Bureau, Free Trade and the Environment, in Brussels, October 1995; the Meetings of Environmental Ministers in Sofia, October 1995; a debate on ISO 14001 organized by the Energy and Environment Studies Institute, Senate Hearing Rooms, Washington, DC, February 1996; the Annual Conference of the National Council of State Legislatures, St Louis, August 1996; the US EPA Working Group on ISO 14001; the CMA (Chemical Manufacturers Association) Annual Conference of State Representatives, Durham, NC, September 1996; the EPA Taskforce on ISO 14001, Washington, DC, October 1996; the Global Environment and Technology Foundation (GETF) /EPA Region 1 conference on ISO 14001 at MIT, in October 1996; a public briefing, in Washington, DC to select USAID staff and consultants and a special briefing to the USAID US–Asia Environmental Partnership, both in Washington in September 1996; the Canadian Environmental Law Association conference, 'Law and the Public Interest' in

Toronto, December 1996; and the National Manufacturers' Association, West Virginia Chapter, Annual Conference, Charlestown, West Virginia, April 1997.

Short papers were published in various trade and academic journals, including *Business and the Environment*; *Corporate Environmental Management Strategy*; and in *Greener Management International*, UK, June 1996, later republished in an edited volume by Chris Shelton; and the *International Environmental Law Review*. Lengthy reviews of the two ISO studies were published in the BNA *International Environmental Reporter*; CEEM *Update*; and other local industry and environmental journals in the US, UK and Germany.

Over the period of research and writing, we have had useful comments from: Arthur Weissman of Green Seal in Washington, DC; Pierre Hausselman, environmental consultant, Pully, Switzerland; Jim Dixon, Ahmed Husseini and Ellen Pekilis of the Canadian Standards Association in Toronto; and Mr I Orhan Türköz, chairman, environmental standards, of the Turkish Standards Institute. To all the above, the authors would like to express their appreciation. Of course, all errors, omissions and opinions remain entirely our own responsibility. Finally, we would like to thank our absolutely marvellous children, Raphael and Miriam, who have for almost two years forgiven us our absorption in this rather obscure topic.

Riva Krut, White Plains, New York; and
Harris Gleckman, Geneva
February 1998

Introduction

SUSTAINABLE INDUSTRIAL DEVELOPMENT

There is currently a great deal of debate on the meaning and measures of global sustainable industrial development. These debates may not be resolved in our genera-tion, but it is important to understand that there is agreement on a common objective – the broad and oft-quoted Brundtland Commission statement that the needs of the present should not compromise the ability of future generations to meet their own needs. That said – and who could disagree with it? – there is lively disagreement on ways to get there and what the roles are of industrial actors, regulators and the public in sustainable industrial development. It is the view of this book that ISO 14001 is in itself an inadequate tool to achieve sustainable industrial development. Moreover, in its creation it ignored a decade of process and content experience in international environmental decision-making that will be very difficult to incorporate now that the standard is in place.

In international environmental decision-making, the key elements of the past decade of intergovernmental work have been those of equity and democracy; a recog-nition of a need to build incrementally on advances already made in other intergovernmental arenas; to broaden participation in environmental decision-making to include non-governmental actors; and to make provision for the uneven terms of entry into these agreements from developing countries. This book will show that, in the process of its development, the creators of ISO 14001 were uninterested in these issues. A private group of industrial representatives created an international environ-mental standard which failed to build on past advances (see Chapter 1). It also used a decision-making structure designed to meet the needs of the most active members of a private club, in order to produce a standard that may have a very broad international use. It failed to involve non-industrial actors in its design of the standard and did not give adequate attention to participation from developing countries (see Chapter 2). Finally, ISO 14001 may have international trade status, but it made no special provision for developing countries. Despite its stated intentions not to be used to create non-tariff trade barriers,[1] ISO 14001 could impose significant trade costs on developing countries without secure economic of environmental advantage (see Chapters 3 and 4).

As regards environmental management systems (EMSs), there is broad agreement that these are a crucial tool towards sustainable industrial development. The debate tends to cluster around two inter-related concerns; how to improve corporate environ-mental performance, and how to demonstrate this, or to show public accountability. Therefore some dialogue is needed between public environmental needs and the environmental impact of the firm. The firm needs to provide information to public bodies so that effective targets can be created, and progress towards them monitored.

A corporate environmental management system, if it is to lead to improved environmental performance and to contribute to sustainable industrial development, must therefore contain publically-disclosed environmental performance information. However, ISO 14001 does not require certified companies either to measure environmental performance (as opposed to systems performance) or to disclose results.

Are these unrealistic expectations of an international EMS? We don't think so. ISO 14001 is inadequate on its own. It will need to be augmented with tools that provide information on environmental performance (see Chapter 5) – what we have called an 'ISO 14001 Plus' approach. But tools to define corporate environmental performance metrics and reporting requirements are still in their infancy. There remains a real question about whether these crucial substantive parts of the sustainable industrial development agenda can be added to ISO 14001 or addressed through ISO 14001, as neither was integral to ISO 14001's concerns. In the meantime, there are more interesting EMS models in play that meet many of the process and substance requirements of sustainable industrial development. This introduction provides an overview of the ISO 14001 series of specifications and guidelines.

ISO 14001: BACKGROUND

Until recently, the general public would have had little interest in the International Organization for Standardization (ISO). This international association of national standard-setting bodies was set up to facilitate international commerce by standardizing technical specifications. It works closely with the International Electrotechnical Commission (IEC). In many areas, from ATM cards to telecommunication bandwidths to plumbing supplies, business and the public experience significant advantages from ISO and IEC activity.

For the most part, ISO/IEC standards provide the basis for international private-sector trade, invisible to the public or the regulatory community. The success of the ISO/IEC work can be illustrated by an example on which they failed to get international agreement: specifications for electrical outlets. Because industrial consensus was not achieved, international travellers are inconvenienced as they move from France to the US to South Africa. Every so often, when an ISO standard favours one firm's technology over another technical approach, ISO standards have raised questions within industry of monopolistic practices. With expanding trade and globalization, such concerns may increase. But by and large ISO meetings and the resulting standards do not attract much public interest. This has changed with the ISO 14000 series. With ISO 14000, the ISO has entered an area that involves normative standards that have deep public and environmental consequence.

The significance of this development from the point of view of sustainable industrial development cannot be over-emphasised. For in developing an international standard for environmental management systems, the ISO has entered a dynamic area of international environmental decision-making and fundamentally changed its character and direction. In a breathtakingly short period of time, it has used a closed system of industrial decision-making to create a standard for EMS that it now argues is equivalent to intergovernmental standards, and best corporate practice in environmental management, both of which were designed to achieve better environmental performance and sustainable industrial development.

From the perspective of public debate on environmental management, the ISO 14000 series is one of several industry responses to the strong general interest in sustainable industrial development precipitated by the UN Conference on Environment and Development (UNCED) in 1992.[2] National governments; local and regional authorities; international organizations, both governmental and nongovernmental; the public and environmental groups – all of these have a deep interest in industrial environmental standards. However, the ISO created ISO 14000 using its normal procedures, working through interested national standard-setting bodies – overwhelmingly from the developed world – and their industry representatives. Consequently, the involvement of other interested parties has been negligible or extremely limited.

Since the ISO was originally established to facilitate international interfirm trade, the process for creating an ISO standard is open only to its members: national standard setting institutions. There is little participation from governments, from non-member organizations or from the public. Whereas the governmental and intergovernmental process of environmental standard setting has progressively moved to integrate public comment, ISO standards can be established in a process relatively insulated from public or non-member input. Nearly a year after ISO 14001 became a draft standard, the head of Sierra Club (US) acknowledged '...most [environmental groups] probably [have] not yet discovered what ISO 14000 is. It is an emerging issue; we [in the environment movement] are still trying to evaluate its implications for us.'[3]

WHOSE ENVIRONMENTAL STANDARDS?

The word 'standard' has several meanings. It can denote a degree or level of requirement, excellence, or attainment; when we refer to a teacher, or a leader, with standards, we mean standards of *excellence*. This is the sense generally used in relation to professional standards. Within environmental policy a 'standard' is a performance level and a limit value aimed at improved environmental protection. In international environmental standard setting, the trend has been to base international public policy standards on the best national standards from leading countries and companies.

Environmental agencies within national governments, for example, set mandatory environmental standards. These generally originate from consumer or public demand; are drafted in debate between the public, scientists, civil servants and the political process; set limit values, for example maximum concentration of pesticides in drinking water; and carry penalties for non-compliance (even though these have become increasingly difficult to enforce).[4] Intergovernmental standards typically take national best practices and elevate them to international standards, thereby encouraging countries to integrate them into national standards. The process of intergovernmental environmental standard setting in the past five years has been characterized by a very high degree of effective involvement from broad sections of civil society, including scientists, industry and environmental activist groups. Intergovernmental standards can be treaties binding on signatory parties or softer recommendations from international agreements such as Agenda 21 or ministerial declarations.

In addition, a host of international specialized organizations negotiate and establish standards of practice for businesses and governments. In the area of environment, health and safety, the prime actors include expert groups associated with the UN Environment Programme (UNEP), the International Maritime Organization (IMO), the International Labour Organization (ILO), the World Health Organization (WHO), and regional organizations such as the Organization for Economic Cooperation and Development (OECD) and the UN regional economic commissions – in particular the UN Economic Commission for Europe (UNECE). In the private sector, most national and international industry associations have set environmental policy and practice standards for member firms. These typically take the form of a voluntary environmental policy, mission, charter, code of conduct or code of practice. In some cases, the associations have moved to implement these standards within their sectors by requiring their members to report against various practice elements. The most notable of these is the chemical industry's Responsible Care® programmes around the world, but initiatives are also in place within other sectors as well, including tourism, banking, and textiles and apparel.

A quite different concept of a standard is 'an acknowledged measure of comparison for quantitative or qualitative value, usually for the purposes of standardization.'[5] When we refer to food of standard quality, or the standard performance of a student, we are referring to standards as *average*. It is in this sense that the term has usually been employed by industrial standard-setting bodies, including the ISO, which set out to standardize or normalize technical product standards to facilitate interfirm commerce. This definition is captured in the names of standard setting organizations around the world: the International Institute for Standardization; the Uruguayan Instituto Uruguayo de Normas Tecnicas (UNIT); Mexico's Direccion General de Normas (DGN); the National Standardization Agency, Indonesia, Dewan Standardisasi Nasional (DSN); the Chilean Instituto Nacional de Normalización; Mexico's Direccion General de Normas (DGN). Finally, there is a question about who should follow a particular standard. Governments and local and regional authorities may set standards for activities operating in their jurisdiction, whether they are building codes or pollutant emission standards. The international intergovernmental process can set international standards of excellence that are recommendations; or it can make binding international standards that need to be followed by ratifying countries. Voluntary international standards for environmental management have been set by industrial associations and by leading international firms with codes of conduct on issues ranging from ethics to environment to labour rights. Other kinds of voluntary international standards are also set by firms and associations. These are usually technical standards designed for procurement so that buyers receive expected quality. Although these standards are voluntary, suppliers regard them as market requirements that are mandatory in order to retain their customers.

STANDARDS FOR ENVIRONMENTAL MANAGEMENT

The very concept of environmental management may be presumptuous. The environment cannot be managed; rather, we can find ways to work with natural laws and natural systems. Consequently, the term environmental management needs to be understood as a shorthand for 'the management of institutions and people that impact the environment'. An environmental management system needs to be thought of as 'an institutionalized system designed for environmental management'. Elements of this system could include:

- current scientific understanding of natural laws and local or ecosystem characteristics;
- society-made standards and laws about how businesses deal with their local ecosystems;
- public/ private sector environmental partnerships to experiment with new ways to fit corporations into their local environment;
- voluntary industry initiatives to guide corporate relations with communities and their environments;
- and organizational management systems in general.

In the early 1990s, a small number of national standard setting bodies began to grapple with the question of how to standardize existing environmental management systems. The concept of environmental management systems was not new, as the term had been used for 20 years; the innovation was setting international standards for future environmental management systems.

The first formally adopted standard for environmental management systems was developed in 1992 by the British Standards Institution (BSI), and BS 7750 became operational for company certification in March 1995. Its goal was to develop a comprehensive environmental management system programme that would be sufficiently generic to apply to all business sectors. BS 7750 was quite successful, with businesses in the UK as well as abroad becoming certified to the standard.

The history and outcome of the BS 7750 negotiations served as the basis for negotiations on environmental management system standards in other fora, including the European Union and the ISO. Denmark and The Netherlands adopted BS 7750 as their national environmental management system standard, while other countries developed their own national standard, such as the French standard X 30–200, the Irish IS 310, or the Spanish UNE77–801. While these initiatives were taking place at the national level, a parallel initiative began regionally. The lead came from the Commission of the European Communities and its Fifth Environmental Action Programme. To help test the concept of environmental management systems within the EU, the European Commission negotiated the Eco-Management and Audit Scheme (EMAS) with industry and environmental groups and other interested stakeholders. EMAS is a voluntary EU regulation, which means that in all member states corporations can try out a specific form of environment management system. It was created for businesses interested in voluntary certification to an environmental management system and to help them evaluate their programmes and work toward continuous improvement in environmental performance.

Under EMAS, certified businesses would integrate environmental concerns into policy, strategy and systems in ways that would meet or exceed the minimum effort required by laws and regulations.

> ... this responsibility calls for companies to establish and implement environ-
> mental policies, objectives and programmes and effective environmental
> management systems; ... adopt an environmental policy, which in addition to
> providing for compliance with all relevant regulatory requirements [includes] ...
> the reasonable continuous improvement of environmental performance.[6]

EMAS calls for businesses to establish and implement environmental policies, programmes and management systems; and to periodically evaluate, in a systematic and objective way, the performance of the site elements and provide environmental performance information to the public. These stakeholder groups are critical to the success of EMAS. In order to fulfil their respective roles, these groups must have access to appropriate information; EMAS therefore includes provisions for releasing relevant environmental information to the public. The 1993 EMAS regulation will be reviewed in 1998, and issues for discussion include better guidelines on verification, clarification of the environmental statement and the inclusion of sustainable development concerns. European Partners for the Environment, a coalition of corporations, think-tanks and environmental groups, has called for the expansion of EMAS to a sustainability management audit scheme (SMAS).[7]

EMAS is an experiment and therefore has some peculiarities. It is, for example, a voluntary regulation: participation in it is voluntary, but it is an EU regulation. Unusually, it does not have to go through national legislation to be put into effect. However, as an experiment, it remains an attempt to take a fresh approach to sustainable industrial development, giving incentives to firms to self-regulate within some tight regulatory frameworks. The emphasis of EMAS is in front-of-pipe environmental solutions or pollution prevention; cleaner technology, life-cycle analysis; and continuous improvement of environmental performance. To create incentives for these approaches, but at the same time secure environmental protection, EMAS firms have to operate 'beyond compliance'; in addition, firms must produce an initial environmental impact assessment and disclose their environmental improvements in annual reports.[8]

ISO INTERNATIONAL STANDARDS

ISO 14001 maintains past practice in several areas and opens up several new ones. On the question of the meaning of standard, the ISO typically understands this as technical standardization and setting performance specifications, not setting ceilings. Ceilings have typically had strict performance requirements that were crucial to consumers – specifying, for example, the width of a specific widget or the durability of a condom. ISO 14001 differs in both these areas. It deals in the normative issues of environmental management, not in the technical issues of engineering; and it standardizes a process, not a product's performance. These departures from the conventional ISO line of business need to be understood.

Founded in 1946, the ISO has some 111 member national and regional standard-setting bodies. National standard-setting bodies are sometimes governmental organizations, sometimes quasi-governmental bodies and sometimes private industry associations, with national firms as members. Some countries have no national representation in the ISO because they have small or no standard-setting associations. The ISO currently has over 200 technical committees that create and review standards. Some of these are indicated in Box i.1. They cover a broad range of areas and issues, and their work generally builds upon existing nationally approved technological standards. TC 176, for example, created the ISO 9000 series for quality management, and this committee based their work on some ten years of action on quality standards at the national level among standard-setting organizations, primarily in the industrialized world. ISO standards have been broadly adopted by industry and in some cases incorporated into government procurement guidelines. Any ISO standard developed by a technical committee results from agreement between its member bodies.

Once approved, ISO standards may be incorporated into voluntary, national-level technical standards specifications and guidelines; in this way they create an international language to facilitate interfirm commerce. Industries and firms that engage in trade with other businesses tend to use ISO standards extensively. The system seeks engineering equivalence or consistency of product or process testing methods and reduces ambiguity in the description of products and processes. If a firm wishes to purchase screws, surgery implants or loading pallets, the product would conform to expectations in terms of size, quality or other components of the ISO standard.

ISO AND INTERNATIONAL MANAGEMENT SYSTEMS STANDARDS

ISO's entry into the public policy arena is new. Its presence within normative standard setting is also relatively new, starting with the precursor to ISO 14000, the ISO 9000 series on international quality management standards.

ISO 9000

ISO 9000 was the first attempt made by the ISO to write normative management standards as opposed to technical specifications. ISO 9001, issued in 1987, is the lead quality management system standard. In terms of external recognition, it has been by far the most successful of the ISO standards. Since June 1996, ISO 9001 has been adopted as a national standard by national standards setting bodies in over 70 countries worldwide, as well as by the lead industry regional trade bodies in Europe, Africa, America and the Middle East. By the end of 1995 some 100,000 certificates were issued in about 86 countries. 75 per cent of these were in Europe, 50 per cent in the UK alone.[9] Since ISO 9001 places an obligation on the certified firm to use certified suppliers, ISO 9001 has had the effect of requiring supplier firms to get certification or lose clients.

BOX i.1 EXAMPLES OF ISO TECHNICAL COMMITTEES

TC1	Screw threads
TC 25	Cast iron and pig iron
TC 26	Copper and copper alloys
TC 51	Pallets for unit load methods of materials handling
TC 76	Transfusion, infusion and injection equipment for medical use
TC 100	Chains and chain wheels for power transmission and conveyors
TC 101	Continuous mechanical handling equipment
TC 125	Plain bearings
TC 150	Implants for surgery
TC 175	Flurospar
TC 176	Quality management and quality assurance
TC 200	Solid wastes
TC 201	Surface chemical analysis

ISO 9001 was established in the wake of the 'quality movement' lead by management gurus Demming, Juran and Crosby. Definitions of quality vary. Like the concept of environmental standards, a quality standard could mean a degree of excellence; or it could mean compliance with specifications. ISO 9001 is not a quality standard but a quality systems standard. A quality system is defined as: the organizational structure, procedures, processes and resources needed to implement quality management.'[10] Quality management is defined as: all activities of the overall management function that determine the quality policy, objectives and responsibilities, and implement them by means such as quality planning, quality control, quality assurance and quality improvement within the quality system.

The roots of several ideas that flourished in the ISO 9000 series were transplanted into ISO 14000 series. The most important was the concept of a standard for the organization's management system, rather than an organizational performance standard. ISO 9000 distinguishes between quality systems requirements and product requirements. 9001 states that quality systems requirements should be satisfied and proscribes processes, not objectives. Objectives are viewed as organizational choices. Following this thinking, quality is *created* by managing the processes in a quality management system; this is done by defining and updating the product in line with market needs; by the quality of the product design features that influence the performance of the product; by consistency in conforming to product design and customer expectations; and by product support throughout the life cycle of the product. For certification, this quality system standard should be established and maintained, and the performance of the system should be reported to management as a basis for continual systems improvement.[11] Following this logic, a company that makes lead balloons can be certified to ISO 9001; and a company making weapons for biological warfare can be certified to ISO 14001.

ISO 9000 is principally concerned with suppliers, so that the quality chain can be maintained. Suppliers are broadly defined to include internal and external suppliers, from contractors to workers. *ISO 9001: Quality Systems – model for quality assurance in design, development, production, installation and servicing* is written as a supplier standard. The term 'supplier' is so central to this concept of quality that the supplier is the firm seeking certification who will impose this same set of concepts on their suppliers throughout the life cycle of the product.[12] The 'multiplier' effect of the supplier condition created a wave of ISO 9001 certifications and a huge market for certification consultants – called (even by its beneficiaries) the 'certification circus'. These same consultants have been active in the ISO 14001 process, arguing for the integration of concepts from the two families of standards. This would keep them in business and expand their market; and also ensure that ISO 9001 firms need not undergo a complete organizational upheaval to incorporate the new standard.

Nevertheless, some elements of ISO 9001 were not transferred into ISO 14001, notably the supplier condition. This is important to note because it is commonly assumed that the 'supplier condition' *was* transferred to 14001. Obviously the implications are enormous for the hundreds of non-certified suppliers to major firms, and the lack of this provision in ISO 14001 needs to be stressed. It was this supplier condition, and the fear of being cut out of the market, that made ISO 9001 so popular – not necessarily the value it brought to quality management. The fear of repeating of the market pressure is being fanned by ISO 14001 consultants, even though there is no equivalent text in ISO 14001.

The effort to build on the ISO 9000 series has, in fact, been far more important to its architects than the need to integrate this new environmental management systems standard with existing international environmental standards or with the movement towards self-regulation and environmental management systems. This is evident in the constant reference to the two standards as a set in official ISO and trade literature, to the inclusion of an annex to ISO 14001 on the overlap between ISO 9001 and ISO 14001 and by the omission in ISO 14001 of any reference to existing international environmental agreements and conventions.

ISO 14000

Like many international decision-making processes, the ISO 14000 series has generated its own language. Acronyms abound, and individuals seeking to be effective in this process will need to understand references to the position of TC 207/SC4/WG1 on CD on EPE (Working Group 1 of Subcommittee 4 of Technical Committee 207's Committee Draft on Environmental Performance Evaluation). Unlike intergovernmental meetings, most ISO meetings and negotiations are conducted in English only. There is, of course, the technical vocabulary as well. In some cases, apparently neutral terms – such as environmental standards – have been given specific and new meaning in this process. In other cases, nuances of English that may appear trivial – such as environmental aspect assessment (rather than environmental impact assessment) and prevention of pollution (rather than pollution prevention) – were the result of intense debate, resulting in different meanings in ISO circles than in common usage, in national regulations or international law.

ISO 14000 Series Specification and Guidance Standards

The ISO 14000 series presents a set of generic standards for environmental management systems – following the ISO 9000 precedent. The goal of these standards is to
give the private sector, and others who may use them, a framework for managing their
environmental issues. The 14000 series consists of over a dozen separate standards.
These standards focus on organizational processes, not necessarily their products or
their environmental impacts. ISO 14001, the standard on environmental management
systems, describes how a firm might manage and control its organizational system so
that it measures, controls and continually improves the environmental aspects of its
operations. It does not assess what the organization produces – its products or services
– nor its environmental performance, nor long-term changes in performance.

   There are two types of standards within the ISO 14000 series: specification
standards and guidance standards. ISO specification standards are prescriptive
documents: they describe what a company must do or must not do in order to get
certification. ISO 14001 is a blueprint for the firm's environmental management
system, and it is the only specification standard in the ISO 14000 series. Negotiations
for this standard began in 1991, and it was adopted as an international standard by the
ISO in June 1996. Non-participating firms and stakeholders must decide if or how
they may use or implement this standard. They may also opt to participate in future
reviews of this specification standard.

   ISO guidance standards are used to clarify requirements and provide definitions.
There are many guidance standards in the ISO 14000 series and they can be divided
into two groups: organizational evaluation and product evaluation. The organizational
evaluation standards cover concerns such as auditing and environmental performance
evaluations. Product evaluation standards include guidelines for ecolabelling, life-cycle
assessment and environmental aspects of product standards (see Annex B). While the
basic framework for most of these standards has already been set, some of the
subcommittees are still in the process of determining the exact details. These standards
are also described further below.

ISO 14001: AN INTERNATIONAL ENVIRONMENTAL MANAGEMENT SYSTEMS STANDARD

The 14001 environmental management systems standard is the cornerstone of the
ISO 14000 series. It is a prescriptive document against which the company will be
benchmarked and receive certification. ISO 14000 defines an environmental management system to include these five elements:

- an environmental policy;
- an assessment of environmental aspects and legal and voluntary obligations;
- a management system;
- a series of periodic internal audits and reports to top management;
- a public declaration that ISO 14001 is being implemented.

Environmental Policy

The environmental policy is the basis for an ISO 14001 environmental management system. It is the only public document that ISO 14001 requires a certified facility to produce. The policy is the statement of corporate environmental mission against which the management system should be designed, implemented, monitored and continually improved. This policy should be defined by top management, who should ensure that the policy:

- is appropriate to the nature, scale and environmental aspects of its activities, products or services;
- includes a commitment to continual improvement and prevention of pollution;
- includes a commitment to comply with relevant environmental legislation and regulations, and with other requirements to which the organization subscribes;
- provides the framework for setting and reviewing environmental objectives and targets;
- is documented, implemented and maintained and communicated to all employees;
- is available to the public.[13]

A weak environmental policy or one that is narrowly defined, even if rigorously implemented, may not lead to any environmental improvements. There are some concerns that ISO 14001 could provide some companies with an easy 'A'. In all events, it will be impossible to distinguish between a good and a desultory environmental performer on the grounds of their ISO 14001 certification alone.[14]

For regulators seeking to provide incentives for corporate self-regulation, or for individuals looking for environmental performance assurances, one key distinguishing feature between companies with ISO 14001 certification will be the contents of their environmental policy. For example, if a firm's policy is committed to environmental performance improvement, to working with local authorities or the government to set performance limit values that are externally audited, and to public reporting of performance against these voluntary standards, then the relationship between the regulatory and private sectors could clearly shift in favor of self-regulation without compromising public policy. ISO 14001 on its own will not be enough. Without additional evidence of corporate commitment and improved environmental performance than is offered under ISO 14001, regulators can choose to retain a stronger environmental infrastructure, and/or to add some of the missing elements to the standard that will make it a more effective— an 'ISO Plus' approach.

Environmental Aspects Assessment; Legal and Voluntary Obligations Assessment

ISO 14001 requires that businesses conduct conformance assessments. In setting their environmental objectives, the organization will establish and maintain 'procedures to identify the environmental aspects of its activities, products or services that it can control and over which [the business] can be expected to have an influence'. Businesses also will establish and maintain a procedure to identify and have access to 'legal requirements, and other requirements to which the organization subscribes'.[15]

Assuming that an assessment demonstrates that these procedures have been established and are maintained, the company can be certified to the ISO 14001 standard. The audit for ISO 14001 certification is an internal audit for senior management. It is not intended as a basis for public reporting – although this is, of course, at the discretion of the firm. It is also not clear whether information discovered on possible illegal activities in an audit should be disclosed to public authorities, or whether public authorities can demand access to the audit.

Management System

A management system must be established to check that the facility is in line with its environmental policy statement. This management system is based on a regular project cycle, with phases for planning, implementation, checking, review and continual improvement. It is characterized by clear lines of authority and responsibility and the designation of environmental officials who should check that the system requirements are established, implemented and maintained. There are stipulations about worker training,[16] communication, documentation and operational control, emergency preparedness and response, checking and corrective action, and record keeping.[17]

Periodic Internal Audit and Top Management Report; Implementing ISO 14001

Periodic audits should check that the management system conforms to plans and policy and that it is being properly implemented and maintained. The results of the audit are reported to top management. This could be an external auditor that the company employs like a consultant, or the company can create an internal system for self-auditing the site's management system. In addition to self-audits, a firm can self-certify that it conforms with the standard, or it can seek certification or registration of its environmental management system by an external organisation.[18]

ISO 14000 Guidance Standards

A host of ISO 14000 guidance standards are under development or have been approved. As noted above, the guidance standards clarify some ISO 14001 requirements or address interconnected themes. Some relate to evaluating efforts by organizations to certify to ISO 14001. Others pertain to evaluating products. One standard provides general guidelines on principles, systems and supporting techniques.[19]

Several developing countries have proposed an additional standard that would provide guidelines on special considerations affecting small and medium enterprises. While part of the original 1993 TC 207 workplan, the standard has not yet been developed, even though 90 per cent of many countries' industry sectors is composed of small- and medium-sized enterprises.[20]

Organizational Evaluation Standards; Environmental Auditing and Environmental Performance Evaluation

In the past, corporate management systems were set up to comply with external regulatory or fiscal requirements and were driven by accountants, lawyers, engineers and auditors. More recently, this has changed, particularly in the developed world. Management systems have become integral to business operations and strategic business management. In terms of environmental management, this meant a shift from compliance audits in the 1960s and 1970s to proactive audits that include a larger range of firms' activities, including products, services, suppliers and investments in the 1980s. In the 1990s, a strategic systems approach has developed. Its strength lies in integrating environmental management into general business functions. Its weakness is that the concept of 'audit' has been enlarged to include routine internal monitoring of performance targets, while abandoning a commitment to audit in the traditional compliance sense. The audit criteria are set by the organization, and not through a public process, and reporting is to management, not a public body.

The ISO definition of an environmental management system audit is as follows:

> ... a systematic and documented verification process of obtaining and evaluating evidence to determine whether an organization's environmental management system conforms to the environmental-management system audit criteria set by the organization, and for communication of the results of this process to management.[21]

Audits are required to ensure that environmental systems standards are met. Since the standards measure system conformance, not environmental performance, an audit need not provide environmental performance information. Information from the audit is presented to management. It does not necessarily need to be verified by an independent third party nor reported to the public. Audits may be performed by personnel from within the organization or by external consultants and registrars. Either can result in a certificate.

The first guidance standards relating to audits were approved in June 1996. They set guidelines for audits and qualification standards for auditors.[22] One standard under the environmental auditing umbrella, however, was deleted at the June 1996 meeting by a 16-to-14 vote.[23] Developing countries wanted a guideline for initial/preparatory environmental reviews to help companies produce appropriate environmental management systems and to better understand those activities that could be damaging to the environment. Because many developing countries were absent when the vote was taken, their position lost to a fairly united block of developed countries. Since no further work was needed on the three other standards relating to audits and auditors, the subcommittee working groups were disbanded.

ISO environmental performance evaluation (EPE) standards are guidelines on how to measure, analyze, assess and describe an organization's environmental management system performance. ISO 14001 defines environmental performance as follows: '...measurable results of the environmental management system, related to an organization's control of its environmental aspects, based on its environmental policy,

objectives and targets'.[24] For many people involved in environmental protection, this
is a highly unusual and circular definition. An ISO environmental performance evaluation is an evaluation of organizational systems performance, not the environmental
impact of the organization, its technology or its products. This systems approach is
consistent with the ISO 9000 approach on quality management. The example is often
given that ISO 9000 certification could be granted to a company that made cement life
jackets – a product unusable by consumers – if the company had a quality system in
place and all products met the self-defined 'error-free' = 'zero-defects' standard. In
the same way, ISO 14001 could be granted to a company that produces dangerous
products, such as persistent organic pollutants, but has a sound management system in
place. On the other hand, 'green firms' producing environmentally sound products
cannot be certified for having environmentally sound products, for using life-cycle
analysis in their product selection process, or for maintaining a sound environmental
audit programme.

ISO has standardized the process for conducting environmental performance
evaluations in a guidance document that is still under review.[25] There are some significant questions and issues which remain. At the June 1996 meeting, for example,
references to life-cycle assessment were eliminated because the representatives could
not agree on the link between environmental performance evaluation and life-cycle
assessment. As a result, non-product output and other references to materials flows
were deleted from the draft environmental performance evaluation standard.[26]

ISO environmental performance evaluations cover the results of an organization's
management of the environmental aspects of its activities, products and services. By
establishing an inventory of impacts such as air emission or wastewater discharge, the
organization should then be able to identify improvement indicators. In this context,
companies would use this standard as an evaluation tool and as a means for setting a
strategy, taking into account the results of the inventory. The drafting committee has
yet (1997) to decide if the environmental performance evaluation would be a supporting document for the ISO 14001 environmental management system standard or a
stand-alone document – the option that most developing countries prefer.

Product Evaluation Standards; Life-Cycle Assessment and Environmental Labelling

At least four supporting standards will provide guidance on conducting a life-cycle
assessment. The current documents focus on principles and practices, inventory analysis, impact assessment, and improvement assessment.[27]

> Life-cycle assessment is a compilation and evaluation, according to a systematic
> set of procedures, of the inputs and outputs of materials and energy and the
> associated environmental impacts directly attributable to the function of a
> product throughout its life cycle.[28]

Life-cycle assessment begins with the extraction of raw materials from the ground,
continues through the various processing, manufacturing and transportation steps,
and concludes with consumption, disposal or recovery – or 'cradle to grave'. By

emphasizing the effects related to all the production steps and the use of products, life-cycle assessment guides decision-makers in selecting actions that minimize environmental impacts. As noted above, the relationship between life-cycle assessment and environmental performance evaluation (EPE) is still under negotiation.

Standards for making environmental claims differ greatly by country. Many businesses use ecolabels as a marketing tool for their products, and some may even make claims without reference to any external standard. The goal of this TC 207 subcommittee is to develop a standard to prevent unwarranted claims, to ensure that claims are accurate and verifiable, to reduce trade barriers, and to set standards for types of labels. It may not be possible to achieve all of these goals through an ISO standard.

A number of separate guidance standards for labelling are still under development. As with other sections of the ISO 14000 series, one standard sets the goals and principles, and other standards cover components, such as third-party labels.[29] Some labels would be limited to environmentally preferable products (analogous to most existing ecolabels), while others would provide information on the environmental impacts of a product (analogous to nutrition labels on food packaging).

REGISTERING TO ISO 14001

A company has a set of options when deciding what elements of their corporate operations should be registered to ISO 14001. ISO 14001 can be applied corporate-wide or it can be applied at the level of the site. It can also be applied to one part of the firm's operations. The exact scope of ISO 14001 is at the discretion of the firm. In one city, a firm may have a manufacturing facility, a storage facility and a retail outlet, each under separate 'management', and it might seek ISO 14001 only for the retail site. For governments, businesses and consumers, it may be hard to distinguish between the geographic scope of certifications. This is something that is especially important to check for those who wish to understand the environmental performance of a specific firm.

For firms that feel ISO 14001 may be a ticket of entry into a global marketplace, it is crucial that they ascertain what sectors this may apply to and what kind of environmental management system is required. There are significant expenses in certifying to ISO 14001. In many cases, global firms already require an environmental management system in place among their suppliers. These may be content with direct inspections, combined with a self-declared environmental management system such as the chemical industry 'Responsible Care®' programmes. Firms who are registering to the ISO 14001 standard will need to have the ISO 14001 system in place before they can be certified. Once a company believes that it has met the requirements, it can self-certify or contact a third-party body for certification and registration as an ISO 14001 site or company. The external certification process under ISO 14001 is not yet clarified. For example, it is not clear whether a consultant firm retained to establish an environmental management system can then certify its own recommendations. At the moment, it appears that this is the case. Some firms and consultants support this, based on the argument that real competence for auditing an environmental management system lies with the existing environmental consultants or lawyers, and confidentiality issues will not arise. Standard-setting bodies often develop their own cadre of registrars, and they perceive specialized environment consulting firms as their ISO 14001 competition.

Once a company is certified and registered to an ISO standard, it receives a certificate and may be listed in a register or directory published by the certification body. As with ISO 9000, the registrar will reinspect the environmental management system on a regular, perhaps annual, basis to look for evidence that the system is still in compliance with the standard. The validity of an ISO 9000 registration certificate typically is three years, after which a full reaudit is conducted. Some registration companies offer ISO 9000 certificates that are valid indefinitely, contingent upon a record of successful surveillance visits. The policies of most national standard-setting bodies and registers on the reviews and reinspection of ISO 14001 certification are still under development.

Registration procedures for certification to the ISO 14001 environmental management system are not yet defined. Nevertheless, even while registration methods were being discussed, international consulting firms were certifying firms in the developed and developing world to the drafts of the ISO 14000 standards, arguing that this investment will bring their clients early market advantage and that it will make eventual certification to the finalized ISO standards easier. However, as of mid-1997, there remained major disagreements about the value of national-level certificates and what cross-accreditation will be negotiated regionally and internationally.[30]

ISO 14001-certified companies should be in conformance with the requirements for the standard outlined above. The most important components of ISO 14001 are the environmental policy statement and a management system to ensure that the facility is in line with its environmental policy statement. The policy statement needs to contain a commitment to comply with applicable laws and regulations. There is, however, no commitment under ISO 14001 to exceed the law, if laws and regulations are deficient. Therefore, an ISO-certified company may be operating at a low standard and can still be certified with ISO 14001. In other words, it is possible to meet ISO requirements and still be out of regulatory compliance, snarled in litigation and embroiled in conflicts with environmentalists.[31]

ISO 14001 AND EMAS: DIFFERENT KINDS OF EMS STANDARDS

ISO 14001 and EMAS are different in kind, not in degree. This is quite obvious, even from their names: a standard for environmental management systems is quite different in concept from an Eco-Management and Audit Scheme. EMAS contains several key elements absent in ISO 14001. In process and in content, the differences between the two standards lie precisely in the areas crucial to sustainable development: public access to information, legal environmental proceedings, assurances of regulatory compliance, and environmental performance assurances and improvements. EMAS was created by a broad coalition of different interest groups and from the way it is being implemented at the national level. EMAS is a standard of excellence, derived and intended to be used in the same way that international environmental standards have been developed and applied. ISO is a method of standardization.

Another crucial difference is, who governs each standard? EMAS was a creation of the Council of European Communities and the government representatives – in this case the environmental ministries – of the Member States. ISO 14001 was created by an international industry association and its participating membership (national standards-setting bodies). In some cases, the industry association of a country is a governmental or quasi-governmental organization reporting to the ministry of trade and industry or the department of commerce. This raises a complex issue about governance of environmental management standards. When EMAS is under consideration in a country, it is under consideration by environmental ministries and requires, amongst other things, compliance to its environmental laws and third-party verification by an accredited EMAS auditor. When ISO 14001 is under consideration in a country, it means its industry association or its trade ministry governs the standard, and it requires compliance.

ISO 14001 and EMAS therefore have different interests. As Table i.1 shows, EMAS takes as its province a much wider definition of the environment and the process by which it is managed. The role of the firm therefore starts with a baseline review of its environmental impact and ends with a public report on performance improvements against that initial review. One part of this is the internal organizational management system that is set up to accomplish these external targets and goals. It is this smaller box that is the province of the internal organizational management system. ISO is concerned with the organizational system and infers that environmental-management systems improvements will lead to improved environmental performance.

The differences in content between the two standards are also illustrated in Table i.1. The first element is the discrepancy in the concept of self-regulation. EMAS was conceived as a partnership between the public and private sectors and gives discretion to the firm on how external performance benchmarks should be achieved; ISO 14001 is an internal management tool that awards discretion to the firm without providing performance or compliance assurances to the public.

ISO 14001 is less rigorous than other environmental management systems. In Europe, the EMAS programme has been open for voluntary participation by businesses and industry since 1995. The European Union devised the system to enhance environmental protection by sharing the onus of environmental impact control with the business community. EMAS includes some supervision and control mechanisms, such as compulsory validation (which has to be renewed at least every three years) of the management system, published environmental policies, and annual environmental reporting through an independent third party accredited by a body within the EMAS system. In this public report the company must cover the various fields of its environmental impact and – most importantly of all – state relevant facts and figures. Such reports keep all stakeholders informed and the publicity ensures that companies are proactive in their approaches. EMAS requires a company to commit itself to continuous improvement of environmental performance; ISO 14001, on the other hand, encourages (the more limited) continuous improvement of the environment management system.

Table i.1 *EMAS Compared to ISO 14001*

	EMAS	ISO 14001
Guiding principles/ terms of reference	'...a Community programme of policy and action in relation to the environment and sustainable development ... protection of the environment ... in particular, to prevent, reduce and as far as possible eliminate pollution, particularly at source on the basis of the polluter pays principle, to ensure sound management of resources and to use clean or cleaner technology ...'	Title: Environmental management Scope: Standardization in the field of environmental management tools and systems
Legal status	Voluntary EU regulation integrated in the legal system of the European Union and the member states	ISO standards are voluntary industry standards and have historically had no relationship to legal regimes; although they are voluntary standards, they tend to become market requirements for international interfirm commerce
Applicability	Currently limited to sites in Europe with industrial activities that choose to use it	Any organization, any activity, worldwide
Legal commitment	Compliance with relevant environmental rules and regulations is necessary for certification	A 'commitment to compliance' is required in the policy; compliance is not essential to obtain or to retain certification
Concept of self-regulation	Supported by a legal framework and by external verification and evaluation elements (role of the EU Commission) – beyond compliance commitments	Left in the hands of the firm (for example, to choose third party certification or not; to choose what to report publically beyond the policy)
Initial environmental review	A pre-condition for the EMS that examines the firm's environmental impacts; this is the starting point for the initial and later audits; registration can be removed if adequate performance improvements are not demonstrated.	Suggested in Annex 4.2.1 but not a specification/ requirement

Environmental statement	Must be verified and made public; has to contain core elements of EMS and continual improvement of environmental performance	Available to workers only; only the environmental policy must be publicly available
Environmental policy	Commitment to continual improvement of environmental performance	Commitment to continual improvement of environmental management system
Environmental performance	Performance improvement against the baseline review is reported publicly; EMAS registration can be removed for inadequate improvements against targets	Continual improvement of the management system must be demonstrated, internally to management
Use for marketing	Expressly forbidden	The ISO itself does not certify a firm to any standard; the firm is certified by a certification body to an ISO standard; in practice, a firm can be certified to an ISO standard and ISO 9001 and 14001 certifications (with the logo) are used for public and customer relations purposes
Audits	Audit of the system and of the continual improvement of the firm's environmental performance against its initial environmental impact review. Maximum frequency of three years. Certification can be removed for inadequate performance	Audit of the system only, against internal benchmarks; frequency not specified; no penalties for no improvements or for limited improvements
Corporate discretion	Limited by safeguards, such as: public environmental policy, third party certification, role of the EU Commission or the member states	The cornerstone of the whole scheme: the good will and faith of the company is the only guarantee that environmental performance is taken into account; the company decides how to have its scheme verified and what information it should disclose
EMS evaluation	Guaranteed by: deadlines, public statement, audits, evaluation and quantification elements	At the discretion of the company

EMS Verification	Third party verification required	Firm may choose to be third party or be internally (self) certified; verification not required
Disclosure	External communication of site-specific environmental information to public authorities and the public is required	Disclosure of information is at the discretion of the firm
Supplier chains	'Provisions shall be taken to ensure that contractors working at the site on the company's behalf apply environmental standards equivalent to the company's own.'	Not included in the standard, although there are strong concerns that this may become a market practice

Sources: ISO *ISO 14001*; CEN *Bridge Document*; EEC *Council Regulation No 183 6/93 of 29 June 1993, allowing voluntary participation by companies in the industrial sector in a community eco-management and audit scheme*; ISO Technical Board Recommendation 2/1993 adopting the recommendation from the SAGE for the establishment of a new technical committee (that became TC 207), January 1993

One of the key differences between ISO 14001 and EMAS is in their environmental policy requirements. EMAS is performance-based, and requires action to protect the environment and to prevent, reduce or eliminate pollution at source on the basis of the polluter pays principle. These performance results are externally supervized: 'this legal framework is…a way of ensuring that self-regulation is not left entirely open to interpretation by the company.'[32] Such controls are absent in the ISO 14001 policy; therefore, environmental officials need to ensure that domestic environmental objectives are achievable – for example, through a proper balance between ISO 14001 and the legal environment.

Another key difference is the quality of audit requirements. ISO 14001 requires audit for certification, and this can be done by an internal department or by an external consultant. Firms can then become certified to the standard, either by a self-declaration or through an accredited certifier. Governments should compare this dual system of auditing with the mandatory external audits under EMAS, or the mandatory external audits of financial statements for most types of corporations. The debate in Europe on the merits of EMAS versus ISO 14001 remains lively. In the UK, the BS 7750 standard was withdrawn in March 1997 and superseded by ISO 14001. The hundreds of British (as well as foreign) firms that were certified to BS 7750 can become ISO 14001 certified, because the British Standards Institute (BSI) considers them to be sufficiently similar.

On the basis of the difference in public access to information between EMAS and ISO 14001, the Danish authorities voted in 1995 against the European CEN ISO 14001 standard until there was clarity on the issue. To eliminate some of the differences, the Danish Parliament has adopted a law saying that all of the most polluting companies have to set up annual accounts of their environmental aspects and make them public. The Danish Environmental Protection Agency noted: 'It is our hope that the companies, being forced to make such annual accounts anyway, then will take the

BOX i.2 THE ISO 14001 ENVIRONMENTAL MANAGEMENT SYSTEM AS A SUBSET OF EMAS

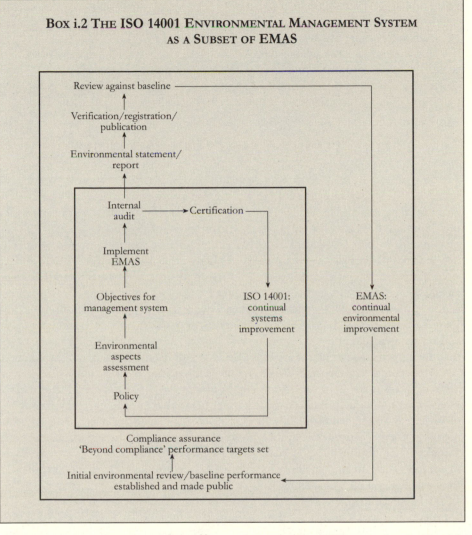

full step to be registered to EMAS.'[33] Another significant difference for the Danish regulators is registration and verification, where EMAS again sets higher standards (see Box i.2)

The Swedish Ministry of the Environment was content if ISO 14001 worked as a subset within EMAS, but made a commitment in March 1996 to 'work to assure that the obligations of EMAS [are] not watered down.'[34]

As noted earlier, the concept of an environmental management system is broadly defined at the early stages of development. Until now, the practical application of environmental management system programmes has been mainly within large enterprises in a few sectors, such as the chemical industry, in industrialized countries. Developing countries and even many industry sectors in the developed world do not have experience with evolving and implementing environmental management system programmes. If ISO 14001 is to be broadly adopted by the business community or regulatory agencies, it will need to adapt to a range of circumstances – or it will need to be amended at the five-year review of the standard in 2001.

In the meantime, the EC asked the CEN to develop a bridging document to span the gap between ISO 14001 and EMAS. The document has now been finalised, but as of January 1998 it is not certain that EMAS registration can be achieved by companies that have ISO 14001 certification coupled with the CEN bridge document.[35]

PUTTING TEETH INTO ISO 14001: ISO 14001 PLUS

The interaction of ISO 14001 with regulatory authorities has produced a range of reactions. As suggested by the Danish and Swedish cases, environmental agencies are creating an new amalgam, an ISO 14001 Plus approach. ISO 14001 Plus generally uses the momentum created for corporate environmental management systems from the proponents of ISO 14001 while modifying the structure and form in new ways. The new ISO 14001 Plus allows governments to say that they have used ISO 14001 but the resulting policy mixture is no longer consistent with strict ISO 14000 standards. The advantage for regulators is that they encourage corporate environmental management in the spirit of ISO 14001 while changing its character in its application. The most frequent fundamental changes are requirements for: conformance with regulatory laws and regulations; and public information and participation. ISO 14001 Plus also means that the implementation of the ISO standard will vary from jurisdiction to jurisdiction.

A corporate version of ISO 14001 Plus is also emerging for similar reasons: an interest in tools for better environmental performance. Corporate interest in ISO 14001 Plus has come principally from global firms that already have environmental management systems in place and often by those that already produce public environmental reports. Their interest in ISO 14001 is strategic: if the new standard becomes a market condition then they need to have a sense of what their firm will have to do to comply. These firms sometimes have invested in consulting advice and have aligned their environmental management system language so that it is consistent with ISO 14001 language in appropriate parts. This has been characterized as a 'wait and see' approach. It is also a no vote to the standard from these global firms, most of whom regard their existing environmental management systems as more demanding than ISO 14001; they will certify to ISO 14001 for market, not environmental, reasons if ISO 14001 becomes a requirement for suppliers.

For firms without current commitments to strong environmental management, some senior environmental and health and safety executives have used ISO 14001 to encourage their chief executive officers to review and alter their existing environmental management systems while introducing their own firm-specific elements into the review process. For public consumption, these firms can state that they are 'supporting ISO 14001', while in practice they have introduced environmental management elements into their own systems that are not part of ISO 14001 requirements.

The corporate ISO 14001 Plus approach is both an alliance with ISO and a substantive challenge to ISO 14000. As an alliance, it creates a public impression that firms have adopted the ISO standard. As a challenge, the demand for an ISO 14001 Plus approach is a demand for non-standardization and for performance assurances. It is a recognition that ISO 14001 certification on its own tells an interested firm or consumer nothing about the environmental performance of a firm: intelligent customers will have to learn what the crucial elements are of the 'plus' in ISO 14001.

THE SIGNIFICANCE OF ISO 14001 AND GLOBAL SUSTAINABLE INDUSTRIAL DEVELOPMENT: FIVE KEY QUESTIONS

There are a set of international currents in play around international standards, environmental management, EMSs, sustainable industrial development and trade. ISO 14001 has linked them together in a quite radical way. ISO 14001 uses terminology that overlaps with the domains of international environmental standards setting and with corporate self-regulation and environmental management, but its process and content are quite different from either. This is an international environmental management systems standard that has been created by industrial actors working through their national industry associations and their trade ministries, creating an EMS standard under the new GATT trade regime. It has sidelined the newly-emerging, dynamic and far more participatory area of international environmental standard-setting that was working towards sustainable development through multi-sectoral partnerships with environmental agencies, intergovernmental agencies, industry, scientists and environmental groups. At the same time, the global picture has changed. New issues – such as the standing of ISO 14001 in relation to the WTO and its authority vis-à-vis older intergovernmental environmental standards – are not yet well understood, and they will continue to be controversial over the next few years.[36] Expectations are being raised that ISO 14001 will become a condition of doing business globally, and developing countries are eager to expand their export markets. In the meantime, ISO 14001 is being presented to the public and regulators as a comprehensive tool that will give firms a new way to control their environmental impact, and therefore should be a basis for a new relationship between industry and the private sector.[37]

This book is arranged around six rhetorical questions. Question 1: does the ISO 14000 series reinforce intergovernmental environmental standard setting or advance trends in sustainable industrial development? Most environmental officials and environmental groups active on the international stage are familiar with the substance and processes of intergovernmental environmental standard setting, and have been participants in some of these initiatives. In many cases, environmental agreements have been based on best practice in one country, and have then become a benchmark for new national regulation in other countries that are signatories to the agreement. In addition, the years before and after the Rio Earth Summit were characterized by an increase in the scope of corporate environmental initiatives. Leading firms have integrated sustainable development concepts – including commitments to pollution prevention, the polluter pays principle, and the application of country standards abroad – into their environmental practices, policies and reports. Many of the assumptions of sustainable development – public–private partnerships and participation, transparency, environmental performance improvement, and accountability – are absent in ISO 14001.

Question 2: could the process within the ISO represent the perspectives of the major environmental stakeholders? The process of ISO decision-making is far more exclusive than other arenas of international environmental standard setting. Developing-country standards officials and environmental nongovernmental organizations (NGOs) who became involved in ISO 14001 came into the ISO 14000 process very late. Very few were involved prior to the summer of 1995, when the key standard, ISO 14001, was voted a draft international standard. They were involved too late to make effective interventions. Some officials were not aware of the decision-making processes and procedures in the ISO. Intergovernmental meetings, for instance, operate differently. Officials from developing countries and NGOs felt frustrated that they could not use their time effectively. As so few developing countries or NGOs participated at all in the process, there was concern about whether the process had allowed for development or environment issues to be adequately represented. Their strong sense was that key procedural issues kept the developing countries, NGOs, and others effectively out of the ISO drafting and negotiation process.

Question 3: does the new GATT agreement change the status of ISO standards? The new and radical element to the ISO 14001 package is the relationship between the ISO and the World Trade Organization (WTO). Under GATT rules, private sector organizations such as the ISO have the authority to set international standards that have legal standing under the GATT Agreement on Technical Barriers to Trade. As a result, ISO international standards may now have greater status through their ties to GATT sanctions than new or existing international standards established through other intergovernmental organizations and processes, such as United Nations agencies and affiliated bodies.

The ISO recognizes the scope of the WTO to encourage the adoption and use of international standards wherever possible, and wishes to sustain its initiative as the leader in standards information services, standards development, and international conformity-assessment programmes. The ISO intends to become recognized as providing a special technical support role in relation to the new and expanded WTO programme.[38] When governments decide to set new standards or revise outdated standards, they now must take the ISO standards into consideration. If governments ignore ISO standards when setting their national, subnational or local standards, then the standard may be challenged by foreign governments as a technical barrier to trade. This is a new hurdle for governments in developing innovative policy options.

Question 4: what are the economic consequences of ISO 14001? ISO 14001 comes at a price and the return on investment is uncertain. The strong perception in developing countries is that ISO 14001 is a ticket of market access, and that not having certification could jeopardize existing and future international contracts. Much of the interest in ISO 14001 is reactive. It stems from a fear that the market pressure that arose from the ISO 9000 quality standards will be repeated and interest is not a proactive sense of environmental management.[39] The price of this admission ticket can be very high. It is unclear that there is an 'added value' of economic or environmental performance improvement. The costs may be higher in developing countries, in part because governments and industries have less experience with corporate environmental management. Despite this lack of experience, developing country regulators are being encouraged to believe that they can leapfrog the so-called command-control phase of regulation with ISO 14001 and move directly into a 'new paradigm of partnership'. Such an attempt may carry enormous risks for environment and public policy.

Question 5: how can ISO 14001 be integrated into public law and policy? ISO on its own will not bring improved environmental performance. ISO 14001 is a process, not a performance, standard. It will not necessarily raise the level of certified firms' environmental performance. Various countries and firms are seeking environmental management systems that will improve environmental performance and provide a new basis for public–private sector trust. Regulators in developed and developing countries are proposing elements that need to be added to the 14001 standard to provide public assurances. ISO 'plus' elements include key aspects of sustainable industrial development.

Question 6 : can something be done to regain the initiative for global sustainable industrial development? A series of initiatives over the past ten years have begun to flesh out the ingredients of global sustainable industrial development. Prompted or catalysed by an emergent public environmental consciousness, firms around the world have developed a new sense of local and global corporate environmental responsibility. This chapter sketches out some of the elements of this new trend and where ISO 14001 fits into this picture. At the moment, firms interested in the global or local sustainable industrial development agenda can choose to absorb all or part of ISO 14001, together with their own additional environmental management standards (the ISO Plus approach); or they can pursue their own standards of environmental excellence and ignore ISO 14001 altogether.

However, the future of ISO 14001 may not be left to rest on the question of environmental standards. Given current scenarios, particularly in Asia, there is a strong possibility that ISO 14001 will be sold and purchased not on hopes for environmental improvement but on fears of market conditions. The fact that ISO 14001 may be implemented for market reasons is a reality that needs to be dealt with by those who remain interested in global environmental standards and sustainable industrial development. This chapter concludes by presenting a 'gap analysis' for stakeholders in global environmental standards who need to understand the new players in this area and the opportunities that exist for negotiation and intervention in the ISO and GATT processes. It is still possible to insist that where the institutions and policies of economic globalization and standardization affect issues of sustainable industrial development, they need to grapple with the processes, institutions and issues that have created and nurtured the concepts of sustainable development and corporate responsibility.

CONCLUSION

On its own, ISO 14001 cannot achieve sustainable industrial development or even environmental performance improvement – for a certifying firm, for its suppliers, for regulators interested in a new public–private partnership, for the intergovernmental community seeking to address global environmental problems, or for communities interested in the environmental impact of industrial facilities in their neighbourhoods. ISO 14001 was catalysed as a consequence of these issues, but chose to address a narrower, and in the end a different, agenda.

The challenge now remains to work out how to develop a model for environmental management that will bring enduring environmental performance improvement and provide enough information to the public to earn the firm's right to self-regulation. This may or may not be possible with a standardized approach to process and environmental management systems. The argument that attention to the environmental process brings environmental improvements has yet to be proven. But whatever the process, refocussing the debate on environmental management systems will require firms to grapple with the 'plus' in ISO 14001 Plus –issues that have been integral to the sustainable development agenda for years. These include transparency, democracy, accountability, partnership, the global application of international environmental standards and of best national practice abroad where regulations are weaker, and so on. These issues, and also related ISO-specific issues such as certifier accreditation and mutual recognition of national standards, will become central to the ISO 14001 debates in the coming months – and will result in 'non-standard' applications of the standard. But without these additions to ISO 14001, there will be no relationship between ISO 14001 and sustainable industrial development. On the other hand, it is possible that ISO 14001 may become, like many ISO standards, a market instrument – in this case with no connections to its original environmental moorings.

Chapter 1

Does ISO 14000 Series Reinforce Intergovernmental Environmental Agreements or Advance Trends in Sustainable Industrial Development?

INTRODUCTION

As a management tool, environmental management systems are a rather new creation. In the 1980s, businesses began to figure out how to organise themselves in response to their ecological, public and legal obligations. By the 1990s, leading firms were continuing to develop and enlarge their environmental management systems. Several new issues became synonymous with leading global environmental policy and practice. International industry associations and many global firms made commitments in their environmental policies to sustainable development, the precautionary principle and community involvement. Many began to explore how to create and impose global corporate-wide environment and sustainable development standards while being sensistive to local ecosystems. Others started to produce public environmental reports. With the advent of the internet, firms are now beginning to post their environmental policies and reports on their web sites. The technology will soon exist for these to be updated in 'real time'. Some firms are already committed to regular – six-monthly – updates, far more rapid than the once-every-one-or-two-years environmental reporting that we have seen in the past.

During this period, environmental managers discovered that sustainable development meant that they had to take into account labour conditions, employees' health and safety, community relations, and other 'soft' social and cultural factors – as well as uncertain environmental science in relation to ecosystems or the global impact of industrial activity on the global climate. They found that simple focus on complying with existing laws and regulations could mean that they missed both the economic opportunities that came from investing in environmental technologies, as well as the dynamically changing public perception of respect for the environment. Firms that initiated environmental management systems in order to ensure compliance and reduce negative publicity discovered that savings and profits could be made from incorporating environmental management systems in early facility or product design. They also found that public expectations required them to learn about, and manage: climate change, persistent organic pollutants; land-based sources of marine pollution; and product take-back – to name only a few of the topics on the current corporate EMS agenda.

Other firms are exploring these issues in an eclectic range of strategic partnerships. Some have formed links with progressive non-governmental organizations that promote various environmental standards and approaches for integrating environment and industrial activity. The CERES principles, which stress public reporting and ecosystem responsibility, have been endorsed by major global firms such as General Motors, Polaroid, Sun Oil and HB Fuller. The Natural Step Principles, based on the assumption of environmental resource limits and closed-loop systems, have been endorsed by international companies such as Electrolux and Ikea. European Partners for Environment in Brussels brings together leading industrial partners with environmental NGOs and government officials to address complex issues on the sustainable industrial development agenda.

ISO 14001 is heralded by its proponents as industry's answer to the challenge of sustainable development. Advertising copy in the Richard Clements *Complete Guide to ISO 14000* is headlined: 'ISO 14000 is the hot new set of environmental management standards that add up to a global Green Stamp of Approval'.[1] The head of the American National Standards Institute (ANSI) delegation to TC 207 presents ISO 14000 as an 'instrument for sustainable development' at various industry meetings around the world.[2] The front page of the ISO newsletter on ISO 14000 in March 1997 had a half-page photo of a tree in Bavaria, Germany, and is captioned: 'Keeping our planet intact and preserving its pristine beauty while encouraging sustainable economic growth by judicious environmental management standards is the ultimate goal of ISO/TC 207.'[3]

The March 1997 edition of the *Smithsonian* has a full-page advertisement from the Japanese electronics firm NEC. In a stunning photograph of flowers and vegetables, NEC comments:

> ISO 14001…environmental standards written in nature's own hand. Nature always has a hand in writing the standards of our own existence, because nature is the standard of all life. Having long embraced measures that preserve and protect the environment, NEC enthusiastically supports the international environmental standards of the ISO 14000 series. These comprehensive guidelines bring a global focus to environmental management issues and allow organizations to compare their efforts against internationally accepted criteria. Written hand in hand with nature, ISO 14000 spells good news for the environment.[4]

Although ISO 14001 started out with a broad mandate, it ended up being written by a small group of business executives, hand in hand not with nature, but often with lawyers concerned about the legal obligations ISO 14001 may create in their home countries. Unfortunately, the ISO international environmental management systems standard was not founded on the best environmental management system in use by transnational corporations. It did not build upon the existing agreed intergovernmental understandings and conventions. This chapter will show that ISO 14001 makes no reference to the substance or process of any of these constructive developments. It will also show how concepts crucial to sustainable development, that were in the initial thinking and texts in ISO 14001, were watered down or completely diluted during the negotiation process. These include pollution prevention, the polluter pays principle, public participation, an initial environmental impact review, and performance reporting. Inferences that ISO 14001 can, on its own, bring sustainable industrial development are just that: an act of faith.

Proponents of the new environmental systems standard ISO 14001 make it sound like intergovernmental environmental standards, although it is not. It is the result of a private-sector voluntary initiative, but the differences are sometimes blurred by the media and general public. The NEC advertisement, for example, that speaks of 'internationally accepted criteria' is referring not to intergovernmental environmental criteria, but to business systems criteria. In contrast to this private-sector standard, intergovernmental environmental agreements have for some years been working to elevate the standard of international environmental performance. The result has been a set of agreements and standards that integrate sustainable development concepts – precisely those concepts that were removed from ISO 14001.

ISO 14001: REVERSING THE TREND TO SUSTAINABLE INDUSTRIAL DEVELOPMENT

While the EU negotiated EMAS and the British defined the first standards for environmental management systems, the ISO conducted their own discussions on the issue of environmental management. ISO recognized that the concepts of sustainable development and environmental protection had evolved to the extent that they were becoming part of legal and business practice. The ISO/IEC Strategic Advisory Group on Environment (SAGE) was established inter alia to 'assess the needs for future international standardization work to promote *worldwide application of the key elements embodied in the concept of sustainable industrial development* (emphasis added)'.[5]

As part of its preparatory work, the ISO secretariat distributed a position paper defining sustainable development and environmental management guiding principles as:

> 2.1.2. The concept of sustainable development is now embraced by many government and business leaders. For business purposes, sustainable development means that operating activities should meet the needs of present stakeholders, (shareholders, employees, consumers and communities) without impairing the ability of future generations to meet their needs.
> 2.1.3. Environmental protection is an important element but only one element of sustainable development. With respect to the environment, the aim is to ensure that current use of environment and natural resources does not damage prospects for use by future generations.[6]

In their subsequent negotiations, the ISO could have built upon this definition of sustainable development as well as advances among some of the leading industry associations and individual businesses in implementing sustainable development. The standard that ISO adopted, however, is far more limited in scope and commitment. Most crucially, the initial interest in standards for environmental management, which was of significance to global firms and to the intergovernmental process for some years, began to focus on standards for environmental management systems. With this switch of language, the focus on performance improvement was replaced with a focus on process and systems improvement, with the inference that these could affect performance. The result is that the ISO international environmental management system standard omits any explicit link between environmental management and sustainable development.

SUSTAINABLE INDUSTRIAL DEVELOPMENT AND VOLUNTARY INTERNATIONAL CORPORATE ENVIRONMENTAL STANDARDS

Over the last 15 years, several industry and corporate initiatives have defined a range of responses to the challenge of environmental management and sustainable development. These have been characterized by strong agreement on the principle of sustainable development, but equally strong debate about its meaning. New terminology emerged from this debate, such as 'economically and environmentally sustainable development', 'sustainable industrial development' and 'sustainable management system'.[7] Advocates of these views stress the compatibility of economic and environmental investments and state that environmental protection makes good business sense. In practice, advocates clearly feel that there are financial costs to better environmental management. This support for sustainable development is usually accompanied by appeals to regulators to provide incentives for environmentally sound practices that go 'beyond compliance', thereby reducing cost or risk for environmental innovators and leaders.[8]

INDUSTRY ASSOCIATIONS

In the absence of a strong national or international regulatory framework, many industry associations have established voluntary guidelines or standards of practice (see Box 1.1). The International Chamber of Commerce produced its first environmental statement in 1965, and in preparation for the Rio Earth Summit later issued a Business Charter on Sustainable Development. As a result of the industrial disaster at the Union Carbide plant in Bhopal in 1985, the Canadian Chemical Producer's Association launched the Responsible Care® initiative, which was subsequently adopted by the European Chemical Industry Council, the US Chemical Manufacturers Association and several other national chemical industry associations around the world. In 1989, an oil tanker accident in Alaska, the *Exxon Valdez*, resulted in the Valdez Principles, an environmental code of conduct defined by public interest groups and stressing public reporting. It was subsequently renamed the CERES Principles, after the drafting group: the Coalition for Environmentally Responsible Economies and Societies.

Industry associations generally try to develop positions on the environment that are acceptable to a majority of its members. Their policy statements represent attempts to soften potentially difficult topics for individual members and to reassure a some-

---

BOX 1.1 SELECTED INDUSTRY ASSOCIATION ENVIRONMENTAL GUIDELINES WITH INTERNATIONAL APPLICATION

Alliance Internationale de Tourism/ Federation Internationale de l'Automobile – ATI/FTA (1992): Charter of Ethics for Tourism and the Environment

Group of International Banks (1992): Statement by Banks on Environment and Sustainable Development

International Chamber of Commerce – ICC (1991): Business Charter on Sustainable Development

International Council on Metals and the Environment – ICME (1993): Environmental Charter

International Federation of Consulting Engineers – FIDIC (1990): Consulting Engineers and the Environment

Keidanren – Japan (1992 & 1996): Keidanren Global Environment Charter; Keidanren Appeal on Environment

World Business Council for Sustainable Development – WBCSD (1992): Declaration of the Business Council for Sustainable Development

World Travel and Tourism Council – WTTC (1991): World Travel and Tourism Council Environmental Guidelines

Source: UNCTAD (1996) *Self-Regulation of Environmental Management* UN Publications, New York and Geneva

---

times skeptical global or local community that there are environmentally responsible firms within the industry. One might expect these statements to be environmentally weak; however, the past decade has seen a proliferation of environmental statements from trade associations that integrate a new language of corporate environmental management. These cover topics as diverse as contract terms for the transfer of potentially hazardous chemical technologies, to the conditions for sustainable tourism. For example, the July 1996 'Keidanren Appeal on Environment' calls for the voluntary action of Japanese industry, directed at conserving the global environment by reconfirming environmental ethics, realizing eco-efficiency and tightening voluntary efforts.

A 1996 UNCTAD report evaluates industry's environmental commitments in relation to the recommendations in *Agenda 21*.[9] This shows that there are areas where industry has been conspicuously reluctant to move, including the issues of public reporting, technology transfer and environmental accounting.[10] But it also shows that industry guidelines tend to make statements on issues that are central to sustainable development, and which represent a significant leap forward in industry's position on self-regulation. The guidelines tend to integrate and make commitments on concepts such as community development, pollution prevention, the polluter pays principle, and the precautionary principle. What is striking is the level to which these codes were responsive to a new set of public issues.[11] In contrast, ISO 14001 makes no reference to any of these concepts in its policy guidelines, or elsewhere.[12]

TRANSNATIONAL CORPORATIONS

There is no magic formula for the perfect global environmental management system. In 1993, the UN Centre on Transnational Corporations released their study

Environmental Management in TNCs: Report on the Benchmark Corporate Environmental Survey.
The study noted the diversity of methods for global environmental management systems and the extent to which management innovations were beginning to appear in the area of environmental management.[13] Since then, this domain has steadily expanded, with numerous corporate efforts at the national, regional and international level.

Global environmental policies are being produced by scores of leading multinational corporations. Some refer to guidelines set by industry associations, others to recommendations or standards made by intergovernmental bodies. Ciba Geigy's 1993 corporate environmental report states that Ciba Geigy applies the same objectives for safety and environmental protection to all countries in which they operate, a statement that is equivalent to the operating standards recommendation in Agenda 21. The Amoco Corporation states: 'Conduct of employees outside the United States may be subject to the criminal laws of the United States…as well as the laws of countries in which you reside and do business… Principles of compliance apply equally to all the laws of all the countries in which Amoco operates.'[14] The *Monsanto Pledge*, originally adopted in January 1990, includes a commitment to achieve sustainable development for the good of all people in both developed and less developed nations. NEC's environmental charter has ten principles, one of which is to 'respect and adhere to national and regional environmental regulations [and to] strengthen and enforce even stricter environmental NEC standards.'[15]

Many global firms now incorporate international environmental reporting with their home-country reporting. NEC, for example, produces mainly national or site-specific environmental data in its environmental report, but produces a graph of 'Changes in the Quantity of Ozone Layer Depleting Chemicals' for its global operations, showing that it abolished ozone depleting compounds (ODCs) well before the 'world regulation' requirement in December 1995.[16] In addition to complying with international treaty obligations, there is a dynamic area of global environmental self-regulation where a firm's policies and practices go beyond complying with home- or host-country laws. Proctor & Gamble produce global data on annual trends in packaging material by region – North America, Europe, Far East, Latin America – and by business sector – health and beauty care; laundry and cleaning; food and beverage; and paper. These are all reported against weight and production figures. They also report data on shipments and manufacturing emissions in various waste categories; effluents (including water); and energy consumption.[17] Dow Chemical have for some years used the reporting structure of the US Responsible Care® programme as the basis for reporting from all their international facilities.[18] Toyota in Japan reports on their global CO_2 emissions; Volkswagen in Germany produces a 110-page environmental report that includes global emissions data and strong environmental requirements of their suppliers and subcontractors, including 'continuous improvement of production and product measured against ecological criteria.'[19] ISO 14000 missed the opportunity to use these leading, relevant and practical examples of international environmental management systems as the basis for the ISO standard.

INTERNATIONAL SELF-REGULATION IN DEVELOPING COUNTRIES

There are very few policy options that would effectively ensure that large private-sector actors and transnational corporations protect the environment, contribute to local economic development, and are sensitive to cultural and social traditions. International regulation will be resisted by TNCs and by governments. Individual transnational corporations (TNCs) are unlikely to move so far ahead of the curve that they take unilateral economic risks, or feel that they do. But without action, economic globalization will continually jeopardize global environmental and social priorities, and sustainable development will be unachieveable. Self-regulation can have a special place, particularly internationally. Private codes and some notion of private-sector environmental responsibility could potentially serve as valuable adjuncts to intergovernmental programmes and public-sector initiatives when transferring environmental technologies and management practices to developing nations. Before ISO 14001 was created, advocates of this concept made the tentative proposition that there could be an opportunity for the ISO to play a pivotal role. In the event, ISO 14001 missed the opportunity to play a role in sustainable industrial development.[20]

One of the most basic ingredients of self-regulation is that a firm is committed to meeting or surpassing existing environmental regulations or standards. The concept of self-regulation, when applied internationally, is that where relevant standards do not exist or are ill-defined, then a voluntary environmental policy should specify what standards will be adopted, and these should clearly be 'beyond compliance.'[21] It is on this basis that national governments in developed countries have offered regulatory relief and incentives towards self-regulation. It is also on this basis that the concept has been extended to the developing world with its relatively less well developed public environmental infrastructure. Nevertheless, ISO 14000 adopted an approach that is two steps lower than a 'beyond compliance' self-regulation framework. ISO 14001-certified firms do not need to be 'in compliance'; they must state in their policy only that they are *committed to compliance*.

The question of how to establish international corporate environmental policy in a way that protects both the firm and the environment is not yet resolved, in principle or in practice. This debate on policy is still in its infancy and perhaps, therefore, is characterized more by heat than by light. However, the heat should not obscure this fact: significant strides have been made at all levels and by all sectors in international environmental policy and practice that moves the agenda of sustainable industrial development forward. Clearly, the ISO could have reinforced trends in business codes of conduct to conform to home country standards abroad, but it did not. The 'commitment to compliance' is inherently a local obligation. Consequently, as a tool for certifying environmental responsibility, ISO 14001 adds little.[22] Furthermore, the ISO could have included commitments such as extending technological and educational support to local industry, reducing levels of pollution and greenhouse gases worldwide, or increasing public reporting and participation, but it did not. These specific performance standards could have been based, in part, on intergovernmentally adopted conventions and could have moved industry towards a stronger definition of a sustainably managed company. It is true that participants in the process were wary of setting performance-based specifications on the grounds that these are the province of national and international regulation. However, the ISO could have referred to performance standards or set them through engineering-based performance specifications, in line with past ISO practices (see Chapter 2).[23] It did not. It only set a commitment to continuously improving the management system.

IMPLEMENTING INTERNATIONAL ENVIRONMENTAL MANAGEMENT

The most visible evidence of managing international environmental impacts is the current generation of corporate environmental reports. Several hundred global corporations now produce annual environmental reports in addition to a corporate financial document. These reports illustrate how members of the corporate community are attempting to implement, as well as influence, international environmental management.

Corporate environmental reports do not follow a standard format. Instead, they are a mixture of policy statements, anecdotes and some data. Often the data is derived from reporting that the firm has to do anyway under national law. In 1994, the UNEP's Industry and Environment Office produced a technical report on company environmental reporting to measure the progress of business and industry.[24] It identified 50 ingredients or building blocks for a corporate environmental report. Five broad clusters are: management policies and systems; an input–output inventory of the environmental impacts of production processes and products, financial implications of environmental actions; relationships with environmental stakeholders; and the sustainable development agenda. Many of these relate to environmental performance (and not conformance), such as materials use, waste output, accidents, product impacts, and environmental liabilities. One component is global development issues – the reporting on 'efforts to address the range of objectives and activities outlined in *Agenda 21*'.

Performance elements have been integral to the major initiatives in corporate self-regulation and to the design of environmental management systems. Responsible Care®, an environmental-management system programme established by the chemical industry, contains performance-based systems established by the national associations of chemical firms. The Responsible Care® standards must be translated into a number of operational or practice areas, with measurable targets set for performance improvement. ISO 14001, on the other hand, does not focus on the environmental performance of a facility or corporation and does not require a public environmental report of any type.

Environmental management systems can operate at the level of the site, nationwide or corporate-wide. For business enterprises with operations in multiple countries, this is an important distinction because an environmental management system committed to comply with local laws could allow the business to have lower standards in places where there is a weaker regulatory environment. As mentioned above, leading global firms have reacted to this issue by adopting worldwide policies in their environmental management system and their corporate environmental ethos (see Box 1.2). Mobil's policy, for example, 'goes beyond compliance and states that Mobil and its affiliates will con-

---

BOX 1.2 PRIVATE-SECTOR POLICY STATEMENTS SUPPORTING GLOBAL CORPORATE ENVIRONMENTAL MANAGEMENT

Industry Associations

CERES: US

We intend to make consistent, measurable progress in implementing these principles and to apply them to all aspects of our operations throughout the world (CERES, introduction). We will conduct and make public an annual self-evaluation of our progress in implementing these principles and in complying with applicable laws and regulations throughout our worldwide operations.

Keizai Doyukai: Japan

Japan should take the initiative in promoting an international framework to tackle the preservation of the global environment, and this should be a major pillar of Japan's international contribution. To do this, Japan should make its basic concept and policies clear both at home and abroad. It must be able to respond flexibly to harmonize economic development and environmental preservation.

ICC: France

To continue to improve corporate policies, programmes and environmental performance, taking into account technical developments, scientific understanding, consumer needs and community expectations, with legal regulations as starting point; and to apply the same criteria internationally.

Companies

ICI: UK, 1994

This policy applies throughout ICI and our subsidiaries worldwide (Preamble). ICI pledges to encourage, through positive interaction within the industry, the worldwide development and implementation of the principles of ... the ICC's Business Charter for Sustainable Development (Policy).

Ciba-Geigy: Switzerland, 1993

We apply the same objectives for safety and environmental protection in all countries where we operate.

Mobil: US, 1994

Our policy goes beyond compliance and states that Mobil and its affiliates will continue to conduct their worldwide activities with full concern for safeguarding public health and protecting the environment in the absence of local laws and regulations.

Showa Denko: Japan, 1993

Participate eagerly in various activities for protection of the global environment and contribute to the good of society by helping restructuring of the economic and social systems into a more harmonious one with the global environment to strive for a global issue of environmental preservation (Report titled: *HFC* 134a, p 2).

Sources: UNCTAD, *Self-Regulation of Environmental Management*, UN Publications, New York and Geneva, 1996; Coalition for Environmentally Responsible Economies, *CERES Principles*, 1989, Principle 1D; Keizai Doyukai, *Kezai Doyukai Report 1993*, p 6; International Chamber of Commerce, *Business Charter for Sustainable Development*, 1989, Principle 3; Mobil, *Protecting the Environment*, 1993, p 30; ICI *Environmental Performance*, 1993, p 16; CIBA, *A Matter of Principle: CIBA's Commitment to Safety and Environmental Protection*, 1993, p 5. CIBA-Geigy and Sandoz merged in 1996/97 to form Novartis.

---

tinue to conduct their worldwide activities with full concern for safeguarding public health and protecting the environment in the absence of local laws and regulations.'

While ISO 14001 allows certification of the site or of a firm, it is expected that most certification will be at the site level. This is reflected in the auditing guidance documents that discuss the definition of site but do not address the auditing issues related to defining a firm.

Intergovernmental Environmental Standard Setting

For decades, governments have been involved in setting international environmental standards and codes of conduct or practice. These standards, typically produced in consultation with business, environmental and other interest groups, provide codes of practice to reduce the potential for negative environmental impacts. The outcome of one discussion or negotiation often influences the basic framework for subsequent meetings.

Some of these intergovernmental standards are 'soft law' – in other words, non-binding declarations, codes of conduct, recommendations, or proclamations. Statements or resolutions to be 'better neighbours' or to do a 'good job' provide flexibility to governments and other parties. Though not bound by them, governments cannot in good faith ignore them completely. And therein lies the power of consensus statements such as *Agenda 21*, or the 1985 FAO Code of Conduct on the Distribution and Use of Pesticides.

Standards set through intergovernmental treaties, in contrast, are 'hard law'. As a convention, they must be ratified by signatory governments, and the standards are then incorporated into national law. Examples of this include the 1991 Convention on Environmental Impact Assessment in a Transboundary Context or the 1990 ILO Convention Concerning Safety in the Use of Chemicals at Work. Such agreements typically build on consensus that has been achieved over time as a result of soft law negotiations and discussions.

ISO standards fall into a separate category because they are adopted by a body whose members include the national standard-setting bodies that are more fully described in Chapter 2. ISO standards per se are not legally binding on any of the parties, though many adopt them within a national framework of standards that is used voluntarily by enterprises operating in that country. However, there are two ways that this ISO standard may, in practice, be involuntary. Firstly, ISO standards are given new status as international reference measures under the new GATT (see Chapter 3). Secondly, ISO standards often become a de facto condition of the marketplace. In the case of ISO 9000, not only did this standard become a market condition; it also became a prerequisite of some government or government-agency procurement contracts. In addition, there are debates emerging about self-regulation within national regulatory regimes that consider how or whether to integrate environmental management systems into these regimes. ISO 14001 plays a role in these discussions (see Chapter 4).

The interaction of international environmental agreements of all types has progressively and incrementally raised environmental, health and safety standards for operations and management. Existing standards are of particular relevance to ISO 14001 because they include a broad range of non-binding guidelines, codes of conduct and mandatory requirements. The International Labour Organization (ILO), for example, has adopted 174 conventions and 181 recommendations. These standards form an international labour code that is used as a guideline for national policy, legislation and practice in all spheres of labour activities, including the 1977 Tripartite Declaration of Principles Concerning Multinational Enterprises and Social Policy.[25] Since its establishment in 1972, the UN Environment Programme (UNEP) has been the forum for many international environmental negotiations. UNEP's Industry and Environment

---

BOX 1.3 SELECTED PUBLIC-SECTOR INTERNATIONAL ENVIRONMENTAL TREATIES, AGREEMENTS AND GUIDELINES

ECOSOC: Recommendations on the Transport of Hazardous Goods (Geneva, 1957)
FAO: International Code of Conduct on the Distribution and Use of Pesticides (Rome, 1985)
ILO: Tripartite Declaration of Principles Concerning Multinational Enterprises and Social Policy, (Geneva, 1977)
ILO: Code of Practice on Accident Prevention (Geneva, 1993)
OECD: Guidelines for Multinational Enterprises (Paris, 1976/1985)
UNEP: Awareness and Preparedness for Emergencies at the Local Level (APELL) (Paris, 1988).
UNEP: Guidelines on Offshore Mining and Drilling (Nairobi, 1982)
UNEP: Guidelines on Protection of the Marine Environment from Land-Based Sources (Montreal, 1985)
UNEP: Montreal Protocol on Substances that Deplete the Ozone Layer (Montreal, 1987)
UNEP: Convention on Environmental Impact Assessment (EIA) in a Transboundary Context (Espoo, 1991)

Office has issued several reports on corporate management systems, such as *Awareness and Preparedness for Emergencies at the Local Level* (Paris, 1988).

The Organization for Economic Cooperation and Development (OECD) provides a forum and framework for setting standards among the 27 more industrialized nations. In 1985 it agreed upon a new environmental chapter in its *Guidelines for Multinational Enterprises*. In 1990 the OECD Council adopted a recommendation on accident prevention with specific obligations for suppliers of hazardous technology. Following the UN Conference on Environment and Development, the UNEP set policies and methods for the safe management of chemicals and for public reporting on the release and transfer of pollutants. The conference itself was a watershed in bringing together nongovernmental stakeholders defined as labour, business, youth, local authorities, environmental groups, women, scientists, farmers, and indigenous peoples. These were all given unprecedented access to the formal deliberations with the annual sessions of the Commission on Sustainable Development. Subsequent to the UNCED, many national 'roundtables' were established to consider how to achieve the goal of sustainable development. Members were drawn from all sectors including industry, and some of their recommendations contain an agenda for sustainable industrial development.

While some new sustainable development initiatives arose out of the UNCED process, many of the recommendations in Agenda 21 were based on pre-existing international agreements or guidelines used at the national level. As environmental, health and safety issues become more important for citizens and workers, many international environmental laws and voluntary agreements are adopted, often based on existing best national practices. The US Toxic Release Inventory (TRI), for example, requires US firms to publicly report on national emissions of specific hazardous chemicals. IBM used this reporting category as the basis for their international disclosure of chemical releases.[26] Used by some large European multinationals, emissions reporting was then included in Agenda 21.[27] Also spurred by the TRI, the European Union, in

September 1996, integrated a Polluting Emissions Register with a public disclosure requirement within its Integrated Pollution Prevention and Control Directive.[28]

These trends have not been continued with ISO 14001. During the drafting process, proposals to have an environmental effects register, based on BS7750, were removed. The register was to be a basis for evaluating environmental improvement. The initial environmental review requirement created 'a procedure to identify the environmental aspects of its activities, products and services over which it can be expected to have an influence, in order to determine those which have or can have significant impacts on the environment.'[29] Noting this and other dilutions in the text, one consultant remarked that 'although ISO 14001 might be a remarkable piece regarding the speed in which it was arrived at – this same speed and all the haggling involved have contrived to render it quite boneless. The whole concept is flawed in the aspect of actually furthering the environmental performance of companies.'[30]

In adopting *Agenda 21*, governments called for specific actions. In particular, the action plan includes 32 provisions for transnational corporations and other industrial actors.[31] *Agenda 21* provisions and guidelines on corporate environmental management, environmentally sound production, and risk and hazard minimization are often based on existing national law or international agreements, while the recommendations in areas such as green accounting are based on a developing consensus, among academics and policy researchers, that action in this area is needed. (see Annex C for a list of the 32 provisions).

ISO 14001 makes no explicit reference to these global and regional environmental, health and safety conventions or to the negotiated conclusions of Agenda 21. For developing countries, this represents a loss. According to a senior official at the Turkish Standards Institution, 'activities of ISO and UN agencies engaged in standardization should not take place in isolation but should be integrated.'[32] By ignoring global best practice, ISO 14001 certification in a country with weak applicable laws and regulations could simply mean complying with local regulation.[33] It does not have a context of better practice elsewhere. International firms operating in such countries, who were moving in the direction of applying sustainable development principles and the worldwide application of home-country or highest corporate standards of environmental management, now have little incentive to maintain this momentum. ISO 14001 could reverse the direction of global environmental standard setting.

There are a number of ways to deal with uneven development and the application of international environmental standards, and each has its merits and flaws. The easiest is to create a standard, or to standardize practice, at the lowest common denominator. This is the route chosen in ISO 14001. Some developed country proponents of ISO 14001 have argued that this route was chosen out of sensitivity for developing countries.[34] It is to be expected that developing countries would be concerned about high performance standards and would have raised this as an issue had they participated effectively in the ISO process. This is not to say that these concerns and realities could not have been taken into account, as has been done consistently in other intergovernmental fora. Moreover, the argument that the bar was lowered out of concern for developing countries may be deceptive. The reality is that the text was softened throughout the process by ANSI (US) negotiators concerned with domestic US environmental regulations and trends and the possible strength of the European Union's EMAS.

Within the intergovernmental community, the regular method of addressing uneven development is to set higher expectations and performance standards in international agreements while creating special conditions that will make room for disadvantaged groups entry on equitable terms. Thus, for example, the Framework Convention on Climate Change has different implementation requirements for developed and developing countries.

> The extent to which developing country parties will effectively be able to implement their commitments under the convention will depend on the effective implementation by developed country parties of their commitments under the convention relating to financial resources and their willingness to transfer technology and to take fully into account that economic and social development and poverty eradication are the first and overriding priorities of the developing country parties.[35]

Similarly, the rules and standards of the FAO International Code of Conduct on the Distribution and Use of Pesticides 'takes into account the special circumstances of developing countries.' The rules and standards of the Vienna Convention (including the Montreal Protocol) for the Protection of the Ozone Layer have special considerations for developing countries. If a developing country 'considers itself unable to comply with control measures because of inadequate financial or technical assistance provided under the protocol, it may notify the Ozone Secretariat and the Parties can consider not invoking the non-compliance procedures against the notifying Party'.[36]

CONCLUSION

A competing international environmental standard has been created without reference to intergovernmental environmental agreements. In terms of policy commitments or practical standards for sustainable industrial development, this new ISO standard is well below the environmental standards used by leading global firms and international industry associations. It is not helpful, now, to have the term 'international environmental standard' cover both a range of public-sector standards and this ISO private-sector standard, without distinguishing between them. One of the complexities that will arise from their competing nature is their standing in international law and practice. This will be of particular significance for the conduct of multinational firms in the developing world.

Obviously, an international firm does not need to conform to international standards if the host country has not ratified an agreement. But the advantage of international soft law is that this practice provides a standard for global firms, even in the absence of equivalent national standards or international interest. Moreover, the recent trend within developing countries has been towards implementing national legislation that applies environmental standards and concepts. Since ISO 14001 did not refer to this whole area of intergovernmental environmental agreements and standards, it missed the opportunity to integrate the substance of these years of work into their new international standard. How this happened is the subject of Chapter 2.

Does the Process Within the ISO Represent the Perspectives of the Major Environmental Stakeholders?

INTRODUCTION

The claim is frequently made that the ISO is a consensual industry body – a 'United Nations'-type federation of national standards bodies[1] – and that ISO 14001 is a consensual international standard. However, for some ISO developing country members who wanted to get involved in 14001, just getting access to information proved elusive. Industrialists in Kenya and the Kenyan Bureau of Standards (KBS) were of the strong impression that ISO 14001 would directly affect their company export drives. Their capacity to influence the process, was in principle, in place: the KBS is a full member of the ISO and a participating member of TC 207. Despite this, the KBS reported in June 1996 that they had received no information from the ISO on the 14000 standards. According to a senior principal standards officer with the KBS, updates on ISO 14001 reached him not through the ISO but through BOC Kenya. BOC Kenya received its documentation from its parent company in Britain, British Oxygen Ltd. Kenyan firms also claimed that they had not seen documentation on ISO 14001 unless it was through a parent company – usually in the UK.[2]

Lack of information is only one hurdle for potential participants. The procedures for setting ISO international standards are markedly different from those used in any other international environmental arena. The ISO does not use the rules of procedure and standards of practice similar to any United Nations agency. Instead, it has different voting procedures, different classes of membership and different methods of adopting final reports.

Public policy academics and environmental groups are sharply critical of the ISO process, observing:

> ISO has moved beyond the establishment of technical standards for goods and entered the realm of public policy-making without any of the tiresome constraints associated with democratic/public accountability; without the demands of listening to dissident voices and without any constitutional oversight.[3]

Consequently, it is not surprising that a broad coalition of environmental organizations has called on developed country governments to halt the creation of any new international industry-based standards until the full democratic implications of these developments have been studied and evaluated.[4]

The same concern that the ISO has extended its reach beyond its mandate has been expressed more recently by some industry groups as well. The US Electronics Industry Alliance (EIA) noted, after the standard was accepted, that they disapprove of the ISO contributing to a proliferation of standards. Claiming that they are trying to deal with the organizational and economic consequences of ISO 9000, which is supplemented by market demands for new standards, the EIA describe a world where standard setting has become a market created by consultants to the detriment of business. They urge the ISO to cease creating management standards altogether.[5]

In the world of international environment and development, efforts have been made over the past several decades to ensure that the policy-making process is more representative and more open. International environmental standard-setting has increasingly involved a wide range of stakeholders in the drafting process – from scientists to environmental groups, and from governments to labour unions and industry. States and intergovernmental bodies have adopted policies and procedures to determine that interested parties have access to the necessary information and the negotiation process. As a private international organization, the ISO has so far been immune to these changes in the international community.

Understanding the ISO process is crucial, then, to assessing its status as an institution capable of environmental leadership in a representative and open manner. The history of the decision-making process in creating the ISO 14001 standard is presented in this chapter as indicative of the overall ISO system. It also suggests where developing countries and public interest groups could invest their resources to be more effective in the ongoing round of 14000 standards and future ISO standards with a public policy impact. Senior developing country officials interviewed for this book identified a number of procedural concerns. The first was the low level of developing country participation in the ISO and in TC 207 (see Table 2.1).This was echoed by a journalist covering the June 1995 meeting of TC 207 in Oslo:

> Whilst many of these [developing nations] delegates remained silent during negotiations at the working groups and subcommittee levels, in private interviews with IESU they expressed concern that, because they had not been actively involved in writing the standards from the beginning, their interests have been ignored ... Most of the delegates from developing nations agree that they will have no choice but to implement the ISO 14001 standards to remain competitive, and are now focussing on strategies for doing so.[6]

In fact, representatives of the national standard-setting bodies who drafted the standard were in the main executives from transnational corporations and consulting companies based in the developed world. For example, four of the seven subcommittees of TC 207 in 1995 were chaired by executives from: KPMG Environmental Consulting, NB Contract Services, Merck and Company and Bayer. The subsidiary working groups were led by executives from Rhone-Poulenc, The Federation of

Table 2.1 *Limited Participation by Developing Countries in TC 207*

---

180 countries belong to the United Nations, of which 141 are developing countries. Of these 141 developing countries:

- 50 are Full Members of ISO;
- 25 are Participating Members in TC 207;
- 5 to 6 participated actively in negotiations between the creation of TC 207 and the third session of TC 207;
- 20 voted at the third session of TC 207 in Oslo (June 1995) when ISO 14001 became a draft international standard; and
- 22 were at the opening of the fourth session of TC 207 in Rio, June 1996.

Sources: ISO membership lists. Roll calls printed in *International Environmental Systems Update*, CEEM Information Services, Fairfax, Virginia, vol 3(7), Annex B: 'Composition of TC 207, Voting and Participation by Developing Countries'.

Swedish Industries, Du Pont and Scott Paper Company. Leaders of other working groups came from equivalent backgrounds.[7]

The second concern was whether the rules leading to ISO standards are representative enough to allow adequate input from the different categories of ISO member countries. Developing country officials noted that, while the ISO has shifted its focus from standards in engineering to normative management standards and standards for other 'soft' technologies, they have not altered their rule-making process.

A third concern was that the costs of attending frequent meetings severely restrict participation. To address this concern, the ISO Developing Country Committee (DEVCO) provided modest resources for officials from developing countries to participate in technical committee meetings and to attend seminars on ISO issues. For the TC 207, DEVCO provided financial assistance to a pair of officials, one from a national standard-setting body and one from a government ministry, from over a dozen developing countries, at key meetings on ISO 14001 in Oslo in June 1995 and in Rio de Janeiro in June 1996.[8] Limited resources meant that DEVCO provided for only one national standard-setting body representative to attend the Kyoto meeting in April 1997.

In spite of these financing efforts, most developing countries are not involved in the process at all. For example, in the development of ISO 14001, the third meeting of TC 207 (Oslo, June 1995) was very important: this was when they announced the postal vote to move ISO 14001 to a draft international standard. Representatives from 92 per cent of developed countries participated actively in this meeting while only 17 per cent of the developing country standard-setting bodies participated.[9] In addition, the Oslo meeting was their first active involvement in the process for the majority of delegates from developing countries. There was broader participation at the fourth TC 207 meeting (Rio, June 1996), when the ISO 14001 and several other standards were adopted as international standards; but developing countries were still under-represented.

This concern about under-representation of developing countries in the ISO process was also strongly expressed by developing countries at the WTO Technical Barriers to Trade (TBT) Committee in 1997. As the Agreement on TBT depends on

ISO standards (see Chapter 3), the TBT Committee noted the 'concerns … expressed by certain Members, in particular developing country Members, on the difficulties they encountered' in international standard setting in the ISO. The TBT Committee however stressed that it 'was important that all Members have the opportunity to participate in the discussions, elaboration and adoption of international standards'.[10]

Even when a national standard-setting body is a member of ISO, it does not routinely involve citizens' groups and other stakeholders in the development of its international position. National standard-setting bodies are, in fact, unknown to all but a specialized public. As a result, civil society and non-industrial interests have little opportunity to air their views at the national or international level. It is against this background that the evolution of the ISO 14000 series has special meaning.

MEMBERSHIP RULES

The ISO has some 120 members in three classes of membership.[11] Memberships are given to national institutions, and there is one member per country.[12] All developed countries have standard-setting institutions that are members of the ISO. In contrast, only 53 per cent of developing countries have member institutions in any of the three membership categories. About one quarter of the world's countries do not have members. All non-members come from developing countries or countries in transition. The level of ISO membership is based primarily on the existence of a national standard-setting body. This institution's strength is, in turn, a function of its country's economic development and its access to financial, technical and professional resources.

The three ISO membership classes are as follows:

- *Full members* are those national bodies that are most representative of standardization. The 85 full members can be Participating Members in technical committees (TCs). TCs are the main governing body for a group of international standards. Participating members have the right to vote, to attend all TC meetings and to receive documents.[13]
- *Correspondent members* are usually standards-related organizations in a developing country that does not yet have its own national standard body. Correspondent members do not take an active part in technical work although they are entitled to be fully informed about any work of interest to them. This type of membership allows them to be Observing Members in negotiations, which entitles them to attend TC meetings and collect documents.
- *Subscriber members* are standards-related organizations from 'countries with a very small economy'. The nine subscriber members pay a reduced membership fee and have limited participation rights. They cannot attend TC meetings and have no formal access to the documents.

ISO members are national standard-setting bodies. They may be a private body, a government agency or a hybrid organization. The hybrid status of some organizations obscures issues of responsibility and public accountability. For those countries (such as in France) where the standard-setting body is essentially a government agency, it is

Table 2.2 *Participation in ISO and TC 207 by Region (proportion of possible country membership by region)*

	UN Member	ISO Member	TC 207 P & O Members	TC 207 P-Member only	Voted in Oslo on DIS	Roll call in Rio	Delegate list in Kyoto
Total	180	120	68	51	40	41	47
Developed Countries	24	100%	96%	92%	84%	87%	91%
Western Europe	14	100%	93%	93%	79%	86%	92%
Other Europe	3	100%	100%	67%	67%	67%	67%
North America	2	100%	100%	100%	100%	100%	100%
Other Developed Economies	5	100%	100%	100%	100%	100%	100%
Developing Countries	141	58%	26%	17%	13%	13%	13%
Africa	49	35%	14%	8%	4%	4%	8%
Latin America and Caribbean	38	55%	34%	16%	16%	26%	21%
Asia	48	79%	29%	21%	20%	15%	14%
Developing Europe	6	100%	33%	0%	0%	0%	0%
Central and Eastern Europe	15	93%	60%	27%	13%	7%	20%

Sources: ISO Web Page, August 1996 (http://www.iso.ch); IESU, various issues; regional classifications from the *1995 World Investment Report* UNCTAD,Geneva; List of Delegates and Observers (Registered), Kyoto, April 19, 1997; ISO/TC207 Fifth Meeting.

fair to regard their positions as governmental. For countries (such as the UK with its British Standards Institution) where the standard-setting body is private, the views of these bodies are strictly the views of their corporate membership or specialized trade associations. For those countries (such as the American National Standards Institute in the US) where it is a private body with technical government experts as participating members, it is difficult to characterize their public position. As an organization, ANSI has a limited staff, but it has participation at the technical level from such governmental agencies as the Department of Commerce, the Department of Energy and, on occasions, the Environmental Protection Agency. But when it comes to arranging staff support and chairs for its committees, ANSI selects outside experts who are largely corporate officials. ANSI's experts are given paid leave time and institutional support by their individual employers to maintain the ANSI's technical advisory bodies.

Of the 24 developed nations, all of their national standard-setting bodies are full members of ISO and over 90 per cent of them are voting members of TC 207.

Table 2.3 *Developing countries are not key players in ISO nor in TC 207*

	UN Members	ISO Full Members	TC 207 P-Memb.	Delegation size: Oslo 1995	Rio 1996	Kyoto 1997
Total	180	120	51	365	335	355
Developed Countries	14%	20%	43%	79%	55%	60%
Developing Countries	78%	68%	49%	20%	44%	38%
Central/Eastern Europe	8%	12%	8%	1%	1%	2%

Source: See Table 2.2
Note: The host delegations from Norway, Brazil and Japan in 1995, 1996 and 1997 respectively were excluded from the calculations to allow for reasonable comparisons between TC 207 sessions.

Participation by representatives from standard-setting bodies in other nations is much lower (see Table 2.2). Only 58 per cent of developing countries have institutions that are members of ISO in a membership category that allows full participation in standard-setting negotiations; furthermore, only 26 per cent of developing countries have institutions that are members of TC 207 and only 17 per cent can vote. In Central and eastern Europe, this proportion is larger – all countries have a member and 60 per cent are involved in the negotiations; however, only 27 per cent may vote on the issues.

Another measure is the number of delegates from developing countries attending international negotiations, a major issue at meetings where several – five or six –negotiating sessions may be occurring simultaneously. The number of delegates from developing countries in Oslo (1995), Rio (1996), and Kyoto (1997) were much smaller than the number of delegates from developed countries (see Table 2.3). And in Rio, three-quarters of the participants from developing countries came from only four countries: Brazil, Korea, Argentina and Indonesia. At Kyoto, four developing countries – Indonesia, Korea, China and Brazil – again accounted for 75 per cent of all developing country participants.

A third way of considering the degree of participation in ISO is to examine the extent to which national standard-setting members of ISO and its key bodies reflect the economic or geographic balances. While the proportion of these economic or geographic groupings is similar between the ISO full members and the UN members, developing country participation is significantly lower in key decision-making bodies – the technical committees. (see Table 2.4). This tight hierarchy of access to ISO decision-making stands in contrast to the process of information exchange and drafting in the intergovernmental arena. In the UN system, all countries have the same formal status and all country members represent their national government. And, in general, no more than two negotiation sessions occur concurrently.

Table 2.4 *Distribution of National Secretariats for Key ISO Subsidiary Bodies (1996)*

National Standard-Setting Body	Secretariat to TC/SC	Convenorships of Working Groups	Total
Per cent four largest of which:	62.4% (477)	68.7% (1346)	66.9% (1821)
ANSI (US)	16.6%	21.5%	20.1%
DIN (Germany)	19.2%	19.5%	19.4%
BSI (UK)	15.2%	17.8%	17.0%
AFNOR (France)	11.4%	9.9%	10.3%
Other developed countries	27.1% (213)	28.2% (552)	27.9% (759)
Developing countries	4.3% (33)	1.9% (37)	2.6% (71)
Countries in transition	6.2% (47)	1.2% (23)	2.6% (71)
Total percentage	100% (764)	100% (1958)	100% (2722)

Key:
TC: technical committee
SC: sub-committee of a technical committee
WG: working group generally of a sub-committee
Source: ISO Annual Report, 1996, p 26

LIAISON MEMBERS

Regional and international bodies that are not members of ISO can liaise with the chief executive officer of ISO and work with relevant technical committees and subcommittees. Organizations that are classified as Category A organizations can be sent copies of all relevant documentation and are invited to appropriate meetings. Other organizations, classified as Category B organizations, are only sent reports of the work of specific technical committees or subcommittees.[14]

Category A Liaison organizations may represent important players in standard setting but they can never become voting members.[15] The Global Ecolabelling Network, for example, represents two-thirds of the ecolabelling organizations in the world. As an A Liaison member, it can participate in expert-level working groups but cannot vote in the subcommittee or committee that is creating a new international standard for ecolabelling.[16]

In the United Nations, NGOs accredited to the Economic and Social Council (ECOSOC), which can range from public interest groups to industry associations, attend meetings, collect documents and distribute their written views to delegations. They may also be invited by the chair to address appropriate sessions. NGOs not accredited to ECOSOC have access to UN documents and can attend some UN meetings as observers. In other words, non-accredited nongovernmental organizations at the UN have more access to information about the drafting process in the United Nations than do subscriber members of the ISO to an ISO drafting process.

SECRETARIAT

The ISO has a small, 170-person central secretariat in Geneva. The secretariat is headed by a chief executive officer, currently Lawrence D Eicher. Secretariat support for each technical committee, however, is provided by the national standard-setting bodies. The ISO estimates that the contributed labour of these national standard-setting bodies is 'three times that of its core staff'. When working as staff to a technical committee, the member body, according to its rules of procedure, 'shall maintain strict neutrality and distinguish sharply between proposals which it makes as a member body and its capacity as secretariat'.[17]

Certain developed country standards bodies have been more active in providing secretariat support to TCs than have others. ANSI (US), BSI (UK), DIN (Germany) and AFNOR (France) – Association Française de Normalisation – alone provide 66.9 per cent of the secretariat support staff to TCs and their related bodies. In contrast, developing countries and countries with economies in transition each provide 2.6 per cent of the support for such bodies (see Table 2.4). In the UN system, the staffing for such negotiations is provided by the designated UN agency with either regular budget or extra-budgetary resources available to prepare the background papers and host the meetings.

GOVERNANCE: SETTING THE RULES FOR INTERNATIONAL STANDARDS

Like all processes, there are a series of steps involved in developing international standards, from inception of the technical work to voting on the standard. The issue of representation is not limited to membership and voting rights for the final international standard. In fact, concerns exist through the entire life-cycle of a standard, from inception, through early development and formal issuance, to implementation and revision.

The first step is the creation of a technical committee by the ISO senior operating body, the Technical Management Board (TMB). This board reports to the governing bodies of the ISO, the ISO Council and the ISO General Assembly.[18] The membership of the technical management board depends on the extent of contributed secretariat support by a national body. According to procedure, the board has 12 members. The four most active member bodies (ANSI, BSI, DIN and AFNOR) are 'automatically appointed to the TMB for three consecutive terms'. Four more seats are reserved for national bodies 'ranking from five to 12' in their degree of support to TCs and related bodies. The last four seats are for all other members that provide at least secretariat support to one TC body.[19]

The Technical Management Board can set up advisory bodies to help decide if a given topic is ripe for action. The board defines the mandate and scope of each individual TC in order to prevent overlapping or conflicting standards. The board also ratifies decisions by a TC to establish subcommittees. In accordance with the ISO rules:

> A proposal for work in a new field of technical activity which appears to require the establishment of a new technical committee may be made .... by: a national body; a technical committee or subcommittee; a policy level committee; the

technical management board; the chief executive officer; a body responsible for managing a certification system operating under the auspices of the organization; [or] another international organization with national body membership.'[20]

A proposal is then circulated to all full members asking them if they agree to establish a new technical committee and if they intend to participate actively in its work. In most cases, ISO standards are developed after decades of debate on a particular issue within national standard-setting bodies. The different levels of economic development mean that some national standard-setting bodies will recognize the need for an international standard sooner than others. This has major significance for developing countries and countries with economies in transition. National firms which see their major market initially as customers in their own country are not concerned with international product standards. With increasing economic globalization, these firms may seek to market internationally. The rules may then already be set by ISO through the efforts of transnational corporations whose initial market focus may be global or regional. Not only are their national experiences unaccounted for when creating ISO international standards, they may be prompted to have national standards because of the international market rather than national needs. In the words of the chairman of environmental standards in the Turkish Standards Institute:

> In developed countries special kinds of activities at local or national levels on the sectoral base start first and then standardization of these activities follows. However, in developing countries the sequence of events is entirely in reverse. Standardization activities in developed countries sometimes force the developing countries to apply them, then the standardization activities start first even though there is no activity to be standardized. This is the case not only for environmental management system standards but also LCA [life-cycle analysis] and environmental performance evaluation and certain types of ecolabelling activities and standards.[21]

With such a low threshold of active participants, when some countries recognize the importance of an issue, they may discover that the technology leaders have already set the rules.

The Technical Management Board evaluates the replies and can decide on establishing a new TC provided that:

- two-thirds majority of the national bodies voting are in favour of the proposal; and
- at least five national bodies have expressed their intention to participate actively...'[22]

The TMB also designates the national standard body that will staff the TC. Since only five members have to express their intention to be actively involved, a small group of countries can have a disproportionate role in the leadership of a new theme and technical committee. Any full ISO members can inform the technical management board if they wish to be in the new TC as participating members (called P-Members). Full members may opt to be merely observing members (called O-Members) on a TC. ISO correspondent members can only be observing members; they cannot participate in the decision to create a TC, to define its terms of reference, or to vote on procedural issues and the adoption of standards.

As noted earlier, only the 85 full members have the right to vote at this stage in the process. Most voting on a new TC is done through a postal ballot. Since a two-thirds majority of those voting is needed, this means that less than 60 national standard-setting bodies can agree to open negotiations of a given topic under the ISO. As the rule is two-thirds 'of those voting', it is quite possible, if some countries do not vote or simply do not reply to the postal ballot, that new negotiations can be started with significantly less than 60 national standard bodies.

In contrast, the UN system generally requires unanimous approval of all 188 countries to open intergovernmental negotiations for a convention and formal approval of all voting countries to establish an intergovernmental expert group. The ISO process reduces significantly the level of representation around initiating international standards. Since the requirements for opening negotiations on standards are lower in the Technical Management Board than in the UN, it is likely that some countries may propose, in the future, to negotiate certain topics under the auspices of the ISO rather than under the aegis of the UN system.

THE CREATION OF ISO 14000

In 1991 the Technical Management Board created a joint ISO/IEC Strategic Advisory Group on the Environment (SAGE) to help the Board assess the need for international environmental management standards and to recommend an overall strategic plan for such standards.[23] The impetus for SAGE was, in part, internal: ISO had a long-range planning team and another advisory board on technological trends that felt that environmental issues needed a fresh look. The confidence to pursue environmental management came from the success of the earlier standard on quality management, ISO 9000. The impetus was, in part, also external: the UN was organizing the 1992 Rio Earth Summit Conference, and the Business Council for Sustainable Development suggested to the ISO that it consider organizing a strategic planning activity 'to achieve … desired environmental results within the voluntary international standardization system'.

SAGE was given three tasks by the Technical Management Board.

- …to assess the needs for future international standardization work to promote worldwide application of the key elements embodied in the concept of sustainable industrial development, including but not limited to consumer information and ecolabelling; the use and transport of resources, in particular raw materials and energy; and environmental effects during production, distribution, use of products, disposal and recycling.
- …to recommend an overall ISO/IEC strategic plan for environmental performance and/or management standardization; including primary objectives, proposed new work areas, timing needs, and guidance for the inclusion of environmental considerations in product standards and test methods within the existing ISO/IEC technical committee system.
- …to report its recommendations to the ISO and IEC Councils.[24]

Table 2.5 *Institutional Background of the SAGE Participants
(third meeting, Geneva, October 1992)*

---

80 participants were included at the third session of SAGE, of which:

33% (26) were from national standard-setting bodies
18% (14) were from industrial trade associations
15% (12) were from the private sector firms
13% (10) were from consulting firms
6% (5) were from governments
5% (4) were from NGOs
4% (3) were from international organizations
3% (2) were from universities
8% (6) participants in the meeting could not be classified.

Note: Numbers do not add to 100% because of rounding.
Source: 'Report of the Third Meeting of the ISO/IEC SAGE', Geneva, 15–16 October 1992; ISO/IEC SAGE Report 57

SAGE met four times from September 1991 to June 1993. The membership drew heavily on corporate environmental officials, officials from national standard-setting bodies and environmental consulting firms (see Table 2.5). At its first and second meetings, SAGE established six subgroups to address different environmental issues and a separate subgroup to encourage industrial participation in future ISO work on the environment. At the third meeting, in October 1992, it was unanimously decided that the ISO should proceed with the formal creation of a regular ISO committee.

Based on this recommendation, the Technical Management Board sent a ballot to the member associations asking for their views. 29 national standard-setting bodies supported the proposal. 20 indicated their intention to be Participating members of the new TC; nine to be Observing Members. As noted earlier, the 'two-thirds of those voting rule' meant that in this case less than 30 members supported any work on an international standard on environmental management systems. The Technical Management Board, with only eight of its 12 members attending, recommended in January 1993 that the ISO council establish TC 207 to deal with environmental management.

SAGE called on ISO/TC 207 to establish contact with other organizations to ensure that ISO's work was known and to promote the participation of interested parties, notably those in developing countries. SAGE also stressed the need for TC 207 to establish the necessary contacts with other groups involved in environmental standardization or related activities. This included ISO Technical Committees on Air quality (TC 146), Water quality (TC 147), Soil quality (TC 190), Solid wastes (TC 200), and quality management and quality assurance (TC 176). External liaisons would be established with international and industrial organizations and associations which might have an interest in the work, including the UN Environment Programme (UNEP), the UN Commission on Sustainable Development (CSD), the Organization for Economic Cooperation and Development (OECD), the International Chamber of Commerce

(ICC), the International Network for Environmental Management (INEM), the Worldwide Fund for Nature (WWF), and others.

Once established, a technical committee would review its mandate and the boundaries between its work and that of other TCs by adopting 'a statement precisely defining the limits of the work of a technical committee'.[25] The mandate for establishing TC 207 and the ISO 14000 series was as follows:

- *Scope:*
  - standardization in the field of environmental management tools and systems.
- *Excluded:*
  - test methods for pollutants which are the responsibility of ISO/TC 146 Air quality, ISO/TC 147 Water quality; ISO/TC 190 Soil quality and ISO/TC 43 Acoustics;
  - setting limit values regarding pollutants or effluents;
  - setting environmental performance levels;
  - standardization of products.

Note: The TC for Environmental Management will have close cooperation with ISO/TC176 [Quality Management and Assurance, TC that prepared the ISO 9000 series] in the field of environmental systems and audits.

The authorizing terms of reference for TC 207 are significant in three respects. There is no continuing reference to the first objective of SAGE to sustainable development or sustainable industrial development, only to 'standardization in the field of environmental management tools and systems'. The second objective of SAGE is also modified significantly. Rather than a 'strategic plan for environmental performance', the terms of reference explicitly exclude both the 'setting of limit values regarding pollutants or effluents' and 'setting environmental performance levels'.[26] The third element of significance is that ISO had already established various international environmental standards. These *environmental* standards were developed as part of other *engineering* standards. For example, the technical committee dealing with air quality has developed international standards for determining performance characteristics for air-quality measuring methods (see Box 2.2). By excluding these performance-measuring standards from TC 207, the Technical Management Board paved the way for removing performance-based elements in the environmental management system.

Even before the standard-setting negotiations had begun, the lack of input from a majority of the developing countries constituted the first brake to their participation later on in the process. 16 of the 19 officers interviewed were unable to participate actively in this preparatory stage. These countries have a range of economic, social and environmental characteristics that will not likely appear in the scope as defined by the TC in its early meetings. Themes that some might wish to see added to the TC are technology transfer; comparative environmental standards; development-related information in ecolabels (not just environment related); a phase-in period for implementation; and commitments to equitable representation of developing countries when creating new standards and in the first review of existing standards.

BOX 2.1 SELECTED ISO TECHNICAL ENVIRONMENTAL STANDARDS

Soil protection: method of measuring environmental quality, emissions and immission, eg ISO11269-1 'Soil quality – determination of the effects of pollutants on soil flora – method for the measurement of inhibition of root growth'

Water purity: methods of measurement, eg ISO 5814 'Water quality – determination of dissolved oxygen– electrochemical probe method'; ISO 6703-2 Water quality – determination of easily liberatable cyanide'

Air purity, emission of gases from stationary sources: methods of measurement, eg ISO 6879 'Air Quality – Performance characteristics and related concepts for air quality measuring methods'; ISO 8518 'Workplace air – determination of particulate lead and lead compounds – flame atomic absorption spectrometic method'

Neutralization of pollutants in the air, water, and soil: control methods, technical requirements for equipment, safety standards and rules e.g. ISO789-4 'Agricultural tractors – test procedures – measurements of exhaust smoke'

Radiation protection: test methods, eg ISO2855 'Radioactive materials – packaging; test for contents and radiation leakage'

Neutralization of dangerous waste: technical requirements for equipment, eg ISO 13617 'Shipbuilding – shipboard incinerators – requirements'

Control of noise emission to the environment: admissible levels, test methods, eg ISO 1999 'Determination of occupational noise exposure and estimation of noise-induced hearing impairment'

Sources 'ECE Standardization List', Working Party on Technical Harmonization and Standardization Policies, ECE, United Nations, 1996 ECE/STAND/20/Rev 4; and *ISO Catalogue of Standards*, Geneva, 1997, section 13 'Environment and Health Protection and Safety'

DRAFTING INTERNATIONAL STANDARDS

The procedural rules used in ISO negotiations are based on an ISO/IEC Directive (Part 1) that sets out the steps to be followed by technical committees in their everyday work.[27] These rules set out a six-stage procedure for drafting international standards.

STAGE 1: PROPOSAL STAGE

Members of an established technical committee or subcommittee (SC) can decide on the inclusion of a New Proposal (NP) in their programme of work. A new proposal could be a whole new standard, a new part of an existing standard, or an amendment to an existing standard. The originator of a new work item has to provide an outline of the working document or a first draft and to nominate a project leader. If a majority of P-Members voting in the TC or SC decide in favour of this proposal, and at least five P-Members declare their commitment to participate actively in the development of this new standard, then the TC can authorize new work and assign the new work item to an appropriate subsidiary body.

Table 2.6 *Technical Committee 207 and National Standards Bodies Serving its Subcommittees*

TC 207 Environmental Management: Standards Council of Canada

Subcommittees for the organization-oriented standards
SC1:   Environmental Management Systems: British Standards Institution (BSI)
SC2:   Environmental Auditing and Related Environmental Investigations:
         Netherlands Normalisatie-Instituut (NNI)
SC4:   Environmental Performance Evaluation: American National Standards
         Institute (ANSI)

Subcommittees for product-oriented standards
SC3:   Environmental Labelling: Standards Australia
SC5:   Life-Cycle Assessment: Association Française de Normalisation (AFNOR)
SC6:   Subcommittee for Terms and Definitions: Norges Standardis-
         regeringsforbund (NSF)

As explained earlier, the decision to create a new TC in the ISO is highly dependent on the commitment of five volunteer members to participate actively. These key members provide the chairs and staff support for the working group and the subcommittee. Once this new proposal is accepted, the members appoint a project leader. One national standards body will be given leadership responsibility for administration. Active participation in the secretariat requires an appropriate and skilled staff as much as financial resources.[28]

For TC 207, there were already a set of subgroups and themes established under SAGE. At its first meeting in Toronto, immediately following the last meeting of SAGE, TC 207 established the same six subcommittees as SAGE. By the ISO directive, such subcommittees must have at least five full members and its staffing provided by a national ISO full member. The SAGE subgroups had been working on texts for these themes and passed them on to TC 207 and its subcommittees as starting points. These TC subcommittees are all chaired by standard-setting bodies located in developed nations (see Table 2.7). The TC 207 subcommittees then established working groups, bringing to 25 the number of subsidiary bodies under TC 207. The multiplicity of bodies can make negotiation quite complex for developing countries. In recognition of this, the UN system seldom has more than two subsidiary bodies that meet at the same time.

STAGE 2: PREPARATORY STAGE WITH NATIONAL 'EXPERTS' PREPARING WORKING DRAFTS

To help carry out its mandate, a technical committee and its subcommittees can establish working groups (WGs). The ISO literally has hundreds of these working groups operating around the world at any time. In January 1997, ISO had 184 TCs, 597 sub-

Table 2.7 *Distribution of TC 207 Subcommittees Secretariats and Working Groups Conveners (number of leading positions held by a country as of February 1994)*

Country	Total	SC	Working Group (subset of a SC)
Australia	1	SC3	–
Canada	5	TC 207	SC1/WG2; SC2/WG1; SC2/WG4 & SC3/WG2
France	5	SC5	SC1/WG1; SC2/WG1; SC3/WG1 & SC5/WG5
Germany	2	–	SC2/WG2; SC5/WG2
Japan	3	–	SC4/WG2; SC5/WG2; SC5/WG3
Netherlands	2	SC2	SC2/WG4
Norway	2	SC6	SC4/WG2
Sweden	2	–	SC3/WG1 & SC5/WG4
United States	6	SC4	SC1/WG1; SC2/WG2; SC3/WG3; SC4/WG1 & SC5/WG1
United Kingdom	3	SC1	SC1/WG1 & SC2/WG3

Key: SC = subcommittee
Source: 'Organizational Structure of ISO/TC 207', Global Environmental Management Initiative, February 1994

committees and 2034 Working Groups. These groups prepare working drafts (WDs) for the standard. The bodies select what they consider to be the best technical document and they present it to the corresponding technical committee or subcommittee.

A Working Group 'comprises a restricted number of individually appointed experts brought together to deal with a specific task allocated to the Working Group'. The experts act in a personal capacity and not as the official representative of the P-Member or A-[class] Liaison Organization by which they have been appointed. In order that the Working Groups 'be reasonably limited in size, the TC or SC may ... decide upon the total number of experts'.[29] The ISO rules of procedure require that, when serving in a working group, experts, like secretariats and chairs, do not represent their national organization but rather function in an international capacity. A national standard-setting body, generally the designated chair of the TC or SC, hosts the secretariat for the working groups of these bodies.

At this stage every possible effort is made to have drafts available in English and French. Working Groups and Subcommittees undertake much of their work by circulating written drafts of texts through the post, requesting comments and positions on a strict timetable. Meetings are held to reconcile differences and to finalize drafts. In this process, the chairs of TCs or SCs 'shall ensure at meetings that all points of view expressed are adequately summed up so that they are understood by all present', following the consensus practice of ISO.[30] The preparatory stage is complete when a working draft is available for circulation to the TC or SC as the first committee draft (CD).

For the ISO 14000 series, the chairs of all the TC 207 subcommittees and the conveners of the TC 207 Working Groups come from industrialized countries (see Box 2.2). In the UN system, the chairs of intergovernmental groups are distributed

---

BOX 2.2 DOMINANCE OF LARGE CONSULTING HOUSES AND TNCs IN THE CHAIRS OF TC 207 BODIES

The organizational structure of TC 207 in 1995 shows that the seven subcommittees are chaired by executives from KPMG Environmental Consulting, NB Contract Services, Merck and Company, Bayer, Standards Australia, NAS and DIN. The subsidiary working groups are led by executives from Rhone-Poulenc, The Federation of Swedish Industries, Du Pont and Scott Paper Company. Leaders of other working groups come from equivalent backgrounds.

Source 'Organisational Structure of ISO/TC 207 Environmental Management and US Participation' Global Environmental Management Initiative (GEMI), Management Standards Work Group, Washington, DC, 1995

---

throughout the geographic or political regions used by the sponsoring organization. The chair of the main negotiating body will also have a bureau representing all of the other relevant regions.

In addition, only some 25 per cent of the TC 207 working group chairs work for national standard-setting bodies. Over half of the chairs are employees of transnational corporations, such as Allied Signal, Bayer, Du Pont Company, Elf Altochem, Henkel, KPMG Environmental Consulting, Merck & Company, Rhone-Poulenc, and Scott Paper.[31] Since these positions do not rotate, working group chairs may have the power to influence the outcome of the standards in a way that could have competitive advantage for their firm or their country.

STAGE 3: COMMITTEE STAGE – NATIONAL BODIES IN THE TECHNICAL COMMITTEE REVISE THE COMMITTEE DRAFT (CD)

The committee stage is the point at which comments from national bodies are taken into consideration and ends when all technical issues have been resolved and a committee draft is accepted for circulation as an enquiry draft and is registered.[32] As in the case of Stage 2, much of this is done through the mail. National standard-setting bodies, that have offered to be members of the TC or SCs, receive written versions of the committee text and then send in their comments to the chair. The chair makes changes in the text, attempting to incorporate the relevant ideas that the chair believes are commonly held. The P-Members then receive the revised committee draft and comments of the other committee members. It is during this phase that key concepts and the structure of the final international standard is developed. Finally, during the second and third stages, the standard acquires its shape and technical content.

ISO standards in the environmental management area are difficult to read and follow, even for those who have English as their first language. Developing country officials on TC 207 reported that communication of information during this phase was usually slow and sometimes happened so late that they were unable to respond and make observations on time. The delays or the incomplete information is, according to most of the officials, due to bureaucratic red tape and slowness of the international postal service. Almost all the correspondence documents were only in English. At

Table 2.8 *Selected TC 207 Subcommittee Meetings between the third and fourth session of TC 207 (November 1994 to June 1996)*

Date	Location	Main Subject
Nov 1994	Johannesburg, South Africa	SC6: Terms and Definitions
Dec 1994	Madrid, Spain	SC4: Environmental Performance Evaluation
Jan 1995	Paris, France	SC2: Environmental Auditing
Feb 1995	San Francisco, CA, US	SC1: EMSs
Feb 1995	London, UK	SC4: Environmental Performance Evaluation
Feb 1995	Berlin, Germany	SC5: Life Cycle Assessment
March 1995	Toronto, Canada	SC3/WG2: Self-Declarations
March 1995	London, UK	SC4: Environmental Performance Evaluation
June 1995	Oslo, Norway	TC 207, Third session
Nov 1995	Vancouver, Canada	SC5: Life Cycle Assessment
Nov 1995	Seoul, South Korea	SC3: Environmental Labelling
Dec 1995	Washington, DC, US	SC4: Environmental Performance Evaluation
March 1996	Washington, DC, US	SC3/WG2 & 3: Environmental Labelling
June 1996	Rio, Brazil	TC 207: Fourth session

Source: International Environmental Systems Update, various issues

meetings, the current draft text was available in English and French.[33] In the UN system, documents are available in six languages. In the European Union, documents are translated into ten languages.

Even if they receive comprehensive information in time, there is still the issue of language and lack of technical skills. Officers from all the Latin American countries and some Asian countries that are P-Members of TC 207 feel strongly that language has been an obstacle to their understanding of the process and their capacity to contribute to the negotiations on the ISO 14000 series of standards. If ISO consensus cannot be accomplished through correspondence, the TC or SC schedule meetings to resolve differences between national standard-setting bodies. The third stage ends when the TC or SC decides that all technical issues have been resolved and elevates the document to an enquiry draft (ED). Successive committee drafts may be considered until consensus is reached on the technical content.

ISO frequently cites that decisions are made by consensus. Consensus decision-making in the United Nations system means that no delegation opposes the proposed outcome. A consensus decision in Quaker communities means that, after full discussion, all the participants support the common view. For the ISO, consensus means:

> …general agreement, characterized by the absence of sustained opposition to substantial issues by any important part of the concerned interests and by a process that involves seeking to take into account the news of all parties concerned and to reconcile any conflicting arguments. Note – consensus need not imply unanimity.[34]

As a practical matter, at the committee stage consensus decision-making means two-thirds of the P-Members of the Technical Committee or Subcommittee are in favour of the proposal.[35]

For ISO 14001, this process began in 1993 and continued through June 1995, when a postal vote was taken to adopt the standard as a Draft International Standard. During these two years, TC 207 held meetings of the SCs and of the WGs and the plenary sessions of TC 207 in Brazil, France, Norway, The Netherlands and the US, just to mention a few. Along with these official WG and SC meetings, informal meetings were held, on an ad hoc basis, for further discussion or information exchange (see Table 2.8). These meetings cause significant travel and postal expenses – one estimate is that the members of Subcommittee 1 collectively spent roughly $14 million for each page of the ISO 14001 standard.[36] Many national standard-setting bodies are simply unable to send staff or appoint experts to attend these meetings on a regular basis.

In addition, there are several other preconditions for effective participation in the ISO meetings. Delegates need to participate in all and not just the plenary meetings. A clause that is negotiated and agreed at a plenary can be reopened at any subsequent meeting if requested by a delegation and agreed by the chairman. Secondly, a national delegation needs several representatives to cover the parallel and overlapping sessions. Sometimes even the work of the working groups of the same subcommittee overlap. Thirdly, delegations need to include members who can follow technical and political debates. Combinations of standard-setting officers and staff from government ministries of trade, environment and industry are needed to strategically deploy a range of skills and to be more effective at meetings. Fourthly, all delegates need to speak fluent English. Fifthly, delegates need to monitor the drafts in sessions and in the mail to check what changes were made and what issues need preparing for the next meeting. All of these preconditions present particular problems for developing countries.

The majority of the ISO members from developing countries were not actively involved in the early stages of the process. Even for the June 1995 meeting in Oslo, many developing countries could only to send two to five people. Furthermore, national standard-setting bodies from most South America were not represented at the TC 207 meeting in Rio.

STAGE 4: ENQUIRY STAGE WHERE ALL NATIONAL FULL MEMBERS VOTE TO APPROVE A DRAFT INTERNATIONAL STANDARD

Once adopted by a technical committee, a Draft International Standard (DIS) is circulated to all ISO P-Member bodies for comment and voting. At this stage, technical comments will no longer be considered; instead, they will be registered for consideration during a future revision of the standard.

One should note here that regardless of the outcome of this vote, a Draft International Standard is a de facto international trade standard under the 1995 General Agreement on Tariffs and Trade (GATT). The GATT states that, if an international standard is imminent, it has to be followed even if it has no formal status at that point. For example, the Draft International Standard status of the ISO 14001 gave it the status of an international trade standard as of June 1995 (see Chapter 3).

The vote to adopt a standard is conducted by postal ballot over a period of several months. At this point, substantial amendments are no longer accepted; only procedural and editorial changes will be accepted. For all the national standard-setting bodies that did not participate directly in the working TC, this is their first chance to review the Draft International Standard. If a national standard-setting body wishes to amend the text, the only procedural choice at this point is to oppose the text in order that it is returned to the previous stage for additional work. The national standard-setting bodies opposing the text need to indicate the areas of their concern or their negative vote will be ignored. To be approved by consensus as a final DIS, there is a slightly different practical definition of consensus. Two-thirds majority of the Participating Members of the relevant TC must be in favour of the standard and not more than one quarter of the total number of votes cast can be negative.[37] As a result, for any decisions relating to a standard in this series, at least 34 must vote in favour of the action, and assuming that all Participating Members are present, no more than 12 Full Members (whether participating in the TC negotiations or not) can vote against it.

Because of this structure, any organization interested in the outcome of an ISO standard must participate in the earlier stages of the process. When the Draft International Standard is circulated to all ISO members for the first time, it is too late for any of them to provide substantive input under the ISO rules, and a de facto international standard already exists under 1995 GATT rules (see Chapter 3). This was a source of frustration to officers surveyed from a number of developing countries.

STAGE 5: APPROVAL STAGE WHERE ALL FULL MEMBERS VOTE ON THE FINAL DRAFT INTERNATIONAL STANDARDS

Once elevated to this level, a final Draft International Standard is again circulated to all ISO members. At this point, the national standard-setting bodies can, again, either vote to return the standard to the relevant TC or SC for further revision or approve it as an International Standard. For ISO 14001 the postal vote elevating it to an International Standard was taken in the spring of 1996 and announced at the TC 207 meeting in Rio in June 1996. Other standards in the 14000 series – the guidance documents – will aid businesses in carrying out the specifications in ISO 14001. As noted earlier, some of these have been approved, and others are still under negotiation.

STAGE 6 (FINAL STAGE): PUBLICATION WITHIN TWO MONTHS OF APPROVAL (THE ISO CENTRAL SECRETARIAT PUBLISHED STANDARD IN ENGLISH AND FRENCH)

After approval by ISO as an international standard, the various national standard-setting bodies each have a separate process to adopt the international standard as an applicable national measure. Sometimes national bodies modify or amend the international standard in light of national technological or market conditions before approving it for domestic use. For most ISO standards, or guidance documents, this is the end of the process.

REVIEW STAGE

The ISO rules and procedures provide for two types of revision. The first type is an automatic process that must take place at least every five years, at which point the standard can be confirmed, revised or withdrawn.[38] The second type of revision process is a review initiated by the ISO chief executive officer or any national standard-setting body. Both processes, automatic or at request, must assess the practical aspects of the standard's implementation at the national level as well as the 'degree to which the standard has been adopted'. If the standard should be revised, it 'becomes a new project and shall be added to the programme of work of the technical committee or subcommittee' and the sequence of stages starts again.[39]

ACCREDITATION AND CERTIFICATION PROCESS

After adopting a specification standard, such as ISO 14001, the national standards bodies have an additional responsibility. For the ISO 14000 series, 14001 is the only standard that requires an accreditation process. Standards bodies need to establish a review system to check whether individual products, processes or firms are in compliance with the new standard. Since there are millions of different products in international trade and hundreds of thousands of different firms and sites, the oversight system is designed to create a chain of authority sufficient to test all the relevant products or sites for a particular standard.

The review structure is a three-tiered process. The national standards body designates a group to accredit other businesses or institutes, which in turn certify specific products or firms. The national standards body also designates a group to receive copies of the successful certification documents. The standards body can select itself, a government agency, or a private firm or a non-profit association as the accreditation body, the certifying body or registrar. The designated accreditation body then needs to announce the rules by which it will authorize the certifying bodies to test specific products or firms, how it will check that these bodies are doing a decent job, what level of specific training is needed by their staff, and how their staff should review specific elements of the ISO standards for subcategories of products or firms.

A domestic certifying industry can be established in each country to provide certification services to firms seeking ISO 14001 certification. Although each national standard-setting body can create its own system, there is no internationally recognized system for mutual recognition of the certificates produced by national systems.[40] This means that it is possible for a foreign supplier to stipulate that a firm needs ISO 14001 certification and that the certifier must be on an approved list. On the other hand, once a certifier has been granted permission by an accreditation body, that certifier can offer its services in any country of the world. When the firm grants a certificate, it is based on the rights of its accreditation body.

The certifiers then evaluate compliance with the ISO standards. In practice, this means that certifiers must design a test in ISO 14001 – for example, a firm must have a commitment to comply with laws and regulation. Thus a US certifier would have to follow advice such as:

> A registration audit is an audit of a management system to determine confor-
> mance to the standard and while compliance is a part of the management sys-
> tem, the registration audit is not an audit of full compliance with all applicable
> regulatory requirements.[41]

The final successful examination is reported to the firm and sent to the registrar so that others can have access to the results.

Of course, certifiers are likely to be commercial entities. In the case of ISO 14001, there are potential market factors that can influence the definition of appropriate certifiers (for instance, can environmental consulting firms also certify their own work?), the training skills of the certifiers (does an ISO 9000 certifier who has attended two non-examination-based environmental courses have sufficient skill to make judgements about environmental aspects of the firm's activities?), and implications of discovering illegal activities (does a certifier have to notify authorities if he or she discovers a serious breach of the law?). Furthermore, since firms are the ones seeking certification, there is strong motivation to use certifiers who have the lowest standards or to discover those certifiers who might be most receptive to bribery. If the certifier can bid on a project – for example, an ISO 14001 documentation system – there will be obvious pressure for a 'supplemental payment' to accept a less demanding documentation system. The accreditation system is the only safeguard against this reality.

An argument could be made that the professional who implemented the system is best placed to certify it. This is not acceptable in the accounting world, where independent outside auditors are called in on a regular basis to confirm that the financial statements 'present fairly, in all material respects, the financial positions' of a business. But for regulators seeking verification and assurances from the certification, this presents a conflict of interest. Consequently, regulators using ISO 14001 as a basis for a coregulation partnership should make stipulations on the independence of the certifier.

CONCLUSION

Over the last ten years there has been a burst of energy in the development of international environmental conventions and standards. These intergovernmental negotiations have had to struggle with the participation of scientific and technical experts, environmental groups and other nongovernmental participants. A series of important accommodations have been made to create expert scientific committees (on climate change), to place NGOs on working groups (on ozone depletion), to address social and economic concerns in environmental agreements (on endangered species) and to have statements from indigenous people at plenaries (desertification). This democratization of the international process and the incorporation of social and economic factors in environmental agreements have been strongly supported by the major governments. The relatively closed ISO system threatens to seriously weaken the growth of public involvement in international environmental and health-and-safety standard setting and to undermine the growing intergovernmental consensus on the economic and environmental aspects of sustainable development.

Indeed, the practical aspects of their participation, together with membership and procedural rules, have made it difficult for developing countries to participate effectively in designing the ISO standards. Existing ISO standards do not fully reflect the economic, cultural, social and business background and other elements that are typical in many developing countries. Even when national environmental regulations are strong, there may be limited enforcement power, limited experience of environmental management systems, or an inadequate environmental infrastructure. Technical skills, knowledge and financial resources may be limited as well. In short, the impression given by those participating in the ISO 14001 negotiations is that developing countries have voted on a standard in which they have had no input, a standard largely prepared and developed by corporate experts from industrialized countries. The ISO rules were initially designed for an industry-oriented organization making engineering specification standards for commercial products and technologies in international trade. With the transition to soft technologies and management systems, the lack of participatory structures for all stakeholders in the ISO is leading to a serious lack of international representation and to the acceptance of standards that will not meet the needs of most stakeholders. As one senior international environmental lawyer commented: 'for a process standard, too little attention has been paid to process in the international institution that is the ISO'.[42]

ISO on its part insists that its international standards are 'voluntary' because they are not for governmental regulatory use and were adopted by their idiosyncratic definition of 'consensus'. But even ISO realises that ISO standards are seldom voluntary in practice. ISO notes that 'companies that do not apply generally accepted standards risk isolation and loss of market share'.[43] In other words, it would be more correct to say that the standards that result from the ISO process are exclusionary and involuntary. For firms and for countries which were not part of the particular technical committee, the results can be imposed with the leadership of the major national standard setting bodies and/or the dominant firms in the particular product area.

The ISO assertion of 'voluntary' standards is important for another reason. It is this double use of the meaning of 'voluntary' that advocates of ISO 14001 are employing when they align the ISO standards with arguments for 'industry self-regulation'. Voluntary environmental management and self-regulation are a crucial battleground in the debate on the paradigm for a new partnership between the public and private sectors, nationally and internationally. When self-regulation is presented as a 'voluntary' standard based on a 'consensus' process, it appears as if the policy base is resolved. Industry advocates for self-regulation claim that self-regulated firms will be 'beyond compliance'. However, the non-performance characteristics of ISO 14001 and the minimalist 'commitment to compliance' in the ISO 14001 policy requirement prevent testing any claims to 'beyond compliance' practices of ISO 14001-certified firms. At the same time some industry self-regulation advocates note that the founding documents for the ISO 14000 series are based on the concept of corporate sustainable development. However, the final ISO 14001 standard took the 'beyond compliance' requirement, removed the sustainable development goals, and restricted public participation. Yet these advocates of 'self-regulation' still expect that the new contract with public authorities should be maintained.

The definition and political ambiguities surrounding 'voluntary standards' have also been given new meanings in the GATT Agreement on Technical Barriers to Trade as outlined in the next chapter.

Chapter 3

Does the New GATT Agreement Change the Status of ISO Standards?

INTRODUCTION

The 1994 General Agreements on Tariffs and Trade (GATT) makes clear reference to international standards set by the ISO. When a country creates a national standard or guideline, then the international community acknowledges that this country is presumed to have avoided initiating an unnecessary obstacle to international trade through the new regulation. Because of these and other clear references in the GATT, standards developed by the ISO have acquired a very important status.

The long-term implication of this formal link between the international trading system and the ISO does not bode well for global environmental protection or for sustainable development. Over time, the misguided wisdom of connecting environmental, health, safety and social standards set by a non-public body to the international trading system will become clearer. In Chapter 2, the exclusion or marginalization of representatives of developing countries and civil society in the ISO standard-setting process was described. With the formal linkage by the new GATT with the ISO standards, a large number of countries are expected to follow rules that they had little or no participation in developing, further weakening the level of public participation needed for a globally sustainable world.

At the same time, the new GATT created obstacles to using the recommendations of UN intergovernmental expert groups as global standards in the international trading system. The consequences for developing country governments, countries in transition, NGOs and standard-setting bodies and businesses are quite significant. Over the next decade, there will be numerous national and local standards whose stature is likely to be challenged as inconsistent with accepted international ISO standards and consequently inconsistent with the obligations of the new GATT.

A hypothetical example illustrates this complex trade issue. In a Latin American country, an environmental group, a university research centre and a group of local manufacturers work together and develop a new environmental approach for their country. In their proposal, the government would require, through laws and regulations, that all manufacturing sites should have an approved accident management system and that this system should provide data on toxic emissions to the public every two years. In its regulations, the government would allow manufacturers to label products or sites with a special green symbol when the storage of toxic chemicals or toxic emission levels drop below a certain threshold for two years in a row. This – the multi-stakeholder group argues – could provide a market-based incentive for firms to reduce their toxic emissions and potential accidents, reward environmentally active firms, and reduce the need for extensive government supervision at some potentially environmentally harmful facilities.

However, other governments might notify this Latin American government that they plan to challenge the innovative law through the WTO dispute-settlement procedures. They could argue that the proposed new law, in their view, does not follow the relevant ISO standards on environmental management, environmental performance measures and ecolabels. And, they could continue, while the government consulted with its domestic constituencies, it did not consult appropriately with its trading partners and the WTO in setting rules that differed from the approved international standard. In addition, these hypothetical government authorities might face opposition from domestic producers with very high emissions who want to obstruct the market advantage that would be given to more environmentally sensitive firms. The domestic challenge could cite, amongst other issues, the potential costs of defending a GATT challenge under new trade rules. Faced with international trade sanctions for, on the one hand, not following ISO standards and, on the other, from domestic industrial opposition to green labelling, the government would be in a weak position to accept the advice of the multistakeholder group on how to improve domestic environmental protection.

PRE-1994 GATT STANDARD SETTING

For nearly 50 years, GATT covered only a very small component of environment, health and safety rules: the safety of food, plant and animal products in international trade. During this period the GATT Agreement on Sanitary and Phytosanitary Measures provided a framework to ensure that all trading partners would be apprised of minimum food safety standards so that shipments would not sit and spoil in cargo ports and customs warehouses. The measures also provided practical minimum health information to countries with fewer safeguards in place.[1] They were not, however, set forth as guidelines, maximum ceilings or requisite standards to be used in national food safety rules.

During these same 50 years, the non-governmental community and the public supported the creation and implementation of intergovernmental environmental, health and safety standards to establish minimum-level safeguards in all countries of the world. Whether set up as voluntary recommendations by UN agencies, or adopted as legally binding conventions, these international standards provided the basis for minimum national standards. For countries without a standard in a given area, agreements such as those described in Chapter 1 became the baseline for de facto standards or starting points for de jure national laws and regulations.

Under the pre-1994 GATT system, there were two principal criteria to evaluate product standards under international trade law. Firstly, national environmental, health and safety standards should not be designed to obstruct entry of a commercial product by another country. Secondly, they should not have this effect, regardless of the official reason for the standard. A country can neither explicitly create a non-tariff barrier to trade nor create a barrier unintentionally based on some other set of concerns. Standards that specified a particular process or production method were not allowed, only standards that pertained to the intrinsic nature of the product. Countries also had to adopt the least trade-restrictive programme possible and to ensure that foreign suppliers had an equal opportunity to compete in the domestic market. GATT did not care how an item was manufactured, only that a product could come into a foreign market on an equal basis.

Countries could also not set product standards that depend on a testing system that is not openly available on the same basis to all suppliers of the same product. When exposure limits are set, an agency or authority often specifies how to measure and document compliance. If a government sets a maximum level for lead in food containers, for example, it might also set a methodology and testing regime to measure the quantity of lead at various temperatures and the levels of exposure to corrosive elements. In GATT language, these compliance-measuring requirements are called conformity assessment systems. At the international level, the ISO has long been active in defining standards about conformity assessment systems for a wide range of industrial products.[2]

If complaints arose under the GATT, the trading partner who felt unfairly blocked by a foreign standard had to prove that the standard or other non-tariff measure posed a trade barrier. When an exporting country challenged a rule or procedure in an importing country as a non-tariff barrier to trade, the GATT dispute settlement panel had to consider, on a case-by-case basis, whether a particular rule should be classified as a barrier or not. With the rapid development of national health and safety rules and regulations, this approach was no longer seen as adequate.

Under the current 1994 GATT agreement, many of these procedures were continued, but some significant changes were introduced. The Uruguay Round of GATT sought to establish an international system of reference standards to be used by all member countries when they crafted or revised national standards, such as those for environmental and health and safety concerns. With a set of rules about how to make national standards and regulations, it might be possible to identify more quickly what is and is not allowed as a national rule.

THE 1994 GATT

The Final Act of the 1994 GATT is a one-page document, followed by an extensive collection of annexes, each a separate individual agreement on issues such as agriculture, textiles, intellectual property, subsidies, trade-related investment measures, and technical barriers to trade. There are two key annexes to the 1994 GATT which are of importance to the ISO 14000 series:

- the Agreement on Technical Barriers to Trade (TBT) – the annex that defines the development and application of product standards.

- the Understanding on Rules and Procedures Governing the Settlement of Disputes (DSU) – the annex that revised the burden of proof for claims regarding non-tariff barriers to trade.

Since these are revised agreements, their legal interpretations must still be developed. In fact, the full implications will only emerge through individual cases before the dispute settlement bodies and decisions of the relevant WTO committees. In 1996 preliminary discussions occurred before the WTO Committee on Trade and Environment on ecolabelling standards.[3] And in 1997, discussions took place on ISO-related issues before the WTO Committee on Technical Barriers to Trade.[4] The following description, then, is based principally on the wording of the final text of the 1994 agreements and the 1997 first triennial review of the TBT, not on formal decisions by WTO dispute-settlement bodies or on adopted interpretations by WTO committees or Council.

The TBT agreement recognizes 'the important contribution that international standards and conformity assessment systems can make in this regard by improving efficiency of production and facilitating the conduct of international trade'.[5] As a result, it seeks to ensure that unnecessary obstacles to trade are not created through technical regulations and standards, including packaging, marketing and labelling requirements or through procedures for assessing conformity with technical regulations and standards.[6] At the same time it recognizes that countries should not be prevented from taking measures necessary to 'ensure the quality of its exports, or for the protection of human, animal or plant life or health, of the environment or for the prevention of deceptive practices'.[7]

In the 1994 GATT, 'standards' are defined as voluntary guidelines approved by a recognized body. 'Technical regulations' are mandatory and developed through government agencies. Most governmental standards (usually worded as 'exposure to' … 'should not exceed') are considered technical regulations and most industry voluntary guidelines (such as developed by engineering trade associations and the ISO) are considered standards.[8] In the GATT agreement, the preparation, adoption and application of mandatory technical regulations follow essentially the same language as those for voluntary standards. For example, when technical regulations are required and relevant international standards exist, central government bodies are obliged to use them, except for 'fundamental climatic or geographic factors or fundamental technological problems'.[9]

The 1994 TBT agreement deals not only with 'standards' and 'technical regulations' regarding imported products, but for the first time it covers rules regarding their process and production methods (PPMs). In the pre-1994 GATT, if an environmental technical regulation or standard differentiated between how products were made, it was likely that the rule would be considered a technical barrier to trade, principally on the grounds that the rule specified something – anything – about the process and production method. Now the 1994 TBT recognizes that environmental rules about products inherently specify some process and production method and that these rules are presumed to be alright if they follow an existing international standard that used process and production methods.

Dispute Settlement Procedures and International Standards

The second new component of the 1994 GATT that relates to the ISO 14000 series is the change in the dispute-settlement procedure. WTO member governments may challenge national standards and technical regulations set by other governments if they consider the standard to be a barrier to trade. Standards cannot pose an 'unnecessary obstacle to trade', meaning that the standard must achieve a legitimate objective that could not be met by alternative means. The criterion used to justify a standard will weigh equally the necessity of the measure from the perspectives of reducing trade restrictions; available scientific and technical evidence; and cost consequences. This system reduces the traditional role of the public-policy process in global decision-making. The new GATT also places the onus on the country with the more stringent environment, health or safety measures to defend the measure on the basis of its trade impact, technical and scientific evidence, and climatic or geographic need.

When there is a dispute, the dispute-settlement body is called in. Under the GATT dispute-settlement process, a dispute-settlement panel may establish technical expert groups to assist in questions of a technical nature or to request an advisory report on issues of scientific or technical concern from an expert review group.[10] The TBT agreement includes an annex which also describes the use of technical expert groups. In the past, however, such expert groups have not been established to assist in fact-finding or deliberations on environmental, health and safety issues before GATT panels. If the dispute-settlement process determines that a country has non-tariff barriers to trade, then the country can be sanctioned by tariffs or other measures.

Under the WTO, governments have a limited number of defences to a challenge, by a foreign government, that a national standard differs from a relevant international standard or draft international standard. As their defence, governments can demonstrate that the standard is based, in fact, on an international standard. Governments can also base a stronger standard on 'inter alia, available scientific and technical information, related processing technology or intended end uses of products'.[11] In addition, governments may ignore existing standards 'when such international standards or relevant parts would be an ineffective or inappropriate means of fulfilling the legitimate objectives pursued, for instance, because of fundamental climatic or geographic factors or fundamental technological problems'.[12] The number of cases brought before the WTO so far are insufficient to describe the full meaning of these provisions. As almost all standards are the result of numerous compromises, it may well be very difficult for any country to produce credible grounds for exceptions to the final regulations.

This new approach to defining and setting an international reference point for measuring standards may challenge the use of consumer protection, safety standards and conservation measures that cannot be defended as essential to product safety. While the WTO agreement could help facilitate the use of standards globally, such as those negotiated by the ISO, these standards may not sufficiently address the concerns of those who were not included in the negotiation process.

Six Key Concerns Regarding the Link Between the TBT Agreement and ISO 14000 Series

There are six key elements of concern regarding the links between the TBT and the ISO 14000 series:

- the definition of 'international standards' in the TBT agreement;
- the potential domestic policy limitations for environmental and health and safety policies under the TBT and dispute-settlement understanding;
- the reduced status of international standards set by intergovernmental bodies and conventions;
- potential ambiguities in the scope of allowed production processing methods;
- the unusually significant status provided for 'draft' international standards; and
- the differences in the treatment of developing countries.

Definition of International Standards in the TBT Agreement

Under the TBT agreement, international standards established by the approved process are very important because they set an international plateau. All national standards that exist for legitimate purposes and that fall at or below the plateau are assumed not to be creating trade barriers or, in the words of the TBT agreement, 'shall be rebuttably presumed not to create an unnecessary obstacle to international trade'.[13] Because of the shift by ISO into the public policy realm, experimentation by countries, provinces, states, and cities will be considerably reduced as the body of international reference standards increases.

The TBT covers national standard-setting bodies, central government bodies and local government bodies in different sections. National standard-setting bodies are those bodies, public, private or mixed, that have domestic recognition to set industry-based standards. Central government bodies are national government offices which have legal authority to set environmental, health, and safety standards. Local government bodies are, for instance, states, provinces, cantons and municipalities under a central government body. The TBT calls on national standard-setting bodies to participate actively in international standard-setting activities. It also calls on government bodies and national standard-setting bodies to use the results of the international standard-setting bodies as the basis for legally binding technical regulations or voluntary national standards if relevant international standards exist in the area.

Under the WTO, the standards set by international bodies are now ceilings which require a country to justify its decision if its practices are more rigorous than an existing international standard. A country that may have higher standards is unlikely to prevail against a challenge on the grounds that the international ISO standard is too weak for the protection of domestic health and safety.

DOMESTIC ENVIRONMENTAL POLICY OPTIONS AND THE TBT AGREEMENT

When central government bodies make environmental rules in the future, they are expected to follow the new GATT procedures. When there are GATT-recognised international standards, governments and national standard-setting bodies are encouraged to use them unless there are compelling reasons to the contrary.[14] When there are no GATT-recognised international standards or where the new standard is likely to exceed an existing international standard, the standards body is required to notify the WTO of their intention to establish a new standard.

If governments or national standard-setting bodies wish to use environmental management in a section of new measures, the ISO 14001 and related guidance standards should be consulted if the authorities want to ensure that their measures are not likely to be considered a technical barrier to trade. Likewise, if and when ISO completes its work to the appropriate level on ecolabelling, environmental auditing, life-cycle analysis, and environmental performance indicators, then governments and national standard-setting bodies will be expected to use these definitions in their new rules. As ISO undertakes new topics in the coming years which affect health, safety and social needs, the TBT is worded to capture these standards as the appropriate international reference standard for trade purposes.

THE SOURCE OF INTERNATIONAL TRADE STANDARDS: ISO OR THE UN SYSTEM?

When describing the process of setting recognized international standards, the GATT describes the ISO system, the standard-setting procedures of the International Electrotechnical Commission (IEC) and the International Telecommunications Union (ITU), not the intergovernmental system. The IEC and the ITU develop specialized standards dealing with electrical components and communications respectively. For example, the preparation, adoption and application of standards must be conducted by standardizing bodies that conform to a Code of Good Practice.[15] This code is 'open to acceptance by any standardizing body within the territory of a member, whether a central government body, a local government body, or a non-governmental body; to any governmental regional standardizing body, one or more members of which are Members of WTO; and to any non-governmental regional standardizing body one or more members of which are situated within the territory of a Member of the WTO'.[16]

The purpose of the Code of Good Practice is to extend to voluntary standards the same obligations that exist for government regulations (transparency, national treatment, non-discrimination, least trade-restrictiveness, and reference to international standards). It also extends these obligations to local and non-governmental standardization bodies. Over the years, for example, the World Health Organization (WHO) expert groups have created guidelines for water quality; the UNEP intergovernmental groups have adopted guidelines for disclosing information on banned and restricted products; and the International Labour Organization (ILO) tripartite expert groups have made recommendations on exposure limits to various chemicals. In addition, as described in Chapter 2, governments have committed themselves to moving their nations to sustainable development as well as formal environmental, labour, health and safety conventions. The TBT does not recognize these intergovernmental actions as acceptable international standards for use by governments or national standard-setting bodies to avoid establishing a non-tariff barrier to trade.

The wording of the Code of Good Practice excludes UN system expert groups from becoming signatories to the code. Furthermore, it excludes UN system intergovernmental bodies from being considered acceptable international standard-setting bodies because the intergovernmental participants in UN meetings are likely to come from government ministries and not from a national standard-setting body which has signed the Code of Good Practice. It is also the case that intergovernmental bodies are not likely to follow the lead of voluntary industry bodies, such as the ISO, when they initiate work on new intergovernmental standards. The GATT language may hinder the development of new standards or guidelines set by other intergovernmental bodies, since these standards do not conform to the TBT definition of an acceptable international standard. Each year, government, international organizations and civil society put considerable resources into drafting intergovernmental standards and agreeing on how to move the world closer to sustainable development. But the TBT Agreement does not mention these intergovernmental undertakings as acceptable international standards. In terms of the TBT Agreement, these standards and agreements are then inappropriate standards for governments to use to meet the TBT test of a presumption against a non-tariff barreier to trade. National standardizing bodies who participate in the negotiations should adhere to the GATT-recognized Code of Good Practice. Standardizing bodies who have accepted or withdrawn from the Code of Good Practice 'shall notify this fact to the ISO/IEC Information Centre in Geneva'.[17] Notification should be sent either directly to the centre, or preferably through the relevant national member of the international affiliate of ISONET – the ISO information network.' This significantly increases the power of the ISO members – all standard-setting activities must work through the ISO network. The ISO Central Secretariat is excited by the new position their work has in international trade law (see Box 3.1).[18]

SCOPE AND COVERAGE OF PPMS

As noted earlier, the 1994 TBT defines a product standard as including its 'production and process methods'. For example, organic coffee could be defined, in part, as coffee grown and harvested using an environmentally sound farm-management system (see Box 3.2). Following this approach, the current ISO 14000 series could be read to establish new international standards for process and production methods for management systems, life-cycle analysis, environmental auditing, and environmental performance measurements. Accordingly, the ISO 14000 series should now be used by national authorities if they cite these elements in their new standards or technical regulations. However, this is not universally clear.

Some delegations at the TBT committee, for instance, are uncertain if a management system used to specify a product standard would be considered a production and

---

Box 3.1 Developing new business – Partnership with WTO

'You are our best allies!' was how World Trade Organization (WTO) Director General Renato Ruggiero greeted the Presidents and Secretaries-General of ISO and IEC when they visited him during the course of the year. The welcome underlined the close collaboration that is growing between the WTO and the three principal international standardization bodies whose technical agreements underpin the political agreements for free and fair trade reached within the WTO.

The GATT Uruguay Round, which gave birth to the WTO, has considerably strengthened the GATT Standards Code which urges governments to use international standards in order to make the free circulation of goods across national borders easier. The new WTO Agreement on Technical Barriers to Trade includes a code of good practice for the preparation, adoption and application of standards.

The transition of ISO from a purely technical organization to one at the forefront of world trade developments is illustrated by the agreement with the WTO according to which ISO operates a joint information system for collection notifications relating to the code of good practice. This system is run through ISONET (the ISO information network) and the ISO/IEC Information Centre in Geneva.

Source: ISO, *Annual Report*, 1996

---

process method. Since PPMs are a relatively new term of reference in international trade law, a dispute-settlement body could interpret the TBT to include or exclude 'management system' from the agreement's scope of coverage. Were it excluded, then a government could develop a technical regulation and a national standard body could develop standards that used management systems to define product categories; these standards could create de facto barriers to trade and be immune from challenge under the current GATT.[19]

The second ambiguity is as follows: if a management system standard were used without a specific product reference, would this be covered by the TBT? It is possible that a government regulation covered the use of an environmental management system to define a specific type of firm. For example, firms with an environmentally sound management practice can get preferential treatment in bank loans. In this case, the environmental management system is not tied to a particular product or class of products but to the enterprise itself. Most of the debate about the applicability of TBT to ISO 14000 is whether the TBT captures stand alone references to management systems or only those management systems used to describe a product's production system.

While governments, firms and citizens' groups wait for a decision from dispute-settlement bodies on how management systems are defined, Canada has another proposal. Canada proposed in its paper for the triennial 1997 Review of the TBT Agreement that 'the TBT committee arrive at a consensus regarding the coverage and applicability of the agreement to these management standards. At present, Members interpret differently the degree to which these voluntary standards are subject to TBT and WTO disciplines'. In the view of the Canadian Government, the TBT committee should 'focus not on clarifying the current coverage and application of the Agreement to these organizations or management type standards, but rather initiate discussion on how, and under which terms, we can explicitly incorporate these standards under the disciplines of the TBT agreement and its Code of Good Practice'.[20]

Box 3.2 Organic Coffee

Under the pre-1994 TBT agreement, rules could be made that differentiated between coffees on their inherent characteristics (bean type, ground, etc). Any such differentiation would be appropriate and would not be a technical barrier to trade.

Under the 1994 TBT agreement, rules could be made about organic coffee – that is a coffee produced using a certain process in an environmentally healthy manner. These rules would not be presumed to be a technical barrier to trade if the national authorities followed an existing international standard definition for 'organic' coffee. Therefore, when ISO adopts the ecolabelling standards, authorities will be able to approve specific ways to label organic coffee which will not be considered a technical barrier to trade. With the approval of ISO 14001, authorities could, if they wished, specify that a part of the organic coffee production system could include that the grower had an environmental management system based on ISO 14001. Such rules on ecolabels and environmental management systems related to coffee would be consistent with the new requirements of TBT.

The New Significance of Draft International Standards

Intergovernmental standards developed through a number of different processes and fora have long been used as a basis for national standards. This has now changed. An international standard created through the procedures defined in the 1994 GATT shall be used by national standard-setting bodies. The WTO agreement also states that, if an international standard is imminent, it has to be followed when preparing national laws, regulations and standards. Draft international standards are considered as applicable as international standards under the TBT.

The Code of Good Practice also uses this language when referring to standards:

> Where international standards exist or their completion is imminent, the standardizing body shall use them, or the relevant parts of them, as a basis for the standards it develops, except when such international standards or relevant parts would be an ineffective or inappropriate means for fulfilling the legitimate objectives pursued, for instance, because of fundamental climatic or geographic factors or fundamental technological problems.[21]

Thus, the draft international standard status given to an ISO standard, approved by the voting members of an ISO technical committee, would have the status of a de facto international trade standard.

Under UN procedure, there is no such thing as a draft international standard. In intergovernmental fora, international standards are considered adopted or approved only after the final vote by the appropriate governing body or after a convention has entered into force. Until that time, the text has no special status and governments do not even consider themselves as following the international guidelines until after final approval. In the ISO, however, there is a formal procedure for establishing a draft international standard (see Chapter 2), and under the TBT rules, national standard-setting bodies are obliged to use the draft as if it were an international standard when there is no other comparable international measures.

Special Status for Developing Countries under TBT

Another key difference between the ISO and the intergovernmental arena is the process by which the agreements were developed. Recognizing the need for greater participation, the TBT requires that government members 'shall play a full part, within the limits of their resources, in the preparation by appropriate international standardizing bodies of international standards for products for which they either have adopted, or expect to adopt, technical regulations'.[22] For private and public organizations in many countries, the 'limits of their resources' are very quickly reached. As a result, a vast majority of the governments did not participate or fund participation of their national standard-setting body in the early stages of developing the ISO 14000 measures. In addition, many countries that have adopted the 1994 GATT do not have national standard-setting bodies who are full members of the ISO and so do not participate in setting the ISO standards.

Developing countries should be aware that they have special status under the TBT agreement. The agreement recognizes that developing countries may encounter special difficulties in formulating and applying technical regulations and standards and procedures for conformity assessment. It therefore includes provisions for technical assistance and transfer of technology, as well as for differential and more favourable treatment. In particular, 'developing country members should not be expected to use international standards as a basis for their technical regulations or standards, including test methods, which are not appropriate to their developmental, financial and trade needs'.[23]

It is also recognized that the special needs of developing country members, as well as their stage of technological development, may hinder their ability to fully discharge their obligations under the GATT–TBT agreement.[24] As a result, they can be granted, 'upon request, specified, time-limited exemptions' from the TBT agreement. A ten-year exemption, for example, would allow developing countries to establish their own national standards for environmental management systems or ecolabels.

If this were granted, then – at the five-year review of ISO 14001 – developing countries could work to ensure that their views were more fully incorporated into the revised standard. In addition, exclusions may need to be available to individual firms that have problems with the ISO 14000 series. With ISO 14000, it is not the developing country that needs the exemption, but rather the individual business enterprises which may have difficulties in terms of certification and meeting the standards imposed for procurement in other countries.

The TBT agreement recognizes that officials in standard-setting bodies in developing countries may need technical assistance from other GATT members. Such technical assistance can be granted 'regarding the establishment of national standardizing bodies, and participation in the international standardizing bodies'.[25] ISO's Programme for Developing Countries provides some technical assistance to national standard-setting bodies. ISO offers regional training seminars, individual fellowships for standardization officers, training for serving as secretariat of an ISO TC, and assistance in establishing standardization programmes for bilateral and multilateral agencies.[26] Assistance is not available to help developing countries upgrade their health, trade or environment ministries, or to assist the government in implementing better rules and regulations.

As prescribed by the TBT agreement, developed country members will, if requested by other members, provide in English, French or Spanish translations of the documents covered by a specific notification, or, in case of voluminous documents, summaries of such documents.[27] The working language of the ISO is English. Even though some material is available in French or Russian, meetings of TC 207 are conducted solely in English and without simultaneous translation.

CONCLUSION

Governments and businesses of all sizes will be affected by the political, social or environmental consequences associated with adopting and using ISO standards as the basis for environmental, safety and health standards in the international trading system. For 20 years the intergovernmental arena has seen a remarkable development of new standard-setting open to a wide range of participants and adopted by a recognised intergovernmental process. This entire body of standards – and future standards set through an interngovernmental process – is now likely to be marginalized through the operations of the TBT.

The link established between 'international standards' in the TBT and the ISO/IEC also means that experts with technical capacities or with vested corporate interests will take primacy over others with expertise in international health, environment and safety. ISO members, national standard-setting bodies, are not specialists in sustainable development, environmental management, health policy, employment effects or other such topics. With the TBT giving to the ISO system the status to determine relevant international standards for the trading system,. the net result is likely to be standards that are weak in these crucial areas. The adoption of non-performance based ISO 14001 as an EMS standard is indicative of the significant weakening of international standards, and of the prospect that ISO standards in this area will also serve, through the non-voluntary TBT Agreement, to undercut efforts at increased global and national environmental protection.

Chapter 4

What are the Costs and Economic Consequences of ISO 14001?

INTRODUCTION

A developing country standard-setting official was ruminating about the disappointing lack of environmental performance measures in ISO 14001. In his view, it was not clear whether ISO 14001 would be a paper stamp or would help improve environmental performance. This, he felt, was an economic question and therefore a political one:

> For example: say we have a company that we [the standard-setting body] feel should lose their certification. But the consequence of this would be bad for domestic foreign revenue. This will put political pressure on us to let them keep their certification. The same applies to a company that is an exporter, for example to the EU. There is strong political pressure for certification to be granted so that the export market is maintained. This pressure is not documented anywhere, but it is the main issue we speak about. My standard-setting body will be asked to make it easy for firms to get certification. Politics may force the prostitution of the system to retain economic stability.

This anecdote is revealing in several respects. Firstly, the issue that ISO 14001 raised for this official was not environmental protection but trade. Developing-country standards officials and firms are concerned not so much with the environmental advantage and economic opportunity that ISO certification may or may not bring, but with the economic disadvantage that they perceive may come from *not* getting involved.

This is not a new issue. For some years, development observers have been concerned that 'the ascendancy of market-based approaches is raising the issue of how market economies can deliver social equity and environmental protection, especially in developing countries.'[1] Now, just as the new GATT and trade liberalization have opened the door to global markets, developing countries feel the door being shut again because they fear that this new 'voluntary' environmental standard will not be voluntary, but become a market-based trade barrier. Many of the government officials surveyed for this book believe that ISO 14000 – particularly ISO 14001 and ecolabelling – will lead to cost increases or discrimination against their exports.[2]

> The economic impact of the ISO 14000 series will be great, as our country is an exporting country. It is feared that the ISO 14000 series will be a trade barrier, if the companies cannot conform to the standards. People see standards as a way to prevent developing countries from exporting to developed country markets (*African Respondent # 1*).

The second issue that the anecdote raises is the discretion allowed to national standard-setting bodies to set the level of the standard. Given the enormous importance of market access for developing world economies and for countries in transition, the inference in this anecdote is that national bodies will make it as easy as possible for their firms to get this ticket of admission to international markets. This means that in some countries, certification will be easier to get or less expensive than in others. In other words, the standard will not be standard. 'Experts stressed that certification and accreditation should be fair and rigorous to safeguard the credibility of the ISO 14001 certificate. Developing countries should be assisted in developing the necessary infrastructure to allow conformity assessment, certification, and accreditation.'[3]

There is a strong feeling that ISO 14001 is not only a market requirement, it is a market creation. Many companies in Asia complain that ISO is being driven by consultants seeking business.[4] As observed earlier, the Chairman of Environmental Standards at the Turkish Standards Institute (TSI) commented that ISO standardization activities in developed countries are imposed on developing countries. 'Standardization activities start first even though there is no activity to be standardized.' In his view, this is the case with ISO 14001 and with standards for life-cycle analysis, environmental performance evaluation and ecolabelling.[5] Like most of his colleagues in the developing world, the Turkish official is concerned that his country may have a limited capacity nationally to service this new need. Since the infrastructure with certification and accreditation capacities will be imported until it can be developed locally, developing countries and economies in transition will have increased costs and dependence on developed world services. Not only has a market been created into which developing countries feel they have to buy; there may be limited organizational or environmental value to be derived from the standard. ISO 14001 will be a market, not an environmental, standard.

More generally, developing country officials are deeply concerned about costs. Just maintaining a standard is expensive. National standardization bodies will incur expenses when creating and operating certification and registration systems; firms will incur costs when operating the approved environmental management systems.

> It is a market driven condition to do business, so the companies who are not ISO 14001 certified will be out of the market. If ISO 14001 becomes a condition to do business in and with the US, then it is a problem because not all companies will be able to follow it (*South American Respondent # 6*).

It is worth commenting on how gloomy much of industry feels about this new market imposition: 'politics will force the prostitution of the [standard-setting] system...' If ISO 14001 becomes a trade standard, then implementation/certification is simply a market cost and the most important issue for firms will be to reduce the cost of this market instrument. ISO 14001 is sounding more like an imposition than an opportunity.

The message that ISO 14001 is an international private-sector trade standard with market consequence has gained the attention of national departments of trade who are eager not to restrict their national economy from competing internationally. It has also created enormous anxiety among the thousands of small- and medium-sized firms, in the developed and developing world, who believe that their big-company customers may be imposing a new supplier condition. There are strong beliefs that ISO 14001 will become a condition of doing business internationally and, specifically, a supplier condition with certified international firms. There is also strong feeling that ISO 14001 will become a condition of major government procurement contracts.

This chapter proposes that the anxiety far exceeds the reality.[6] There is simply no evidence, at this time or in the foreseeable future, that ISO 14001 will become an international condition of doing business along the lines of ISO 9000. Nevertheless, this perception is taking root, fueled by the strong sales efforts of consultants and other service providers. This sales hype is escalated by the fact that some of the negotiators in the process of creating the standard are also consultants who sell services into the ISO 14001 market. When they endorse the product, they do so as experts rather than just as salespeople. The result is that firms dependent on international customers feel pressured to invest in what they understand is a customer requirement. Such investment costs are relatively higher for small- and medium-sized firms than for large ones, and higher for firms in countries with weak environmental infrastructures than for those in developed countries. In environmental terms, the return on investment is uncertain. The economic return depends on whether the assumptions, such as those cited earlier, are correct. The first part of this chapter will show that these market assumptions lack a factual basis, and that investment decisions based on these inferences could be very costly.

The second part of this chapter turns to a related question: if ISO 14001 is perceived as a market, not an environmental, standard, then what avenues must firms and governments, particularly in the developing world, pursue to get market access? The chapter will show the kinds of costs that are involved in making this investment, particularly for standard-setting organizations and governments in developing countries and countries in transition. It also argues that, faced with this high market entry cost, developing countries and firms are faced with strong pressure to reduce costs – in other words, to make ISO 14001 certification easy and inexpensive.

There are important implications for developed country and global firms if a trend towards adopting ISO 14001 certification begins for market reasons. If ISO 14001 certificates are issued in large number by national standard-setting bodies with different standards for certification, and whose prime interest is market access rather than environmental management, it could empty the standard of any meaning. Certainly, for global companies who consider using ISO 14001 as an indicator of environmental assurance, an ISO 14001 certificate could become a paper tiger. The flexibility demanded of ISO 14001 certification by developed country interests will become its curse. Pressures on developing country suppliers to demonstrate ISO 14001 certification could result in barriers to trade and/or detract from the environmental objectives of setting up an EMS. Companies in developed countries should establish a supportive cooperation with their suppliers in developing countries in the area of EMS implementation. Transnational corporations (TNCs) could play an important role in this regard.'[7] If developed country firms are interested in using ISO 14001 as some form of environmental assurance, they will need, at minimum, to give increased attention to cross-accreditation and mutual recognition between different national standard-setting bodies.

Most of the debate about the effects of ISO 14001 assumes that it will become a market trade barrier. This assumption comes from experience of ISO 9000 and a belief that this history will be repeated. The assumption that ISO 14001 will become the passport to participation in global trade is very strong, especially outside Europe.[8] Officials from Jamaica, South Africa, Israel, and most Asian countries firmly believe this to be true. Most think that certification to the standard may become a de facto requirement of doing business in certain countries, as has been the case with the ISO 9000 standards for quality management.

WHAT ARE THE MARKET ASSUMPTIONS ABOUT ISO 14001?

SUPPLIER CONDITIONS

ISO 9001, the ISO quality-management systems standard, is referred to continuously as a precedent for ISO 14001. ISO 9001 had a significant effect in certain sectors and certain countries, taking off slowly and gradually becoming more popular. Firms and their governments in countries that did not respond to ISO 9000 (particularly in Asia and the US) feel that this standard became a de facto ticket of admission to European markets. They feel that their lack of interest and activity in ISO 9000 placed them at a market disadvantage in European markets. They fear that market share could be lost again, if national standardization bodies, accreditation companies and developing country firms do not respond quickly, this time to the ISO 14000 series.

Is this assumption true? ISO 9000-certified firms make certification a condition of their suppliers because it is required by the standard. This one feature alone creates a multiplier effect with each new ISO 9000 firm. In principle, this condition is helpful because the customer firm can get a quality system assurance or performance specification, as was the intention of this ISO series of standards. In practice, these conditions have complex market implications by creating closed customer–supplier chains which preclude new entrants or bidders for those contracts. As already indicated, this has imposed significant financial hardships on firms that were late to certify.[9]

If ISO 9001 is a precedent, then there are grounds for concern with ISO 14001. ISO 9000 became a stipulation in some sectors when governments required certification for some procurement contracts. In Hong Kong, ISO 9000 certification was necessary for those businesses bidding for government projects that exceeded US $1.25 million.[10] An official in Israel noted that the Israeli Department of Health made ISO 9000 a condition of procurement within the food industry. He also felt that ISO 9000 was a requisite for trade: 'Try to get any EU government assignment without ISO 9000 nowadays!'[11]

In an expert group meeting on the potential effects of ISO 9000 and ISO 14000 on the trade of developing countries, the UN Industrial Development Organization (UNIDO) found that entrepreneurs were intimidated by the substantial human and

---

BOX 4.1 REASONS FOR RELUCTANCE TO ACCEPT FOREIGN ISO 9000 CERTIFICATES

Most countries:	Lack of confidence due to little knowledge of local certification schemes
Pakistan, the Philippines:	Lack of good reputation and a well known name
Sri Lanka:	Domestic certification bodies are indeed unreliable
Pakistan (one respondent):	Fear of the unknown
Brazil (one respondent):	Protectionist motives

Source: Trade Implications of International Standards for Quality and Environmental Management Systems, Survey prepared by UNIDO Industrial Sectors and Environment Division. UNIDO doc: ISED.9(Spec.) 12 February 1996

---

financial resources needed to comply with ISO 9000.[12] UNIDO also conducted a survey of businesses on the trade implications of international standards, focusing on the ISO standards for quality management and environmental management systems. Released in February 1996, the report stated that, within the developing world, businesses have been reluctant to accept foreign ISO 9000 certificates, in part because of protectionist motives but primarily because businesses were unfamiliar with the requirements for local certifying bodies – or the equivalency of 'standards' in the international standards (see Box 4.1).

However, unlike ISO 9001, ISO 14001 does not include a certification requirement for suppliers. This has not prevented the trade press from predicting that requirements for ISO 14001 certification may follow the route of ISO 9001. One should note that these claims are often made by groups that have a large stake in the ISO 14000 process.[13] The inference however, that interfirm purchasing requirements will be made is clearly assumed in developing countries and such exaggerated market claims can only heighten anxieties. An UNCTAD report pointed out that environmental-management system requirements, such as ISO 14001, will place significant financial burdens on small- and medium-sized enterprises and developing country firms.[14]

The perception that the history of ISO 9000 as a trade barrier will be repeated with ISO 14001 may be incorrect. Firstly, the issues are different. Quality is a generic business issue, while environmental concerns may be of relevance in specific sectors.[15] Secondly, ISO 9000 requires a certified company to have certified suppliers. The European Union's EMAS states that registered firms need to 'ensure that suppliers and those acting on the organization's behalf comply with the company's environmental policy as it relates to them'. However, supplier certification was rejected in the drafting of ISO 14001. The text ISO 14001 requires only 'communication of relevant procedures and requirements to suppliers and contractors'.[16] This means that firms, citing a supplier condition for their ISO 14001 certification, are imposing an extra condition on their downstream suppliers.

Transnational corporate intentions towards ISO 14001 certification are still unclear. According to studies and informed opinion in the US, Canada and Europe, the large companies are taking a wait-and-see approach. There is some movement in some sectors but not in others. In 1996, the international management consulting firm

Arthur D Little reported in a survey that most big firms are sitting on the fence. They are putting environmental management systems in place and establishing what it would take to obtain ISO 14001 if it ever became a market condition; however, there is no trend among the global firms towards ISO 14001 certification.[17] In 1996, Digital Equipment, based in Boston, surveyed 10 per cent of their several thousand customers internationally. They found that not one required Digital to be ISO 14001 certified at that time.[18] As most firms are still undecided about their own certification or implementation of ISO 14001, they are unlikely to have made policy decisions on supplier conditions.

In terms of making ISO 14001 a supplier condition, there is scant evidence that this will happen. As of May 1997, a survey of manufacturers in Asia found that none had any intention of requiring ISO 14001 certification of their Asian suppliers in the foreseeable future.[19] Another survey in July 1997 of global US-based firms found that business are not rushing to certify themselves, are not being asked to certify by their customers, and are not intending to make ISO 14001 a supplier condition.[20] The reasons for the lack of interest in making ISO 14001 a supplier condition are numerous. Firstly, firms are reluctant to place additional financial burdens on their suppliers beyond complying with environmental laws in their key markets. Secondly, global firms are interested in nurturing long-term relationships with their key suppliers. Firms are unlikely to impose draconian options, such as certify or lose our business. They are far more interested in working with such suppliers. Thirdly, environmental partnerships are likely to include ISO Plus features, particularly performance assurances.[21] The prognosis of one international standards expert is: 'ISO 14000 will not fly like ISO 9000'.[22] On the contrary, there is significant concern in some industry sectors about the proliferation of standards and the additional burden this puts on their operations.

One of the reasons that big firms are not rushing to certify with ISO 14001 is precisely because of the history of ISO 9000. Some companies are still trying to absorb the new processes and requirements of ISO 9000. They have spent a great deal of money on consultants, have not yet achieved their return on this investment, and are still too exhausted from organizational change.

This reality, however, is not driving the market. Instead, it is the perception that major customers will make ISO 14001 a supplier condition that is driving much of the interest in ISO 14001. These investments will be expensive at several levels – particularly if firms find that ISO 14001 is not enough to provide environmental assurances to their customers. If firms place environmental-management system criteria on their suppliers, these will probably include performance specifications. If supplier firms invest in ISO 14001 certification with the belief that this will bring market advantage, they may find that this is not enough: they may have to invest yet again to meet ISO Plus requirements from their customers.

Under the product stewardship code of Responsible Care®, for example, firms can ensure that their suppliers implement environmental safeguards and can request information on storage, handling, use and disposal practices, environmental management systems, audit systems, and so on. The US-based company Dow Chemical insists on conducting an audit before it agrees to supply a new customer with hazardous material and routinely audits its distributors. This audit involves visiting the distributor's operations to examine handling, transportation and storage, and prescribing improvements aimed at achieving 'beyond compliance' environmental standards.[23] Volkswagen expects, from its suppliers and subcontractors, a declared commitment to environmental protection; continuous improvement of process and production measured against ecological criteria (tools could include EMAS and the 'ecological balance sheet'); identification and documentation of the chemical composition of material supplied; recycling and disposal concepts for products supplied; and the development of 'new approaches and methods for attaining our common environmental objectives.'[24]

There is some interest among global firms in greening the supply chain or in developing standards for supplier environmental management. General Motors commissioned a benchmarking study of best practice in supplier environmental management. Among the 20 companies surveyed, it found three models of supplier environmental management: an integrated and comprehensive approach that expects beyond compliance activity; a compliance-based approach; and an industry standard approach seeking screens for supplier selection and industry associations or other groups to provide technical assistance. Corporate leaders in this area ask their suppliers for information about their compliance histories; their environmental management systems; eco-efficiency measures (pollution prevention, energy efficiency); and indicators of design for environment (life-cycle assessment, recycling practices). Environmental performance data is requested as a basis for maintaining the business relationship. Most of these companies work with their key suppliers to improve their environmental performance but will end the relationship if suppliers repeatedly fail to meet environmental performance expectations.[25]

A new standard of environmental practice for suppliers has been developed by a group of some 20 global computer firms based in the US, together with the Pacific Industry Business Association (PIBA). They seek to promote this standard across industries, within the US and internationally. CIQC Standard 0014 was driven by a concern to reduce risk and enhance supplier relationships while standardizing customer queries and supplier management regarding non-product-related environmental performance. It expects suppliers to have an environmental policy, compliance plan and compliance audits, and 'a commitment to continuous improvement and performance objectives with implementation plans and measures'. A second part of the standard, intended for critical suppliers, seeks more information about the suppliers' environmental risk management across the range of environmental media.[26] Like the public sector, large firms may create an ISO Plus requirement for environmental assurance. Given this reality, supplier firms need to survey their customer needs and intentions because each choice could have quite different cost implications.

GOVERNMENT PROCUREMENT CONDITIONS

There are inferences in the trade press that some government ministries are considering ISO 14001 certification as a condition in government procurement bids. Closer examination indicates that this may happen only in some ministries, and that generalizations should not be transferred from one ministry to another.

One clear difference between private- and public-sector procurement is that governments cannot set purchase requirements which stipulate production methods. Under GATT rules, government procurement contracts in agreed areas can differentiate only between products on their intrinsic, or product, characteristics. Since ISO 14001 is an environmental management system, two identical products made with or without ISO 14001 certification are not intrinsically different. As a result, governments need to examine if GATT would allow a government to require a specific type of management system when it purchases products. An ISO 14001 requirement might be seen as a non-tariff trade barrier.

As noted in Chapter 3, government procurement requirements can be non-tariff barriers to trade if they make stipulations that bias purchasers in favour of domestic suppliers. There are several ways that such a stipulation could become a trade barrier. Since there is no mutual recognition of registrars between countries, there may well be pressure on governments to define, in the procurement agreement, a specific national or regional certifying body. If the stipulation says that the certification to ISO 14001 has to be through a specific agent, such as their own national standard-setting body, then this would be a traditional form of a non-tariff barrier.

While there may be legal issues with respect to international trade barriers, this has not stopped government agencies from considering ISO 14001 as part of the procurement process. The UK government, in a 1995 bidding round for North Sea oil and gas-lease rights, awarded 10 per cent of the evaluation points to bidders certified with one of the existing voluntary standards for environmental management. Some governments in Latin America and Asia are considering making ISO 14001 a condition of entry for foreign oil exploration and production operators; they argue that this is a low-cost way to ensure responsible environmental management among foreign and locally owned natural resource industries.[27]

These incidents naturally create a fear that ISO 14001 will become a market condition for those who want to do business with governments. As a result, both the developed and developing world feel that they may need to build the necessary infrastructure for ISO 14000.

THE MARKET EFFECT OF ASSUMPTIONS ABOUT ISO 14001

COSTS

Surprisingly, the business participants in the ISO process did not forecast the anticipated cost of implementing ISO 14001 within industrial sectors or even for individual firms. While the business community has often called for cost-benefit analyses of new government standards and regulations, no such analysis has been done for the ISO 14000 series of standards.

In general, some costs are known and others can be approximated. The first economic cost of ISO 14001 to developing countries and CIT countries was the cost of participation at meetings (see Box 4.2). As already demonstrated, this cost was too high for most developing countries, and it is for economic reasons that developing coun-

---

BOX 4.2 BRAZIL – THE COST OF PARTICIPATION

Brazil created an Environmental Standardization Supporting Group (GANA) linked to the Brazilian Association of Technical Standards (ABNT). They have engaged in a number of activities, including financing participation and technical support. The costs of participating in TC 207 meetings through May 1996 has been US $550,000. The Brazilian Ministry of the Environment and the Ministry of Industry and Commerce supported these initiatives. The National Confederation of Industry serves as head of the organization. There have been seminars and workshops organized in all the main states of Brazil for disseminating the ISO 14000 series. Low interest lines of credit are offered for this.

A consortium of Brazilian industry groups has also been promoting ISO 14000. The consortium comprises the Brazilian Institute of the Environment (IBAMA), the Small and Medium Companies Supporting Service (SEBRAE) and the Herbert Levy Institute, with support of the United Nations Educational, Scientific and Cultural Organization (UNESCO) and the National Confederation of Industry. This group distributed a set of folders free in the main Brazilian business newspaper. 100,000 folders were distributed each week over an eight week period, for a cost of $900,000.

Source: South American Respondent #1

---

tries participated so little and so late. Costs are also a major constraint on small- and medium-sized firms and on environmental NGOs. Even if these groups had wished to attend the meetings, they could not afford the continual travel demands as the negotiating sessions moved between the major cities of the world.

In addition to costs borne by national standard-setting bodies, other entities, whether governments or businesses, also incur expenses in efforts to review and appraise the applicability of the ISO 14001 standard to their needs. A small number of companies have become certified to the draft international standard and subsequently to ISO 14001. This is particularly true in Asia, and especially among companies that feel that ISO 14001 will be a ticket of admission to international markets.

COSTS FOR FIRMS

Businesses considering certification must appraise if it is more cost-effective to self-certify, use a local accreditation firm or use an international firm. A self-certified firm can employ an internal resource or a mixture of internal resources with some external consulting. It might ask for external consulting advice on just those technical areas where the company lacks internal capacity.

Alternatively, the firm could apply to register as an ISO 14001 firm through a national or international certifying body. In the developing world where the national standard-setting body may not, or may not yet, have this capacity, international consulting houses provide certification services and registering firms. The authority for international consulting houses can be from a national certifying body or from an authorized certifying body in another country, generally the home country of the firm. This capacity to certify internationally, based on the authority of a national certification body, gives the international industry a market leadership position. Developing country firms who take this route to certification should be wary of high-cost certification services and should, at a minimum, survey their major customers to see if they have, or plan to develop, an environmental management system or ISO 14001 requirement for suppliers; they should then determine what kind of system they require.

There is a third alternative, emerging strongly in developed world firms with an environmental management system, or part of a system, in place. They have taken a 'readiness' approach. Not yet convinced that ISO 14001 will be a market issue, they are unwilling to make an investment in a non-performance-based system; nevertheless they want to be prepared in case it becomes a market issue, so that they can become certified quickly. This option – being 70 to 80 per cent ready for a market standard in case ISO 14001 becomes a market condition – means that firms establish a basic environmental management system so that a transition to ISO 14001 is achieved with little delay. In many cases, this 'readiness' is not difficult for leading firms, since their existing environmental management systems are so far ahead of ISO 14001's requirements; the 'gap' is usually in some of the documentation control areas. This readiness is not the same as preparing for certification. Rather, it indicates the opposite: these firms do not see enough environmental value in certification to support its costs and they are not being asked by their customers to become certified.[28] They will only get certification if it becomes a market condition.

Some businesses in developing economies have invested time and money in certification to ISO 9000. Others have been struggling to implement the ISO 9000 standards and now may have to simultaneously develop ISO environmental-management system standards.[29] In Indonesia, financial aid programmes have been set up to help small- and medium-sized enterprises get certified for ISO 9000, and funds for environmental management systems are being made available as well. In general, however, companies wanting ISO 14001 certification will have to carry the brunt of the short-term and long-term costs. Not only will they have to pay to implement and certify an environmental management system – they will also have to pay for a multitude of other consulting services on the side, such as competence and awareness-building within and beyond the firm. These very high costs are a major reason for the appeal to regulators for regulatory relief and infrastructure support. Developing country standard-setting bodies and industry associations feel that ministries of trade, industry or environment should pay for the creation of national infrastructures for certification and training.[30] Governments are, in effect, being called upon to subsidize their national firms' entry into the global marketplace with support for ISO 14001.

Subsidies for ISO 14001 implementation could come to affiliates of international firms through their corporate parents, from wealthier industrial associations or through the developing country office of the ISO. International and intergovernmental organizations also provide training, such as the environmental management system training programmes of UNIDO and a joint initiative of UNEP and the International Chamber of Commerce (ICC). As of 1997, most businesses estimate their costs based on their ISO 9000 experience. As more businesses become certified to the 14001 standard, an increasing number of determinations will be possible. The care taken by drafters to construct ISO 14001 in such a way that it builds on the ISO 9000 structure will obviously mean that it is less expensive for firms that already have ISO 9000 to put ISO 14001 in place.

Developing country firms must decide on how to get certified: through an international or a local firm. This choice is forced on firms in the absence of a system which mutually recognizes ISO certifiers for the 14001 standard. The firm's choice is based on a perceived price or market value trade-off. A national certifying firm or self-certification may be less expensive, but the ISO 14001 certificate may not be recognized by the international customer. On the other hand, an international firm with the authority to issue ISO 14001 certificates, provided by a standard-setting body in a major country, will most likely be more expensive.[31]

ISO 14001 describes a management system that is in tune with contemporary organizational models in the OECD world. In these countries, there are theories of corporate management, each with its own school of adherents. Businesses in developing countries may be at a disadvantage in terms of their cultural approach to such systems. In developing countries the methods of corporate management may be based on local historical practices that have not yet been transformed into an explicit management systems. Certain characteristics of developing country firms, such as the limited attention traditionally devoted to procedure documentation and records, have represented an obstacle to ISO 9000 implementation.[32] It is considerably less expensive to add an environmental management system onto an existing system than to formalize an overall management system before 'adding in' the environmental component.

Even for firms with a sophisticated environmental management system, there are additional operating costs to meet (training, documentation, monitoring, scope of policy). Many of the global firms questioned in the US–Asian Environmental Partnership (USAEP) survey, all of whom had existing environmental management systems in place, for instance, lacked an adequate ISO 14001 level of documentation. Even for large firms with environmental management systems in place, the costs were time and again cited as being too expensive for the anticipated return. The ISO 14001 documentation-control requirements are seen as involving significant costs on their own, and global US companies such as Georgia Pacific, Union Camp (paper industry), Dow Chemical and Motorola cite the documentation control aspects of ISO 14001 as a cost they will not incur unless pushed.[33]

Many countries are afraid of the serious economic impacts of the ISO 14000 series on small- and medium-sized enterprises (SMEs).[34] In developing and developed countries, SMEs and micro-enterprises constitute a major part of the national economy, employing more people and paying more wages overall than the bigger companies. In China, Mexico and Thailand, more than 90 per cent of all businesses are SMEs.[35] These businesses have significant constraints in meeting environmental standards and regulations, including those that are endemic to the nature of their operations, because of cost, lack of information or technology, etc.[36] Small- and medium-sized enterprises may bear the brunt of the 'obligatory' implementation of additional management standards. The costs involved in running an environmental management system may prove to be too high for SMEs. The fear is that this could result in economic failure.[37] Even in industrialized countries this is recognized as a major problem.[38] In some countries there are already programmes to identify the problems faced by this group of enterprises.[39] TC 207 has belatedly recognized this difficulty and begun a discussion group on implementing ISO 14001 in SMEs.

Subsidiaries of transnational corporations may be relatively better off because they have access to financial and technical assistance from their mother companies. The start-up costs of ISO 14001 implementation for an affiliate of a transnational corporation could be far less than for an independent national firm of comparable size. The affiliate can draw on corporate documentation and systems methods, and may be able to share joint resources that will reduce the cost of systems implementation and registration. SMEs do not have these networks. This is a specific reason why Agenda 21 called on TNCs to 'consider establishing environmental partnership schemes with SMEs' and to 'organize environmental training programmes for the private sector and other groups in developing countries'.[40]

Since the prices for ISO 14000 services are mainly based on consultant or registrar fees, they vary widely depending on the market price for consultant fees in each country. In an example used as the basis for the UN Development Programme (UNDP) calculations for ISO services, a US consultant charged $1800 per day plus US$200 per diems, including weekends. This may be too high an estimate. Indications in the US are that consultants who charge this kind of fee are losing out to consultants charging less than US$1000 per day. Based on the Malaysian public-sector baseline, one would expect Malaysian consultants to charge less than the US fee, or around US$600.[41] If local consultants were available in Malaysia, the professional fee to implement an ISO 14001 environmental management system in an SME could be significantly less than the fee of a US consultant, even assuming that the same travel expenses were incurred.

In the UNDP study, the consulting fees for a small US-based firm with no existing quality or environmental management system was calculated to be around US $92,000, plus US$20,300 for registration costs and US$10,150 for periodic (typically yearly) registration maintenance. The fees were based on 1995 fees for ISO 9000 registration by a private standard-setting body, NSF-International.[42] Under most circumstances, there would be no difference between the fee or per diem costs of US or European consultants in or outside their home country. Not only are the per diem costs of foreign developed-country consultants higher than for their developing country equivalents, the developing country firm would need to absorb travel costs – so the total bill may be even more expensive than for a developed country firm.

Local services in developing countries can result in reduced fees. An Argentinean official gave an estimated cost for certification of between US$10,000 and US$20,000, depending on the size of the company.[43] Based on the Malaysian fee for certification work, the estimate for registering would be US$3225 for 7.5 days of professional services to certify a small firm, or US$5160 for 12 days to certify a large firm. To this should be added the cost of the Malaysian registration fee; this still results in a far less expensive process: US$3440 for an SME and US$5375 for a large firm.[44] Obviously the Malaysian investment in training local providers of ISO 14000 services will result in a far less expensive service provision for local firms.

Some of these costs could be ameliorated by a slower phase-in option, and by offers of technology transfer from developed country firms or industry associations. Historically, the rules and standards of international environmental agreements have recognized uneven development, and made provision for developing countries to delay implementing changes in the new agreement or to make changes contingent on technology transfer from developing countries.[45] An official from the Instituto Colombiano de Normas Técnicas y Certificación suggested a phase-in period and subsidy to business as a way of helping developing countries if ISO 14001 becomes a contractual condition. This kind of request is consistent with past experience in international environmental standard-setting and with the GATT provisions but is lacking in ISO practice.

COSTS FOR ACCREDITATION BODIES

Many countries have consultants and professional networks to provide ISO 9000 certification. In some cases, the ISO 14000 standards will be added to this existing certification system. These networks have the increased costs of adding environmental competence to the existing quality-control certifiers, registrars, and inspectors. A combined or integrated certifying system could reduce the overall level of fixed costs. Of course, the competence of a product or process quality-control auditor, who was responsible for ISO 9000, is quite different from that of an environmental auditor, who is required to check if the system is consistent with environmental laws and regulations and whether the company policy addresses the significant environmental aspects of the firm's activities.[46]

The perceived market pressure is obviously felt by national standard-setting bodies concerned with national economic health. At the same time, international company consultants are active in all countries, providing ISO 14001 certificates, regardless of the activity of the national standard-setting organization. It is possible that, from the perspective of the local firm, the foreign consultant has a greater value because of his or her international status. Nevertheless, outside firms may not provide other needed services which are unrelated to certification or registration, such as training a body of national auditors. As a result, foreign competition may not reduce the need for a national standard-setting body to establish 14000 services, but it may significantly reduce the size of the market that can be serviced by national certifiers. An official from the South African Bureau of Standards (SABS) referred to the increasing number of foreign firms who are registering companies in South Africa as his competitors.

Several certification companies based in the developed world have been certifying companies internationally to ISO 14001 or to DIS/ISO 14001. This has occurred in South Africa (through SGS),[47] in Zimbabwe (through DNV Zimbabwe, an affiliate of a Norwegian company and through SGS), in Argentina (through Bureau Veritas's Argentinean affiliate),[48] in Brazil,[49] and elsewhere. Capacity building in terms of national ISO 14001 accreditation and certification bodies will require significant effort on the part of governments or private industry – in some countries the government is taking the lead role and in others it is the private sector. Guidelines for accreditation bodies or the terms of condition for the registrars are being formulated or just beginning to be implemented. How these criteria are used at the national level is an important issue. Some developing country officials are concerned that overseas customers will be reluctant to accept ISO certificates issued by their domestic certification bodies.[50]

The costs for setting up an accreditation body and a system of registrars can be very high. Many of the investments for a national accreditation body are fixed: capital costs; membership marketing costs; other ongoing expenses; support staff and support services; document production; the design of training and audit services and the maintenance of these capacities; and recruiting and training sufficient numbers of high-calibre staff to deal with environmental management and pollution prevention. In the US, the Registrar Accreditation Board (RAB) exists as a strong accreditation agency for other standards, including ISO 9000, and the RAB reportedly spent over US$1 million just in start-up costs for its ISO 14001 registration programme.[51] This figure does not include the costs that sister institutions in the US have incurred in establishing their programmes.

The estimated start-up costs in Brazil, a country that has taken large steps in the past two decades towards industrial infrastructure development, were released by the Associaçao Brasileira de Normas Técnicas (ABNT). ABNT has been active in the TC 207 process, spending US $550,000 to facilitate participation in the meetings to draft the ISO 14001 standard (see Box 4.2). It also worked domestically in Brazil to promote experimentation in the use of the draft ISO 14000 for small- and medium-sized businesses. The Standards and Industrial Research Institute of Malaysia spent US$93,600 just to set up an environmental-management system certification unit for the institute, and this figure covers staff time and development only – not other costs. Initial costs for certification through the Singapore Productivity and Standards Board ranges from US$8500 for firms with fewer than 100 employees to US$11,500 for firms with 100 to 600 employees, followed by annual certificate and surveillance fees of US$3570 and US$4280, respectively.[52]

In order to ease financial strains, the establishment of regional or multinational bodies of accreditation and certification should be taken into consideration. In addition to financial benefits, it should also be easier to achieve mutual recognition from other international accreditation bodies. For example, the European Accreditation of Certification (EAC), composed of 17 European accreditation bodies, recently signed a memorandum of understanding to affirm that the accreditations from any of the signatories will be recognized by the other accreditation bodies.[53] In September 1996, the EAC approved guidelines on criteria for accreditation bodies that may well be used in designing measures for other regional accreditation foundations.[54] Draft international accreditation criteria are currently being developed by the International Accreditation Forum, based in part on the criteria used by the Joint Accreditation System of Australia and New Zealand.

Despite the competition, there is a need for international recognition of national accreditation and certification bodies. Without it, certification in a developing country might not be well regarded by a company based in the developed world. Or companies in one country may spend hundreds of thousands of dollars on a certificate that could be obtained for a fraction of the cost at similar facilities in another country. Currently there are different means of assessing conformity within developing countries. The criteria for registrars to certify companies are not harmonized internationally, and auditor training standards vary between countries. A global system of mutual recognition is being considered by the ISO Committee on Conformity Assessment (CASCO).

However, this ISO committee has to consider mutual recognition for all ISO standards, not just the ISO 14001 series.

ADDITIONAL COSTS FOR COUNTRIES WITH WEAK REGULATORY SYSTEMS

Governments and businesses will face increased costs in countries where new and additional regulations are needed. Developing countries do not have a large cadre of trained environmental managers. They do not have professional networks that provide continuing education. And they do not have computerized legal and regulatory information systems allowing easy access to a compendium of 'applicable laws and regulations'.

A significant problem for developing countries is the shallow pool of knowledgeable experts. For this reason, *Agenda 21* recommends that the international business community needs to 'have a special role in promoting cooperation in technology transfer and in building a trained human resource pool ... in host countries'.[55] Such training is required not only at the senior executive level of large enterprises, but also among small- and medium-sized enterprises. An official at the Colombian Environment Ministry noted, for example, that developing countries may need significant support for training in ecology among their largely illiterate citizens if ecolabelling becomes a condition contracts.[56]

The potential cost saving from an environmental management system in developing countries may not be as easily seen or measurable outside OECD countries. In most European countries for example, a waste management system resulting in a reduction of waste or sewage water directly pays off because of the reduced cost of waste disposal.[57] These environmental costs are lower in many developing countries.[58] Only in countries where the cost of disposal or liability is high is it likely that an environmental management system will be welcomed as a possible source of economic gain.[59] In other countries it may be difficult to get companies to participate in a voluntary process for pollution prevention if they do not see the short-term cost benefits.[60]

ISO 14001 requires that firms review the significant environmental aspects of their activities. Environmental assessments and environmental analyses are routinely required by regulatory agencies in developed countries. Significant industrial expansions, transportation projects or other development activities all start with the preparation and public review of environmental impact statements. In non-OECD countries there is considerably less experience with environmental impact assessments or EIAs. It may be difficult to recruit or train an inhouse environmental health and safety manager, and there are few domestic environmental consultants available for the specialized preparation of these reports.

ISO 14001 requires that a firm's environmental policy state that the company is committed to obeying relevant laws and regulations. In developed countries, environmental rules and regulations, although criticized as legion, are available through well-used channels. In many firms, the environment, health and safety officer already has full knowledge of these rules and regulations as part of the firm's general compliance activities. This may not be the case in the developing world, and firms (as well as government agencies) may need to go to great lengths and expense to establish a compendium of applicable environmental laws and regulations. According to a UNIDO survey of officials in government, standards and accreditation bodies and industry associations, the greatest interest among small- and medium-sized enterprises for ISO 14000, is in demonstrating conformity with legislation; however, one third of the respondents admitted that they themselves were only partly aware of such environmental legislation.[61]

A 1995 study by UNCTAD noted that applying product environmental standards can impose severe costs on developing country economies.[62] The ecolabelling scheme is especially important since it refers directly to product-related issues and therefore pertains to immediate market relevance.[63] These standards are in many ways regarded as having an even higher potential for economic impact than the ISO 14001 series. Ecolabelling schemes are capable of exacerbating current global market trends; as a result, the share of international markets for developing countries shrinks and, within all countries, the share of both national and international markets for small businesses diminishes. Ecolabelling schemes may need to be accompanied by aggressive affirmative policies to facilitate the participation of small firms and developing country exporters.[64]

Of course, one should note that costs to one sector of the economy may be income to another. Some companies, such as SGS (Switzerland) and Control Services Singapore Ltd, are confident that the demand for environmental management system consultancy and certification services will expand significantly in the next few years.[65] A study of environmental management in the Malay palm oil and timber industry suggests that the distributional effects of compliance may be more important than the international competitive effects.[66] ISO 14000 may help to circulate money within the national economy and create new business opportunity – especially if the work can be conducted by local businesses who will find or train qualified staff.

CONCLUSIONS

The economic costs of the ISO 14001 standard will largely depend on the international marketplace. ISO 14001 is being sold and bought on the basis of its implied trade advantage, not its environmental benefits. The trade argument is supported by reference to the history of ISO 9001 and a prediction that this will be repeated. This chapter demonstrates that there is no evidence to support this prediction. Unlike ISO 9001, ISO 14001 does not have a requirement for supplier certification. If large firms cite ISO 14001 as requiring certification, this is a non-standard application of the measure.

In all cases, the rationale for these expenditures is market access: environmental performance improvement is not a necessary consequence of this investment. This means that countries and companies considering such an investment should be sure either that ISO 14001 is critical to their particular international market or that it would provide other benefits. A performance-based environmental-management system programme might lead to fewer fines for non-compliance with existing laws and regulations. It could lead to better relationships with local authorities and public-interest groups. In the meantime, developing countries and their businesses should not be expected to invest in environmental-management system improvements at the same level as governments, standard-setting bodies and businesses in the developed world.

If firms in developing countries and countries with economies in transition are considering ISO 14001 because of its implied trade consequences (rather than, for example, for internal organizational reasons), then they should be aware that this issue may emerge in some sectors and not in others. They should, like Digital Corp, query their customers on whether they plan to make ISO 14001 a supplier condition. In addition, they should be aware that large firms are unlikely to be satisfied with a non-performance environmental assurance. Such firms may want to add a requirement to the standard. It may be that for firms, as for governments, the ISO 14001 standard on its own will not be enough and that some form of ISO Plus will be required. For firms in the rest of the world, particularly in the case of major global firms, this trend towards certification should be watched closely and with caution. The proliferation of subsidies to this market, by lower regulatory floors, or by lower standards in some national standard-setting organizations, could result in lower standards for corporate environmental performance. Firms that consider imposing ISO 14001 as a supplier requirement may find that they are offered a set of paper tigers which trumpet environmental achievements but have little substantive value. These firms therefore have an interest in sponsoring cross-accreditation and mutual recognition of national standards to some agreed level; or, like the Computer Industry Quality Conference, may decide to work with their sector on performance-based supplier standards.

There are, however, several ways that trade officials and the standard-setting bodies in the developing countries can avoid some of the negative economic effects of these standards. Within the ISO 14000 series, several standards are still being negotiated. As a result, developing countries still have the opportunity to influence the format and potential costs of these standards. In some working groups there may only be 30 voting participants, so several additional voices can have an impact on the outcome. Important issues, such as creating a guidance standard for small- and medium-sized enterprises, were voted down by a majority of one vote. Increased expenditures in the participation process may significantly reduce the future cost of implementation.

A standards institution establishing an infrastructure which will support ISO 14000 certification may want to conduct a 'needs assessment' in the country. This should determine the requirements for environmental management systems, and ISO 14000, in different sectors and businesses. Conformity assessment plans should also be developed. For businesses, those only operating nationally may not need certification, and those firms exporting to international corporate customers may be able to create a combination of self-regulation and customer audits at a lower cost than ISO certification.

ISO 14001 is an international standard on EMS. It therefore has implications for both trade and environment. This chapter and the last described some of the trade consequences. However, ISO 14001 is also being marketed to the environmental regualtory community as an international environmental standard that will bring environmental improvement and therefore merits regulatory relief. This is the subject of the next chapter.

Chapter 5

How Can ISO 14000 Be Integrated Into Public Law and Policy?

INTRODUCTION

A conference for regulators and businesses on ISO 14001 was held at the Massachusetts Institute of Technology (MIT) in late 1996. During the keynote presentation by Joe Cascio, head of the ANSI (US) delegation to TC 207, an EPA officer observed that ISO 14001 required a 'commitment to compliance'. He asked, therefore whether a firm had to be in compliance to get an ISO 14001 certificate. Cascio's answer was no, ISO 14001 could be given to a firm if it was not in compliance. The officer persisted: if the firm remained out of compliance, could the certificate be retained? The answer was yes.[1]

Here lies the rub for the regulators. The rationale for self-regulation, as seen in Chapter 1, is that the firm is operating beyond compliance. It is on this basis that the regulators have in the past considered regulatory relief. The reason that this concept is appealing on a global level is that voluntary, beyond compliance activities by global firms in the developing world can help to rack up environmental standards without placing onerous costs on developing countries or smaller firms. It is the concept of leading by best practice.

The rationale behind Cascio's answers is that ISO 14001 is a process by which the firm can evaluate its environmental aspects and bring it under control while maintaining its business activities. If, therefore, a major event ocurred in the year meant that the firm ended up more out of compliance than earlier, this is not a basis for removing its ISO certification, since the firm may still be strongly committed to compliance. The question, then, of how to integrate ISO 14001 within government regulation must be handled with caution.

Clearly, it is crucial that new ways are established to achieve a partnership between the private and public sectors on environmental management. Many governments are unable to comprehensively and consistently enforce their own environmental legislation. Given the strong trend toward deregulation, there is renewed interest in the concept of public and corporate coregulation. Within this area, environmental management systems and ISO 14001 have become a lively topic of debate. ISO 14001 and self-regulation are being presented as essential elements of the new paradigm. On its own, corporate self-regulation is an oxymoron.[2] The challenging issue is how a new relationship can be forged between the public and private sectors to ensure that firms contribute to environmental improvement and sustainable development. This issue is particularly crucial for global firms operating in developing countries.

This chapter advances the position that some environmental management systems provide a potential for a public–private partnership but that ISO 14001 on its own does not. Additional elements, present in some other models of environmental management systems but not in ISO 14001, need to be added to secure the public interest – these include a baseline environmental assessment, evidence of compliance, environmental performance improvement, public reporting and public participation. A non-performance based ISO 14001 alone cannot provide the basis for regulatory rollback because it has no compliance assurances. In countries with low levels of environmental regulation, for instance, ISO 14001 alone cannot provide an alternative to a regulatory infrastructure.

Proponents of ISO 14001 present a case to firms that ISO 14001 can relieve some of their administrative burden, improve environmental results and increase the competitiveness of national firms in a global marketplace.[3] On the government side, there are possibilities for EMSs to be a condition of government procurement contracts; a condition for fast-track permitting; and a condition for reduced penalties in cases of self-discovered incidents of non-compliance. Once again, this is an example of turbulence in public environmental policy thinking, with ISO 14001 positioned as a simplistic solution to a complex problem.

A long series of attempts have been made in many countries towards an environmental regulatory system that incorporates a partnership between industry and national and provincial-level government. Most of the experiments in this area are in developed countries. In developed countries, regulators have found that there are diminishing returns on direct regulatory controls; as a result, regulators are looking at more flexible policy options, emphasizing incentives for coregulation. In the developing world, such options must be treated with the utmost caution, since regulation and enforcement may be non-existent or ineffective.

The trilateral North American Commission on Environmental Cooperation (CEC), an organization established as a side-commission to the NAFTA, makes recommendations for environmental management in an area that includes developed and developing countries. Its view is that it is the job of governments to set industrial environmental standards (including voluntary programmes) and verify and enforce compliance. As a private voluntary effort, ISO 14001 could make a contribution to better environmental management; but as it does not guarantee compliance or performance, it does not diminish the role of governments.

> Governments must retain the primary role in establishing environmental standards and verifying and enforcing compliance with laws and regulations... ISO 14001 is not, however, a performance standard. Adoption of an EMS pursuant to ISO 14001 does not constitute or guarantee compliance with legal requirements and will not in any way prevent the governments from taking enforcement action where appropriate.[4]

In developed countries, some experiments with public–private partnerships involve a version of ISO 14001. A frequently cited example is the US Department of Energy notice in March 1996 that it might make a comprehensive environmental management system a requirement for procurement contracts. As of February 1998 they had no policy on ISO 14001 for suppliers. But this initiative has sparked off notices from several other federal and state government agencies regarding the benefits that can arise from greater use of environmental management systems – with the recognition that there are many different types of environmental-management system programmes currently in use among US firms. As described later in this chapter, the evidence is, certainly in the US, that federal and state-level regulators are approaching the question of ISO 14001 with an open mind, interested to see if an environmental management system with environmental protection assurances can be helpful as a component of coregulation. Other government agencies are also experimenting with this choice. In Japan, the Ministry of International Trade and Industry (MITI) has advocated third-party registration to ISO 14001, although this is not a regulatory requirement.[5]

A second development that was characterized as a precedent was a court case in Canada between Prospec Chemical Co, a company being prosecuted for non-compliance, and the Province of Alberta.[6] The company, which manufactures mining reagents, was in violation of its operating licence for sulphur emissions. A negotiated settlement between the prosecution and Prospec included a fine of Cdn$100,000 and a requirement for the firm to become ISO 14001 certified. A bond of Cdn$40,000 had to be posted to guarantee that ISO 14001 certification was achieved within the specified timeframe. At the time of the violation, the business did not have ISO 9000 certification or an environmental management system, nor did it participate in the Canadian Chemical Manufacturers' Association's (CCPA) Responsible Care® programme. This was also a second offence in two years. However, the judge accepted a number of mitigating factors: Prospec had a demonstrable organizational commitment to compliance; had reported the offending emissions without delay; had rewritten standard operating procedures for the activity in question; had demoted key offending managers; had become a member of the CCPA; had made, in this incident, an error in judgement; and had continued to make major capital expenditures designed to solve the problem of excess emissions.

The judgement is interesting in several respects. Firstly, the maximum fine for an infringement such as the one being prosecuted had, until late 1993, been Cdn$25,000. In its previous prosecution, the company had been fined Cdn$40,000 for two offenses. In 1993, the threshold was raised to Cdn$500,000, in recognition of 'increased awareness in the public and … in the judiciary and in the legislature concerning the seriousness of these kinds of violations'. But there were few cases where this new limit had been tested. In addition, the firm's lawyer anticipated that installing an environmental management system would cost the company between Cdn$100,000 and Cdn$200,000. The case suggests that an environmental-management system programme such as ISO 14001 could be part of the due diligence and reasonable care expectations of the court.

It is also not clear what kind of trend this decision will create in Canadian law. The Canadian Standards Association and lead office of TC 207 notes: 'this case is not a blanket precedent for substituting ISO 14001 certification for a fine, but as a precedent for alternative sentencing where the company has shown good faith in actively attempting to improve its performance by improving management systems'.[7] In contrast, it should be noted that the Environment and Natural Resources Division of the US Department of Justice (DOJ) has indicated that ISO 14001 is not a sufficient guarantee of improved environmental performance. The DOJ viewpoint is that the standard is not performance-based and provides no assurance of improved environmental performance. 'Such a process [ISO 14001] will often be valuable in [helping] a company meet its environmental goals, but it will not guarantee that a company complies with the standards that DOJ enforces, which, in this country, are the standards set by environmental statutes and implementing regulations.'[8]

Countries with lower compliance requirements than in the US and Canada obviously have to employ these strategies with caution. Co-regulation cannot be achieved in the absence of regulation and enforceable sanctions. This makes the consideration of ISO 14001 quite different for regulators in the developed and developing worlds. Despite assertions by ISO 14001 advocates that the standard will bring regulatory relief, regulators in the developed world are not embracing ISO 14001 on its own. This caution should be emphasized for developing country regulators.

KEY ELEMENTS OF COREGULATION

In order to establish a concept of coregulation between the private and public sectors, some elements of an environmental management system act as crucial indicators for regulators. The five elements are compliance; measureable improvements in environmental performance; third-party verification of the audit; public reporting; and public participation. All five are used in most environmental-management system programmes, including EMAS. None of them are required under ISO 14001. With regard to their environmental protection assurances, therefore, ISO 14001 and EMAS are not equivalent. Consequently, the kind of public–private partnership that would be appropriate for one environmental management system is not necessarily appropriate for the other.

Regulators using ISO 14001 as a basis for co-regulation will need to add elements to ISO 14001 that will provide environmental protection assurances. Evidence is that this may be contested by ISO advocates. For example, a concept of ISO Plus presented to regulators at the MIT conference excited some interest among the regulators in the audience. As a result, an ISO 14001 consultant commented in anger that the concept of ISO Plus was untenable because ISO 14001 was *the standard*. His concern was that if one allowed the concept of ISO Plus, then 'you would get ISO Plus Plus Plus.'[9]

Governments might use voluntary programmes if integration provides concrete benefits to the environmental performance of the enterprises, or furthers environmental protection in the country. By integrating performance-based standards into specific elements of national law, it also might be possible to reallocate overburdened or weak enforcement powers and promote higher company involvement in the effort to enhance environmental performance. This method has been used in Denmark and The Netherlands and is proposed in several developing countries. On the other hand, if a good system of environmental regulation and control is lacking, there is a large potential for 'free riders'. This could result in a loss of respect by the public at home and abroad for ISO 14001, for businesses using it, and for governments advocating it.

COMPLIANCE

As already noted, ISO 14001 does not require compliance but requires that the environmental policy carries a 'commitment to conformance with applicable laws and regulations' in the environmental policy statement. This element of ISO 14001 stands in contrast to EMAS, which requires compliance (see Introduction, Table i.1). Regulators looking for the tools to work with industry initiatives in beyond compliance self-regulation need to understand that ISO 14001 on its own will not provide a basis for regulatory flexibility.

The US Environmental Protection Agency (EPA) has no intention of absorbing ISO 14001 into its regulatory process or reducing compliance responsibilities, although some relationship between environmental management system programmes and ISO 14001 or ISO 14001 Plus will eventually be hammered out in a spirit of partnership.[10] This includes incentives for 'self-policing,' which 'offer regulated entities powerful new incentives to discover, disclose and correct violations of environmental law'. After an 18-month public review period, the EPA has agreed that it will eliminate or substantially reduce legal penalties to firms that self-police and correct environmental violations. In principle, therefore, the EPA could support the position taken by the Crown Counsel in Alberta in the Prospec case. Like Canadian policy, the EPA retains the right to prosecute in the case of repeated or wilful violations. It also has other provisions ensuring public access to information if penalties are mitigated.[11] In other words, the EPA is interested in using self-policing, not self-regulation, as an instrument in compliance assurance and regulatory rollback.

In the US, at the state level, there is also a multistate research pilot project underway. Its objectives are to:

> ...test the hypothesis that the use of an ISO 14001 environmental management system has a positive effect on environmental performance, with compliance as the starting point. The idea is to encourage a system that will maintain not only compliance but enhance overall environmental performance, while making environmental protection more effective and efficient.[12]

In working with ISO 14001, these EPA initiatives will stress non-ISO factors: compliance, compliance audits, and the public right to know.[13]

If ISO 14001 is to have any measurable environmental results, applicable environmental regulations need to exist, and they need to give a very precise framework for the management system. Regulatory systems in most industrial countries have, for example, a set system of limit values and a number of options for dealing creatively and effectively with corporate self-regulation. Countries with weak or poorly enforced environmental legislation need to think about environmental management and corporate self-regulation in very different terms.[14]

ENVIRONMENTAL PERFORMANCE

It can be argued that the question of compliance is not as relevant as environmental performance. Several experiments in coregulation have taken performance outputs as

their starting point. The Dutch Government is establishing covenants, which are negotiated agreements that have been discussed with industry associations and agreed in
parliament. Noting that the environmental load in The Netherlands is higher than in
other developed countries, the government has embarked on a vigorous campaign to
reduce polluting substances by 90 per cent in high-polluting industry sectors – such as
chemicals, construction, etc. Science-based, long-term targets were presented to industry round tables, inviting industry to find the creative means of reaching these goals.
Government agrees that the targets will not be changed for a set period, thus providing a measure of regulatory certainty. The intention of this approach is to have a relationship between the state and the private sector that is positive and confident; where
companies and regulators are not passive and defensive in relation to each other but
are active and collaborative.[15]

> The company creates the trust [between itself and the government] by having
> an adequate environmental management system, which guarantees implementa-
> tion of the company environmental plan as effectively as possible and [pro-
> vides] some understanding of progress being made in environmental perfor-
> mance. From the government's perspective, this trust is achieved by giving legal
> guarantees to the company regarding the objectives for the next four years. This
> ties in with the cycle of company environmental plans and the updating require-
> ment. But this confidence is also substantiated by creating more scope for the
> company itself to decide how to satisfy these objectives.[16]

EMAS requires an initial environmental impact review, and then continual improvement of environmental performance. As discussed in the Introduction, ISO 14001
explicitly excludes environmental performance:

> It should be noted that this standard does not establish absolute requirements
> for environmental performance beyond commitment, in the corporate policy,
> to compliance with applicable legislation and regulations and to continual
> improvement. *ISO 14001, Introduction*

In ISO 14001 there are only two references to the actual environmental performance
of a company: one is the commitment to a continual improvement of the environmental management system 'to achieve improvements in overall environmental performance in line with the organization's environmental policy'[17] and the other is the
commitment to comply with relevant legislation and regulations and the requirements
of the firm's voluntary obligations.[18]

   In early drafts, ISO 14001 contained many components, usually drawn from other
models of environmental management systems such as EMAS and BS 7750, that
would have advanced the environmental performance of companies. During the negotiations, however, the original text was diluted considerably. ANSI (US) representatives,
for example, have been steadfast in their opposition to a public environmental audit
requirement. They altered the original requirements that stipulated continual improvement of environmental performance to continual improvement of the management
system, and chose not to impose maximum rates of emissions. They reduced proposals for a standard of 'viable and achievable technology' to a provision that 'the envi-

ronmental management system should encourage organizations to consider implementation of best available technology where appropriate. In addition, the cost-effectiveness of such technology should be fully taken into account'.[19]

All the developing country officers surveyed for this book understood well that ISO 14001 is a process and not a performance standard.[20] This is also understood by participants in the TC 207:

> While we enthusiastically endorse the environmental management system approach to help facilitate improvement in environmental performance ... an environmental management system in and of itself is not indicative of an organization's level of environmental performance, nor does it guarantee the realization of environmental improvement.[21]

But from the point of view of the public or regulators, a sound ISO 14001 programme will give the certified firm the capacity to measure and monitor the environmental aspects of its operations and the performance of its environmental management system – not the firm's environmental performance or the environmental aspects of its products. It does not matter how much waste an ISO-certified firm dumps into a river. What is important is that the company's environmental management system knows that it happened.[22] Moreover, ISO 14001 certification will not distinguish between a company that makes solar heating panels or one that makes toxic chemicals for warfare. It certifies the process, not the product.

The ISO 14001 standard tracks systems conformance, not environmental performance. There is no guarantee in the standard that an ISO 14001-certified company will be a good environmental performer.[23] No penalty exists in the standard for non-compliance or bad environmental performance.[24] Nevertheless, many advocates infer that ISO 14001 will help improve environmental performance in the long run.[25] Their view is that the more information management has about their EMS, the more likely they are to make the 'right' environmental decision. Unfortunately for regulators, there is nothing to distinguish a mediocre environmental performer with ISO 14001 certification from an outstanding environmental performer with the same certification.

The issue of a relationship between ISO 14001 and regulators is especially important where there is little substantive regulation – for example, in export processing zones and free trade zones (FTZs). These are areas where foreign investment has been encouraged by lowering or waiving certain measures, including environmental and social regulations. In these areas, where regulations are lax, firms have generally not integrated sustainable development into their corporate philosophies.[26] In FTZs, the requirement, in ISO 14001, to conform to applicable regulations would be very limited. Indeed, few regulations are applicable given the prevailing goal of attracting foreign investment. Conforming to host-country or home-country regulations rather than applicable regulations could impose future conditions on firms. Nevertheless, if these firms wish to become certified with ISO 14001, they may find it relatively simple to do so in the absence of an environmental regulatory infrastructure. It is also not clear what the institutional arrangements would be with the host-country standard-setting institutions, since these institutions may have less authority over firms in a FTZ. Furthermore, the price advantage of getting certified in a FTZ may create trade barriers for local firms based outside the zone, yet competing in the same market. The potential for free riders in FTZs on ISO certification is significant.

EXTERNAL VERIFICATION

A third issue for regulators is the quality of the data itself or the verification of the information being generated for the environmental management system. Self-regulation without disclosing verified information to the public or to public authorities provides no safeguards for the regulators. The EU's EMAS, therefore, requires that data in the environmental management system is externally verified. EMAS certification is granted only by qualified third parties. Independent verifiers operate, in theory, in the same fashion as outside financial auditors. ISO 14001 audits do not verify or seek performance information.

PUBLIC REPORTING

Public reporting is a key element in corporate accountability. Thus, for example, the Toxics Release Inventory in the US and in other countries relies on public reporting to induce firms to lower emissions. But even where the regulators are unable to provide effective command-and-control regulations, a requirement for public reporting can have a strong effect on corporate performance. In Indonesia, for example, the environmental agency publishes a list of corporations that are rated on a scale from 'green' to 'black'; this is having some success at changing corporate environmental performance .

Of course, it is not certain that public reporting is sufficient to make the firm a good environmental performer. However, 'shaming' national firms in Indonesia does appear to have an effect. However, even if it is hard to establish the precise relationship between public information and corporate behaviour, it is clear that public reporting on environmental performance is highly controversial for international industry. A recent report showed that commitments to public reporting are unusual among industry associations. Firms, too, prefer to make commitments to internal reporting, or reporting to an industry association that publishes aggregated industry figures, as opposed to public reporting.[27]

ISO 14001 has no requirement for public accountability. The intention of the data generated by the standard and its reporting elements is to provide information to senior management. The only element of the standard that needs to be made public is the environmental policy statement. One of the key requirements for good environmental public policy is that firm-level data is provided to affected communities. If this is not provided as part of the voluntary corporate environmental-management system, then it needs to be required in public laws and regulations.

PUBLIC PARTICIPATION

Principle 10 of the Rio Earth Summit Declaration states that 'environmental issues are best handled with the participation of all concerned citizens, at the relevant level'. This captures a trend in environmental decision-making, at all levels, from international to local, towards integrating the public. As already mentioned in Chapter 1, environmental NGOs are increasingly integrated within international environmental policy formulation. This has been the case nationally and locally. The argument is that environmental improvements and sustainable development cannot be achieved without the participation of citizens. Citizens are stakeholders in the environment and need to be involved as stewards, from policy inception to implementation. This 'right' is increasingly viewed as consistent with democracy and with pragmatism – if citizens' views are not taken into account in the formulation of environmental policy, then they are likely to dissent later.[28]

The concept of public participation in environmental decision-making is most longstanding in the US, where – since 1969 – legislation has regarded consultation with affected citizens in environmental assessments as fundamental. Requirements for public involvement are central to US federal and state experiments using environmental management systems as a basis for regulatory flexibility.[29] This method of involving affected citizens and communities has been replicated in Canada and, more recently, in European environmental policy and regulations. As an environmental management system, EU's EMAS is consistent with the spirit and substance of this set of explorations. In October 1995, an official background paper to the European Environmental Ministers Meeting in Sofia, Bulgaria, called for:

> …the commitment and involvement of all major groups identified in *Agenda 21*. In view of the restructuring of Europe towards sustainable development, which is the objective of the European Partners for the Environment (EPE), all major groups – local authorities, NGOs, women, youth, trade union organizations, farmers, the business and industry community (including finance organizations) – will have to deliver a significant contribution, both in western Europe and in the countries in transition.[30]

The UN Economic Commission for Europe's *Guidelines on Access to Environmental Information and Public Participation in Environmental Decision-Making* were released at the Sofia meeting and endorsed there, with particular support from environment ministries in France, Belgium and The Netherlands. They represent a high point in the formulation of regional policies to integrate the public in environmental decision-making, and have been supported at the national level in a number of European countries, notably Belgium, The Netherlands, the UK, France and Norway.

This new paradigm for state involvement in environmental protection emphasizes stakeholder participation, conflict resolution between different interests, and voluntary corporate environmental management. Public participation is a key element of working with firms towards a new paradigm of coregulation. Evidence is that the road to implementing public participation has been rocky and uneven. ISO 14001, however, makes no reference to broadening participation in environmental decision-making – to the state or to the public – yet asks both to confer their trust to certified firms. Regulators seeking an accommodation with ISO 14001 may want to explore the possibility of adding public participation.

DIFFERENT OPTIONS AND WAYS FOR GOVERNMENTS

Because of the national and international debate on the application of ISO 14001, some governments and agencies have begun reviewing their options with respect to environmental management systems and to ISO 14001. Over the past several years, there have been many press accounts on ISO containing headlines such as 'country X or government agency Y is considering a programme to incorporate the ISO 14001 into a regulatory programme or into their procurement requirements'. While this has been good public relations, most governments and firms have made no decision on ISO 14001 one way or the other. As already indicated, some governments are experimenting with a number of ways to achieve coregulation, using environmental management systems and an ISO 14001 Plus approach.

Governments should recognize that one option is to take no formal action and to let the private sector determine the value and usefulness of ISO 14001. Indeed, a no action option is a legitimate response for governments. An international lawyer and leading member of a US delegation to TC 207 said that ISO 14000 'should not be adopted by regulators, should not be dropped into the next piece of legislation that comes down the pike [and] ISO 14000 should not be a condition of government procurement, which is a very serious issue, not just in the US but also internationally, in terms of creating trade barriers'.[31] This no action option would be consistent with previous government practice with respect to ISO standards. If ISO 14001 has a use as an internal organizational tool, companies can select it or leave it. Environmental ministries could then concentrate on environmental protection and leave management-system standard setting to the market.

The use of any environmental management system as part of a law or regulation might be driven by the search for a complement to traditional environmental laws, regulations and enforcement. The ISO 14001 standards are but one of many ways in which environmental management systems might be used. There are various degrees of embracing environmental management systems in law and policy, including domestic standards and voluntary national initiatives; standards and initiatives from local and regional authorities; procedural or sentencing guidelines in the judicial branch; financial accounting and reporting; and environmental auditing.

REACTIONS TO ISO 14001 FROM DEVELOPED COUNTRY REGULATORS

Governments in developed countries can incorporate an environmental management system into their national, subnational or local laws and regulations. It is important for regulators to realize that ISO 14001 is silent precisely in those areas where regulators need assurance: in requirements for compliance, public reporting and environmental performance. As governments consider integrating environmental management systems into national standards, many recognize that 'ISO 14001 is not a magic wand that can resolve environmental management problems' for regulators.[32]

Some governments are aligning their standards with EMAS. The Irish national environmental management standard was recognized by the European Commission in February 1996 as satisfying the requirements of EMAS.[33] That same month, Ireland's standard-setting agency rejected the ISO 14001 draft because it did not include components of EMAS – most importantly the lack of transparency and information dissemination and the absence of requirements for improving environmental performance. In late 1997, the Irish Standards body dropped EMAS in favour of ISO 14001 as its reference standard. Germany remains a strong proponent of EMAS; as of July 1996, over 220 sites in Germany were participating. In Austria 14 sites have been accredited.[34]

Like the Irish agency, the Danish Government agency responsible for participation in the ISO 14001 negotiations had concerns about the limited nature of the standard, compared to EMAS. The Danes were concerned with the components of environmental statements; external verification; registration; and public reporting – some of the same issues highlighted earlier in this chapter. They voted against a European (CEN) version of ISO 14001, hoping 'that the industry and their market will show the need for a mandatory use of these elements, and thereby prepare the way for a later change of ISO 14001 to reach the long-term goal of an international agreement on these elements'.[35] In TC 207, the Danish standards delegation did, however, vote to approve ISO 14001, 'not because it is the "best" environmental management system standard, but because it is what we, having taken part in the international negotiation process of the standard, find is the best possible international agreement for the time being, and thereby a good starting point for a long-term process'.[36]

At the national level, the Danish Government has adopted a law stating that all the most polluting companies in Denmark have to set up annual accounts of their environmental measures and make them public as a way of eliminating some of the differences between the European Union's EMAS programme and ISO 14001.[37] Thus they can ensure that all companies have to provide public information on their environmental impacts, something that is lacking in ISO 14001.[38] This is an excellent example of developed country legislation that effectively achieves a symbiosis of a voluntary environmental-management system programme and the legal requirements.

Large heavy-industry companies that implement an environmental management system for the first time and commit themselves to complying with applicable regulations will almost invariably achieve better environmental performance. Governments can build on this linkage. Some developing countries can rely on their current or planned environmental regulatory system to ensure that conformance to national laws and regulations also leads to greater environmental protection. For countries like South Africa, which in 1996 embarked on a major review of its environmental legislation in a broad public process, there were opportunities for creating a system of coregulation as an integrated idea.[39] Carefully handled, this could eradicate those elements within the historic regulatory infrastructure that have had little current value for regulators and are expensive for firms.[40]

Regulators are also clear that ISO 14001 certification should not exonerate companies from regulatory responsibilities. The key concerns cited by developing country officials are the lack of public reporting, compliance requirements and follow-up audits. These would need to be part of any hypothetical new regulatory system.[41] The current position of the US Environmental Protection Agency is that, even if a firm is ISO 14001 certified, and receives some privileges, the EPA will prosecute companies for non-compliance with applicable laws and regulations. Grounds for prosecution could be repeat violations or patterns of violation; if there is an imminent and substantial danger, even if hazards are self-disclosed; criminal conduct; or violations of specific terms of consent orders or agreements.[42]

In the US, state governments are also seeking ways to advance self-regulation and integrate corporate initiatives within environmental management systems. The Multi-State Working Group is one part of this. And in each state their are different experiments. For example, the Michigan Department of Environmental Quality has proposed rules for an ISO 14000 Plus programme called Clean Corporate Citizen Program. Participants will be eligible for benefits, such as waivers to commence construction and operation, quicker permit processing and plantwide-applicability limit permits. Participation will depend on the following: that participants have an environmental management system such as ISO 14001 in place; that they develop and implement an effective pollution prevention programme; that they are in compliance; and that their application for participation is opened to a 60-day public review of the application and related documentation.[43] California, similarly seeking to explore the 'utility of ISO 14001 environmental management systems as a tool to augment or replace elements of the current command-and-control regulatory system' is committed to public participation, compliance and performance improvement.[44] No current US state is giving regulatory relief on the sole basis of ISO 14001 certification. However, ISO 14001 Plus programmes are being actively considered as part of what is needed for corporate coregulation.

In the developed world, legislation is evolving because of the new demands placed upon it by industries, citizens and other interested parties. As long as companies are achieving the limit-value regulations set for them, regulators can encourage corporate flexibility on how they get there. In many developing countries, however, the environmental legislation is not yet firmly in place or is non-existent.

REACTIONS TO ISO 14001 FROM DEVELOPING COUNTRY REGULATORS

Even before ISO 14001, preliminary discussion had begun in some developing countries about national standards for environmental management. The Bureau of Indian Standards developed an Indian version of BS 7750 but did not implement it because ISO 14001 was by then under discussion; officials preferred to wait for the creation of the international standard. The South African Bureau of Standards (SABS) produced a South African Standard Code of Practice for Environmental Management Systems, also based on BS 7750, in 1993.[45] No sooner was this published than the SABS began to participate in the ISO international standards.[46]

In general, developing country regulators seem convinced that ISO 14001 will become a ticket of admission to global markets for their exporting firms (see Chapter 4). Given this assumption, they are understandably keen to provide an accommodating environment for their national economy. In many countries, the standard-setting bodies are part of the state apparatus or have some public-sector connection. In many cases, such as in The Philippines or in Malaysia, the standard-setting or certification bodies were governmental and are in the process of being privatized.

There is a major problem in transferring lessons in environmental management from developed to developing countries. Developed countries start from a context of high levels of environmental regulation and face a trend towards deregulation. The question needs to be completely reframed for developing countries who come from a low level of environmental regulation but already feel the pressure to deregulate. In addition, economic pressures are felt acutely by state entities. Developing country regulators may want to explore the range of experiments and options being tried or debated by regulators in other countries, many of which have already generated a literature that could be useful. But, equally, they may need to work towards a different paradigm of private- and public-sector partnerships; sharing experiences, particularly regional experience, may be more useful than transferring developed country examples.

A review of activity in developing countries shows that developing country regulators, like their counterparts in the developed world, are wary of integrating ISO 14001 into their regulatory infrastructure. Given the ongoing nature of the debate on ISO 14001, such a review cannot be comprehensive but, rather, is indicative of the types of discussions currently underway in developing countries.

ASIA

In The Philippines the Bureau of Product Standards (BPS) was in charge of ISO 9000 and will take the lead on ISO 14000. BPS reports to the Department of Trade and Industry, along with other agencies such as the Board of Investments (BOI). The department has recently increased its interests in environmental matters and elevated its environmental subcommittee to report directly to the under-secretary overseeing the BOI. This interest reflects a growing preoccupation with environmental management in the Philippine Government. In 1996 the government formed TC 55 (Technical Committee 55), a multisectoral committee on environmental standards. Participation is from a wide range of governmental agencies and industry associations, including the BOI, the National Economic Development Administration and the Department of Science and Technology. It is co-chaired by BPS and the Philippine Quality and Productivity Movement (PQPM), a non-profit business organization. The role of TC 55 was to formulate technical guidelines rather than policy; it had been examining BS 7750 as a template. This was deferred when ISO 14001 gained attention.

Philippine industry feels the pressure to adopt ISO 14001 compliance not from government or internal corporate financial incentives, but from their sense that some element of environmental management, or ISO 14001, will become a requirement for export to developed country markets in order to attain the status of a 'green tiger'. Therefore, BPS is actively considering how to work with ISO 14001. For industry, BPS will be setting up a certification process and then opening up accreditation opportunities to private applicants. On the regulatory side, the Philippine Department of Environment and Natural Resources (DENR) sees ISO 14001 as a way to leverage limited resources, and is considering ISO 14001 as an alternative to quick compliance with end-of-pipe controls, following a closure order. A possibility under consideration is the use of ISO 14001 to replace regular and less than effective inspections.

In Taiwan, the Environmental Protection Agency is developing a five-year environmental management system promotion plan. The national strategy includes reviewing current environmental protection policies, setting national standards and national accreditation and verification systems, promoting Taiwan's ecolabelling system, and establishing an environmental audit and performance evaluation technology. Such action at the national level will encourage industries to 'voluntarily adopt the environmental management system to strengthen competitiveness and to avoid trade barriers'.[47]

In Indonesia, regulatory enforcement can be another means of shifting the onus of environmental performance control from public bodies to private industry itself. Weak enforcement powers (especially in developing countries) can then be moved away from 'good' performers and directed towards those businesses that need the oversight. In order to guarantee a certain level of environmental performance, legislation needs to set a specific standard. The Indonesian Government agency responsible for all environmental programmes, the Environmental Impact Agency (BAPEDAL), is discussing with all stakeholders how to go beyond the written word and to ensure that the system improves the environmental performance of companies. The implementation of an environmental management system should not be the end for the companies – continual improvement is necessary. There have been very bad experiences with environmental impact assessment (EIAs) in the past: everybody wants them fast, the demand is high and there are no good results. With ISO 14001 they want to ensure that industry does not go all out to acquire the certificate. Their preference is to proceed with caution.[48]

Hopes for better enforcement were expressed by an Indonesian official from the Standardization Council of Indonesia.[49] There is the belief in Indonesia that a voluntary environmental management system like ISO 14001 will help weak and inconsistent enforcement of the existing legislation. Indonesia's view is that the environmental impact of the ISO 14001 will be great: Indonesia has a very tight environmental legislation and companies will be under pressure if they have to comply with all the laws. A governmental official stated: 'Indonesia is so large – the government just does not have the resources to enforce the laws. Therefore, they want to promote voluntary measures. The environmental management system/ISO will, nonetheless, stay voluntary; government has no plans to implement it into laws.'[50]

A similar view was taken by officials in other developing countries. Few want to incorporate ISO 14001 into national legislation. In Vietnam it was understood that ISO 14001 will not replace environmental legislation but may have a useful role in assisting a more efficient allocation of regulatory resources through its commitment to compliance.[51]

In Malaysia, standard setting takes place under the Standards and Industrial Research Institute of Malaysia (SIRIM) that was recently privatized. SIRIM was previously a semi-governmental organization operating under the Ministry of Science, Technology and Environment (MOSTE). Once SIRIM was privatized, MOSTE established a standards department, the Malaysian Accreditation Council, with divisions for standards development and for accreditation. An official of the Department of the Environment in Malaysia was of the opinion that if all companies had ISO and environmental management systems, then ISO 14000 would do a lot of good. One path towards better performance is a proposed amendment to the Malaysian Environmental Quality Act that will, among other things, drastically increase fines for non-compliance to existing laws and regulations. If all businesses complied with national legislation, than they would automatically have a better performance.[52] This view was echoed by officials in governments, standard-setting bodies and international development banks.

On a similar vein, the Ministry of Environment in South Korea introduced the Environmentally Friendly Companies in the summer of 1995. In South Korea, businesses must have a general environmental management system, an overall environmental assessment of the manufacturing process, a record of environmental improvement and a plan for the improvement of environmental parameters – activities that are consistent with ISO 14001 Plus. After reviewing the applications, the ministry inspects the sites and if they pass, they are accepted as environmentally friendly. Facilities must submit annual progress reports and an improvement plan, and after three years the company has to start a new assessment process cycle. Members of this programme should have less need for enforcement action; therefore, the businesses are exempted from surprise compliance inspections.

In Singapore there was no organized activity to implement environmental management systems prior to ISO 14001, although ISO 9000 was very popular and some 1,000 firms were certified under the Singapore Institute of Standards and Industrial Research (SISIR), a statutory board under the Singapore Ministry of Trade and Industry. The Ministry of the Environment is supportive of ISO 14001 and participates on the national technical committee under SISIR. However, as of late 1996 there were no discussions about incorporating ISO 14001 within regulatory standards or making compliance a condition of government procurement contracts.

From the point of view of Singapore industry, there is a belief that the standards, in particular life-cycle assessment and ecolabelling, do have the potential to influence business practice towards more environmentally sound production. While the specifications are voluntary, they move the issues into business discussions and product specifications. A Singapore consultant maintained that the standards will ultimately have an enormous impact just due to the fact that they get people thinking about environmental issues. In this consultant's view, the competitiveness among countries in the Asian region will bring about an impact: environmental-management system programmes will be adopted as soon as businesses realize that better environmental performance brings about economic advantages, such as reduced costs of waste disposal.[53]

AFRICA

In Zimbabwe, officials are taking a comparable position in terms of incorporating ISO into their national regulatory system. An official from the Standards Organization of Zimbabwe acknowledged that they are fully aware that ISO 14001 does not set up performance criteria and cannot achieve environmental protection by itself.[54] Although viewed as insufficient on its own, ISO 14001 could provide an overall approach when used together with a very strong set of regulations set up by legislation and an effective control system. The Zimbabwe concept, therefore, is to use ISO 14001 Plus combining it with good legislation and a tuned-up monitoring system. As part of the tune-up, the Ministry of Environment and Tourism is to update the regulatory infrastructure.

A similar approach is being used in South Africa, starting from a threshold of low or uneven environmental legislation and enforcement. The South African Department of Environmental Affairs is a young agency and is going through the policy formulation process. In the absence of a strong environmental regulatory system, the government has relied on industry self-regulation. The new environmental programmes will be based on three legs: regulation and enforcement; economic instruments; and elements of self-regulation, such as environmental management systems. According to Diane Soutter, a private consultant and South Africa's representative on ISO/TC 207/SC1, ISO 14001 could be a means for companies to demonstrate their environmental responsibility; but the ideal way forward, in her view, 'is to promote a concept of coregulation'. However, that partnership would take time, particularly in South Africa at the moment, with its political and economic volatility. Until such a partnership can be put in place, she feels that any environmental management system will have a positive effect and should be encouraged. It cannot but have environmental advantage, 'even if it only takes out the sloppiness'.

CONCLUSIONS

For sustainable industrial development, each society needs to develop a long-term strategy for integrating the state (the public and private sector) into a constructive dialogue on environmentally sound industrial structure, performance, products and processes. To work towards this goal, some countries have created roundtables of major actors; other countries have experimented with public–private environmental agreements. These efforts have each found their own way to integrate economic, social and environmental concerns into their multi-stakeholder efforts. The diversity of options and forms for managing the transition to a sustainable industrial society is indeed a healthy development, as there cannot be one standardized package for all countries and regions.

The use of voluntary environmental management systems as a tool of public policy has confronted governments with a crucial set of choices. Any policy tool that is exclusively an environmental tool cannot effectively integrate the social and economic dimensions of sustainable industrial development. But any government would welcome a tool resulting in improved environmental performance, particularly if it offered environmental benefits with reduced reliance on public resources. A recent report from the Global Environmental Management Initiative (GEMI), a business non-profit group made up of 25 US-based firms, noted that there is, alas, no shortcut around legislating for pollution prevention.[55] As a non-performance standard, ISO 14001 leaves the public and regulatory authorities uncertain about the possibility of using ISO 14001 certification alone as a cost-saving public policy tool.

At the same time, regulatory agencies around the world continue to grapple with the problem of how to create a new model of co-regulation that harnesses the energies of industry's voluntary commitments as a component of a functioning regulatory environment. In this context, experiments using ISO 14001 as part of this new relationship tend to emphasise the importance of non-ISO elements, creating a working version of an ISO 14001 Plus model. To save state enforcement resources and time, the public and regulators are introducing measurable environmental performance indicators, public accountability and reporting, community involvement, and local economic planning. The results of these experiments in OECD countries are well worth observing. It is a separate question whether these ISO-plus experiments are directly transferable to the public and regulators in countries with weak environmental regulatory systems.

While the public policy debate continues on sustainable industrial development and environmental management systems, there are a number of concrete steps that can be taken to strengthen the overall participation of key constituencies in this process. Some of these strategies and tools are introduced in the following chapter.

Chapter 6

Can Something be Done to Regain the Initiative for Global Sustainable Industrial Development?

INTRODUCTION

The key concern for global environmental management is: how can we create an integrated approach to sustainable industrial development that will secure 'our common future'? In its broadest vision, this would result in a world where businesses contribute to the 'triple bottom line' of sound economic, social and environmental health. In this context, the management of corporate performance and its impact on nature takes on a pressing urgency.

In the face of these global challenges, ISO 14001 has been presented as a solution – resolving the question of sustainable industrial development, voluntary environmental regulation, a new paradigm for public–private partnership, and so on. This book cautions that the emperor may not have any clothes.

There is no doubt that there was a role for ISO in this debate – the initial terms of reference starting ISO work on the environment certainly defined sustainable development as the context for creating the ISO 14000 series. But the authors behind the ISO 14000 series chose not to face up to this challenge. Instead, they reduced their sights and created an instrument for environmental management systems. They addressed none of the isues integral to sustainable industrial development and even retreated from preexisting efforts to integrate corporate, intergovernmental and nongovernmental experiences within this area. In short, the ISO missed the opportunity to contribute to the issue of global sustainable industrial development.

The result is a standard that, on its own, is neither necessary nor sufficient for the achievement of its initial aim. ISO 14001 is a low bar that will be promoted mainly on fears of market, not environmental, requirements. Stakeholders in the issue of global sustainable development will still have to grapple with the complex issues of international environmental standards for broadening participation, assuring environmental performance improvement, and going 'beyond compliance'. Buyers of ISO 14001 for market reasons should be wary of the sales hype. They should confirm with their customers what environmental assurances they require and work with them to achieve these results. Buyers of ISO 14001 should also be wary of casual inferences from environmental consulting houses about public-sector intentions to reduce regulatory oversights. There is a commitment among regulators to work on a new paradigm of public–private partnership, but there is no evidence that the regulators' flirtation with ISO 14001 will break their commitments to enforcing environmental laws and regulations.

The messages within this book are as follows. Global and local environmental management systems are a sound idea, and corporate, public and environmental group innovation in this direction should be encouraged. ISO 14001 does not represent a leadership model. It ignored public-sector, private-sector and environmental group precedents in this area that could provide good models and could have been building blocks towards sustainable development. These models all strive to integrate sustainable development concepts such as public participation, accountability, social development and cultural diversity in a new balanced relationship of economic and environmental performance.

A thriving sector of small-business consulting houses – and small divisions of larger consulting houses – has developed in response to these issues, often collaborating with academics. The academic sector around the world offers a broad array of courses and conferences in this subject area. Examples of centres of excellence are at the Universtiy of Dundee (Scotland), University of Keele (Canada) and Lowell Center for Sustainable Production at the University of Massachusetts (US). A small number of organizations bring together firms and business groups to address sustainability and the greening of business practice: in Geneva there is the World Business Council for Sustainable Development; and in the US the Aspen Institute Program on Energy, the Environment and the Economy.

On a sectoral basis, there is at any one time, a set of industry working groups grappling with issues related to sustainable development. The Electronics Industry Environmental Initiative in the US has been working on methods for closed-loop production and design for the environment. The Computer Industry Quality Conference (CIQC) in the US, with the Pacific Industry and Business Association (PIBA), is promoting an international standard for supplier environmental practice in the computer industry, which they feel could be utilized internationally and in all sectors. Since natural diversity did not develop in a decade, sustainable business management practices will also need to take a longer evolutionary period before standardization makes any sense.

Ironically, the success of ISO 14001 internationally may depend not on the hopes for environmental improvements but on the fears that this voluntary standard will become a mandatory market condition. Given this reality, stakeholders in sustainable industrial development cannot ignore ISO 14001. This chapter makes several broad suggestions for re-injecting the issue of sustainable industrial development into the new institutional WTO and ISO context for international standard setting. It then sets out some practical recommendations for activities for different groups of stakeholders to promote sustainable industrial development.

STRATEGIC APPROACHES IN RELATION TO THE ISO 14001 SERIES

- Further environmental or public policy work within ISO's current structure should be discouraged.
- ISO rules for standard setting that have public policy consequences should be changed. New ISO 14000 series standards should not be supported unless they contain sustainable development as an explicit component.
- The existing approved ISO 14000 standards should be revised to reincorporate sustainable development.
- The GATT Technical Barriers to Trade Agreement should be modified so as to exclude public policy standards as technical regulations.

DISCOURAGING FURTHER ENVIRONMENTAL OR PUBLIC POLICY WORK WITHIN THE ISO'S CURRENT STRUCTURE

ISO is excited about the recognition of ISO 9000 and ISO 14000 by the general public, the WTO and the international trading system. Part of this excitement is that ISO sees itself as an institutional alternative to the intergovernmental system for setting global environmental standards. Within ISO, the rules allow a limited number of national standard-setting bodies to declare a new work area, the results of which can set limitations on national public-policy bodies. There are a healthy number of multilateral institutions that should be involved in setting these standards in an open, democratic and public fashion.

Until ISO restructures its rule-making system, governments, intergovernmental bodies, NGOs and the general public risk having ISO move into areas of public policy that politically belong to governments and the intergovernmental system. One ISO proposal for a standard on 'occupational safety and health management systems' was stopped by a combination of economic and political forces in the labour arena. Standards Australia and New Zealand did issue, in 1997, a standard for their countries on occupational safety and health management. The ISO in 1998 is canvassing for support to merge ISO 9000 certification with ISO 14001 certification. ISO needs to be restrained from venturing into other new terrains with broad public policy impacts.

CHANGING ISO RULES FOR STANDARD SETTING THAT HAVE PUBLIC POLICY CONSEQUENCES

Public participation in governmental and intergovernmental environmental rule-making is the accepted way of working today. This process is not easy to achieve or manage, but the intergovernmental environmental community feels that these difficulties are intrinsic to the legitimate objective of democratizing decision-making in international standard setting. The private sector can be expected to be ambivalent on the issue of public participation and community development in corporate environmental decision-making, but there have been some conspicuous successes, particularly with the chemical industry's community participation programmes.

ISO has to start a process to revise their working procedures to catch up with the rest of the international community. Governments are currently negotiating a formal convention on national-level public participation in environmental policy-making. All intergovernmental negotiations attract international media and international NGOs as observers, lobbyists and sometimes as participants. Under their unique definition of 'consensus', the ISO has created a blinder, preventing it from easily understanding the extent to which its rules and procedures inappropriately exclude the effective participation of key stakeholders.

The ISO can convene an advisory body, similar to its expert meeting of SAGE and occupational health and safety management, to start a thorough review of its rules and procedures on matters which may have a significant public policy consequence. The ISO should consider a lesson from the intergovernmental arena. Broader governmental, industrial and social participation in the development process of international agreements significantly increases the political reception of the final product. ISO should not be surprised if governmental and non-governmental participation in national standard-setting bodies will increasingly put pressure on the ISO to reject tabling new work items that belong within the public policy arena, unless there is a changed preception about the fairness of ISO procedures.

In the final stage of ISO approval, all full national standard-setting bodies are polled on upgrading a draft international standard to an international standard. At this final stage, ISO requires negative votes with substantive rationales if it is to reject the Draft International Standard's promotion to a new International Standard. Since the goals of sustainable industrial development, reflected in SAGE's original terms of reference, disappeared from the text, national standard-setting bodies can vote 'no' to upcoming standards in the ISO 14000 series. They can provide, as a basis for this vote, the observation that the standard represents a lost opportunity for sustainable industrial development. If as few as 15 national standards bodies reject the approval of work from TC 207, this sends a strong message that sustainable industrial development cannot be ignored or forgotten by the ISO.

REVISING THE EXISTING APPROVED ISO 14000 STANDARDS TO REINCORPORATE SUSTAINABLE DEVELOPMENT

ISO routinely reviews each standard after five years to see how it has been accepted in the market and if it is still current with technological and other developments. ISO also allows a standard to be reviewed whenever significant other developments have occurred. It would be appropriate to request an expedited review in order to bring the ISO process back in line with efforts to create a sustainable industrial community. During the course of this review, some of the weaknesses of the standards might be removed. It will also permit other firms with more sensitive environmental management systems to share their wisdom with others. The review procedure may also discourage some firms from unnecessarily imposing the limited ISO 14001 system on their suppliers until after the results of the review are completed.

Modifying the GATT Technical Barriers to Trade Agreement to Exclude Public Policy Standards

The GATT Technical Barriers to Trade Agreement was not a major focus of negotiators during the Uruguay Round. Most delegations probably thought that the agreement dealt, as its name suggests, with only technical trade barrier issues. However, the modifications greatly expanded the potential impact of the agreement. It is one thing to require that all definitions of, for example, screw heads and band widths by national standard-setting bodies follow a common international approach. It is another thing to require that public policy tools, like environmental, health and safety labelling, must follow an international standard that is set without government involvement or active public participation.

Every three years, the Technical Barriers to Trade Agreement is reviewed to see if it should be modified.[1] The agreement should be altered to exclude from coverage those product, process and production choices that are necessarily part of an individual country's health, safety, environmental, gender, racial and social policy areas. These matters are not technical but, rather, crucial elements of a vibrant democractic system. Should the TBT discover that some public policy standards were being used as disguised barriers to trade, then the TBT committee could well request an appropriate intergovernmental body to develop relevant international standards in that area. The agreement should also be modified to give at least equal standing on technical matters to the conclusions of existing intergovernmental expert bodies, convened under the United Nations system.

Toward Better Stakeholder Strategies for Environmental Management and Sustainable Industrial Development

Achieving sustainable industrial development now depends on a high degree of interaction between all the diverse stakeholders in this field. This is a challenge that cannot be met in a short period or by a single training programme. It will require not only national capacity-building but new links at regional and international levels, including new partnerships between stakeholders and new 'paradigms of environmental management and new strategies for sustainable industrial development'.

The very fact that this issue is relevant internationally opens up intervention points for all stakeholders. This chapter lays out some of the new opportunities for a broad range of community stakeholders which may make a difference. Recommendations are presented for:

(a) officials in national standard-setting bodies concerned with ISO 14000 implementation;
(b) government officials concerned with domestic environmental management;
(c) government officials dealing with trade and environmental policy in the UN system and WTO;

(d) government officials dealing with ISO standards and environmental issues;
(e) members of environment and development NGOs;
(f) media professionals who cover economic and environmental issues;
(g) executives in exporting businesses affected by ISO 14000; and
(h) executives in charge of environmental, health and safety policies at global firms.

Many of these constituences may need some form of technical assistance to prepare them for this new international arena. Technical assistance for governments with weak environmental infrastructures, and executives in small- and medium-sized entreprises, is being offered by many international organizations, including UNEP's Industry and Environment Programme, UNIDO, ITC, the ICC, and the ISO's special programme to assist developing countries, DEVCO, and the proposed new assistance through the WTO's Committee on Technical Barriers to Trade. Some bilateral aid programmes, such as the US–Asian Environmental Partnership (USAEP), are also offering technical assistance to developing countries in these areas.

OFFICIALS IN NATIONAL STANDARD-SETTING BODIES CONCERNED WITH ISO 14000 IMPLEMENTATION

Officials in national standard-setting bodies concerned with ISO 14000 implementation have already taken steps to promote knowledge and awareness of the ISO standards. Since each major industrial sector may have different concerns and needs with respect to ISO and the ISO 14000 series, their educational awareness campaigns will need a sectoral prespective. Given the pressure that developing country standard-setting bodies are under to react to the wave of ISO 14000 interest, officials are concerned that ISO 14000 will be sponsored because certain industrial sectors feel that ISO 14000 is an admission ticket to international markets. Standard-setting bodies, therefore, feel under pressure to create infrastructures to service this need, and to make certification as easy and simple as possible.

This report has shown that the demand is varied, both in terms of the kinds of certification required and across sectors. Standard-setting bodies should do a proper needs analysis across sectors before making a large investment. In those sectors where ISO 14000 certification and registration is appropriate, the national standard-setting body will need assistance in establishing competent, viable certification, capable of reliable environmental auditing. The national standard-setting body or its designated certifying body will have to adopt standards for ISO 14000 auditors. These standards must specify, for example, the level of environmental training of the certifiers, the separation between certifiers and consulting businesses, the supervision process for a certifier, and the schedule for maintaining ISO 14001 certification.

In the short term, a certifier industry may convince some suppliers and customers to accept certificates, even if they are given to businesses with poor environmental performance and without a commitment to sustainable industrial development. However, if the image of an 'easy A' certification process persists – giving a certificate to all who merely pass a very low set of hurdles – then suppliers, customers and governments may no longer accept them. National standard-setting bodies should be aware of this trend and should educate themselves about the approaches adopted in other countries.

A standards institution establishing an infrastructure to support ISO 14000 certification may want assistance in the following areas:

- national environmental-management needs assessment and scoping of potential market demand for varieties of EMS and for ISO 14000;
- conformity assessment plans;
- relationships with regulatory infrastructure;
- relationships with domestic trade associations;
- rules governing certifying firms
- levels of environmental training needed for ISO 14000 certifiers;
- relationships with ISO 9000 certifiers;
- education and outreach programmes; and
- translation and re-publication of ISO 14001-related standards and guidance documents.

In this regard, multilateral recognition of the accreditation bodies, and the certificates awarded through national or regional accreditation bodies, would be helpful to developing country economies. If a company in a developing country is forced to employ a certifying firm from an OECD country in order to receive an internationally recognized certificate, the financial strain is clearly more significant than if it could make use of a local auditor. This would be reduced if countries mutually recognized the certificate awarding body.

In order to reduce financial strains for standard-setting bodies in developing countries, the establishment of regional accreditation and certification organizations should be considered, for example, on the lines of the model of the Joint Australian and New Zealand national standards body. Regional bodies could use more efficiently the scarce financial and human resources by sharing with neighbouring countries the costs of such programmes. A regional body could arrange for consistent approaches for product data and safety, based on relevant scientific research on regional ecosystem or geographic considerations. A joint laboratory could be created, supplemented by agreements on the cross-acceptance of data from national testing laboratories.[2]

GOVERNMENT OFFICIALS CONCERNED WITH DOMESTIC ENVIRONMENTAL MANAGEMENT

ISO 14001 itself provides a compelling need for governments to have a clear set of laws and regulations on the effective operation of corporate environmental management systems. For ISO 14001 certification, firms will include in their environmental policy statement that they are committed to complying with applicable laws and regulations. Without a clear set of laws and regulations, firms cannot know what is required of them by law and they cannot design a management plan to act within these laws and regulations. Many developing countries will need assistance in developing specific rules and to make these rules easily available to all potential users.

No government can fully enforce all of their environmental, health and safety laws and regulations. At the same time, the expansion and diversity of national economies brings more demands on regulators to monitor ever more complex industrial processes. Regulators seek information and assurance from good self-monitoring systems, sound environmental management systems, and active worker and community consulting systems. For these purposes, a non-performance based ISO 14001 certificate is an ambiguous report. It provides regulators little actual information on the actual impact of management decisions or the firm's activities.

These government officials will need to judge the relative risks emerging from certain types of firms against their environmental management systems. In this situation, there may be lessons from developed countries or regions with more experience that could be worked into relevant case studies. These practical case studies could demonstrate how ISO 14001 Plus tools may help allocate scarce enforcement resources for regulatory agencies.

Training and negotiation skills may be especially important in recognizing the limits and opportunities created by the new GATT when setting national public policy standards. Formulating national standards in line with ISO standards will be a completely new area for policy and regulatory officials. National environmental management officials and parliamentary committees may need technical assistance in incorporating environmental management systems, life-cycle analysis, ecolabelling and environmental auditing concepts within their laws and regulations. Furthermore, many developing country environmental rules are based on the standards in OECD countries or on the recommendations of international environmental experts. In the future, country officials may need to base their rules and regulations on standards such as those in the ISO 14000 series.

Finally, the concept of coregulation in developing countries with low levels of environmental regulation needs to be thought of in different terms than coregulation in contexts of high regulation. Developing country officials may need assistance to devise programmes that complement industry-based voluntary schemes. Regulatory programmes in some OECD countries already require a public environmental report containing the most salient facts about a company's environmental performance or a toxic release inventory. Training for governmental and non-governmental officials of developing countries who are concerned with domestic environmental management could emphasize:

- establishing a working set of effective environmental rules and enforcement arrangements;
- appraising the potential use of environmental management systems and ISO 14001 in an enforcement regime;
- evaluating the potential limitation on national policies from the scope and coverage of the ISO 14000 series and the GATT Technical Barriers to Trade Agreement;
- supporting voluntary industry efforts to use environmental management systems;
- creating regional structures to develop standards and conformity assessment procedures for products, processes, and services and taking into account regional ecological and economic realities;

- incorporating public environmental reporting for emissions, accident-data reporting, and other innovative, best practices from leading national and international regulations, into national legislation;
- examining alternative enforcement systems used in other countries for their potential applicability; and
- establishing a phase-in process for environmental management systems, environmental performance indicators and ecolabels.

GOVERNMENT OFFICIALS DEALING WITH TRADE OR ENVIRONMENT POLICY IN THE UN AND THE WTO

Officials in countries with weak regulatory infrastructures may wish to arrange adequate negotiation training on environmental, health and safety matters for their trade officials. In addition to the WTO Committee on Technical Barriers to Trade, related negotiations are taking place in the WTO Commitee on Trade and Environment, the WTO Committee on Trade and Development, the UN Commission on Sustainable Development (CSD), the UN Conference on Trade and Development (UNCTAD), the UN Environment Programme (UNEP), and the UN Industrial Development Organization (UNIDO).

The current work of TC 207 does not incorporate the environmental standards developed by governments through negotiations, such as those conducted under the auspices of the CSD, UNEP, the WHO or the ILO. In this context, strategic training programmes are needed for officials who can use them to negotiate, in a coordinated fashion, with the ISO, national standard-setting bodies and intergovernmental fora, while developing effective international links with global environmental management and sustainable development.

Other proposals that could be considered include:

- ensuring that references to existing policies and standards set by UN bodies and other organizations are included in ISO standards relating to environment, health and worker safety;
- incorporating explicitly in the revision of ISO 14001 all 32 items in *Agenda 21* governing the conduct of international business;
- modifying the regional standard-setting body concept in the Technical Barriers to Trade Agreement to include national standard-setting and regulatory bodies;
- arranging for the establishment of new international environmental, health and safety standards by UN bodies for those products, processes, and standards important to groups of developing countries; and
- identifying those newer items on the intergovernmental agenda (such as desertification and hormone disruptors) that should be built into the ISO 14000 series.

GOVERNMENT OFFICIALS DEALING WITH ISO STANDARDS AND ENVIRONMENTAL ISSUES

For government officials dealing with ISO standards and environmental issues, the negotiation process for the ISO 14000 series is far from over. ISO is proposing a number of new ISO series with public policy implications. Within the current framework for the ISO 14000 series, work is ongoing for a number of guidance standards including ecolabelling, life-cycle assessment and environmental performance evaluation In addition, there is an automatic five-year review process for existing ISO standards.

One area of action for officials dealing with ISO standards is inherent to the ISO system itself. The ISO 14001 specification standard for environmental management systems is followed by guidance documents on how to implement this system, including special circumstances. These guidance documents give valuable help in addressing the problems companies have in implementing an environmental management system. A guidance document designed for small- and medium-sized enterprises has been considered. It should also be possible to devise a guidance document pertaining to sectors important to particular groups, such as those concerned with tropical forests or specific export commodity markets.

Other proposals that could be considered include :

* increasing the number of active developing country members in ISO by requesting significantly increased financial resources to increase participation in all future TC 207 committee, subcommittee and working group meetings; taking advantage of training programmes offered under the ISO DEVCO, particularly those that train developing country officers as ISO committee chairpeople;
* elevating the class of a country's ISO membership to allow participation from more diverse technical committees; these countries could also recommend that a regional standard-setting body from a developing-country economic association is granted P-membership on behalf of their combined economies and industries;
* establishing regional environmental, health and safety standard-setting bodies to jointly represent the interests of a number of developing countries in ISO fora; arranging to divide the burden of covering the multitude of SCs and WGs by assigning a G77 group representative to selected meetings;
* obtaining resources to retain consultants and other experts to evaluate texts and proposals under consideration in the more than two dozen working groups dealing with environmental management under TC 207 and other technical committees;
* proposing a special ISO standard in the ISO 14000 series relating to the sustainable development concerns of developing countries in line with the 1994 GATT Agreement on Technical Barriers to Trade which proposed integrating developing country views; and
* proposing neutral and geographically balanced secretariats and chairs of TC 207 subcommittees and working groups; rotating leadership positions and arranging to increase the translation of working draft documents into the six United Nations working languages.

MEMBERS OF ENVIRONMENT AND DEVELOPMENT NGOS

Environment and development NGOs have been at the forefront of international environmental efforts over the past three decades. Some of these organizations have made issues related to trade, investment and environmental protection a significant focus of their international efforts. However, fewer NGOs have so far joined ISO as liaision members. The Global Ecolabelling Network, the WWF and Consumers International have been active 'Liaison A' organizations seeking to alter the form and content of the ISO standards. Over time, more international and regional NGOs should apply for liaison status with ISO.

As with each new forum, the international NGO community will have to learn new rules of procedure and new organizational styles. Support for these efforts could include seminars on topics to:

* learn new participation techniques in order to influence ISO meetings;
* assist NGOs from countries with weak regulatory infrastructures to participate effectively in the ISO arena;
* challenge the rule-making decisions of the chairs of the working groups;
* apply for liaison relationship with the correct technical committees;
* develop different negotiating styles for working groups, subcommittees and technical committees;
* push to have full and public distribution of all relevant ISO documents;
* develop foundation grant proposals to cover the high costs of effective participation.

MEDIA PROFESSIONALS COVERING ECONOMIC AND ENVIRONMENTAL ISSUES

Since ISO and other organizations are interested in expanding their standard-setting activities into more public policy areas, media professionals will need to figure out how to cover the multitude of the private and semi-private international meetings. The challenge will be to identify those meetings where there is sufficient public interest in the outcome to provide a basis for a sound story. Journalists will then need to explain, in non-technical language, what public policy issues are at stake.

The ISO, on one hand, is now seeking broader public recogniztion of its new role in policy-making and its new association with the WTO. This self-interest will provide a basis for good journalists to gain some access to the relevant working papers of the technical groups and introductions to key ISO delegations. Media representatives could be assisted if they:

* requested daily press summaries of all ISO meetings;
* asked for open press credentials to all technical committee, subcommittee and working groups;
* informed the chairs of the technical committees, subcommittees and working

groups that the press needs the relevant documents in advance of the scheduled meeting;

• asked for briefing packets on related issues before international meetings;

• held seminars to develop approaches on how to cover technical discussions that will interest and inform the general public.

EXECUTIVES IN EXPORTING BUSINESSES AFFECTED BY ISO 14000

There are benefits to be had from an environmental management system for medium-sized and larger firms in terms of ongoing, effective supervision of the environmental impacts of their firms, products and practices. The impact of the non-performance based ISO 14001 system series on exporting firms will largely depend on the international market of ISO 14001 in specific sectors. One would expect that certain sectors and subsectors may adopt ISO 14001 while others will not. Executives in exporting firms should check with their customers and suppliers to see what interest or benefit there is in ISO 14001 certification. It is very important for firms to see how this standard and certification process might be accepted in their particular market before they assign resources to a non-performance based environmental management system. If ISO 14001 starts to acquire the same importance in a given sector as its quality management cousin, the ISO 9000 series, then a firm with an operating environmental management system (EMS) will be a step ahead of those without an EMS in place. Current indications are that, while ISO 9000 had general applicability, ISO 14001 may have more limited applicability; nevertheless, there is more liability involved where environmental management is important.

In sectors where customers create environmental conditions, there are other approaches that a firm might adopt. One approach is to negotiate specific environmental standards and conditions in purchase or delivery contracts with customers. The timber products and the offshore oil and gas industries have been using this option as a means of controlling a discrete and limited set of environmentally hazardous chemicals and activities. In many industries, environmental and health and safety standards are already written explicitly into contracts. Some multinational corporations and their affiliates, for example, specify the process for disposing of certain hazardous wastes. Firms using chlorine gas set very precise working safety standards and conditions for the safe transfer of chlorine gas from tank to production lines.

When international suppliers wish to reassure themselves that a particular supplier is environmentally safe, it may make sense to agree on tailored performance standards for their product or sector, rather than require a more generalized environmental management system that does not contain performance requirements. This would be consistent with current customer–supplier relations, where inspections are made by customers of their suppliers. Current environmental and quality obligations placed on suppliers are understood to have benefits for the customer.

There is some potential for suppliers to negotiate how this environmental management system is set up so that it meets customer requirements but does not pass all the costs onto the supplier. One option is to negotiate a phased-in time period acceptable to the customer. It may also be the case that the customer is prepared to help the supplier develop an environmental management system or assist in obtaining some sector-specific environmental monitoring technology. A second approach is for firms in countries with weak environmental and social infrastructures to develop their own coherent monitoring and compliance systems. As with firms that operate a sound management system, businesses with an effective monitoring and compliance system are ahead of the game when they need to meet explicit environmental and social objectives.

A third approach is for the firm to select an environmental management system that is appropriate to its size and environmental complexity and to put this environmental management system in place for its own management reasons. If a supplier or customer enquires about the environmental practices of the firm, there will be a clear and practical answer available. Executives of firms may need assistance in determining the level of voluntary environmental management programmes that would fit their overall corporate management system. Smaller firms that have a business link with larger enterprises can ask for their assistance in selecting the most appropriate environmental management system. Larger firms may also wish to get advice on these issues. Within a corporation, the wisdom of self-selecting an environmental management system may be complemented by reductions in disposal costs, liability insurance, and worker and community satisfaction.

If it is appropriate to get ISO 14001 certified, an exporting firm may want assistance with:

- appraising the relative advantage of an internationally accredited certifier versus retaining a domestic certifier;
- evaluating and selecting a specific certifier;
- examining the benefits and limitations of self-certification; and
- developing a national trade-association environmental policy statement so that firms within the sector accept broadly the same definition of environmental protection in their own environmental management system.

EXECUTIVES IN CHARGE OF ENVIRONMENTAL, HEALTH AND SAFETY POLICIES AT GLOBAL FIRMS

Executives responsible for environmental, health and safety matters within international firms should continue to review and improve their corporate environmental management systems and benchmark themselves against leaders in their sectors. Global firms are showing that good environmental practice can be synonymous with integrated and responsible environmental management. Some have shown that it is possible to take best national environmental practice in their home countries and apply it to all their countries of operation. Others have shown that investments in environmental technologies can bring significant economic advantage. Leading firms partipate in a range of think-tanks and policy fora that involve non-industrial actors. Some have put issues of social, community and job security into their strategic thinking and policy-making. These firms are sketching new standards for global environmental management.

For global firms that are already committed to environmental management, ISO 14001 may have a utility. Many global firms are experimenting with implementation in a small number of sites and will use these pilots as benchmarks for cost-benefit evaluations. For firms not committed to environmental management, ISO 14001 can be used to garner internal or top management interest in the broader issues of integrated environmental management and environmental management systems. But indications are that ISO 14001 on its own may not bring enough return on investment. The return will come when firms move beyond an ISO 14001 approach, and start to grapple with the triple bottom line of sustainable industrial development.

In relation to ISO 14001, global firms may want to consider the following:

- developing environmental policies with commitments to sustainable development principles;
- appraising, on a yearly cycle, the sustainable development issues on the intergovernmental agenda and evaluating the most constructive responses to those issues that affect the firm's future production and markets;
- benchmarking voluntary environmental management practices against other leaders within and across sectors in order to remain cognisant of what 'leadership' is;
- posting the company's environmental policy and report on the web site and keeping it updated;
- reinventing ways to integrate community and ecosystem considerations into global and local environmental management; and
- reviewing with corporate staff, on loan to ISO and national standard-setting committees, the positions taken in light of the need to move toward sustainable industrial development.

CONCLUSION: THE EMPEROR'S CLOTHES

Most existing ISO international standards are not important to the public. But ISO has made clear that they want to take on more and more issues that are of broad significance. Other industry-based organizations have started setting their own environmental and social standards. As the ISO and these other industry-based organizations are private organizations, they can circumvent the need to respond to the views of the public or other non-member organizations.

The ISO, as a matter of priority, needs to grapple with the implications of entering the public, non-technical arena in terms of its own processes and outcomes. They should either withdraw from drafting ISO standards with public policy consequences or revise significantly their procedures to incorporate civil society and government in a more democratic decision-making system.

With the new ISO standard being presented to the world, there are a number of critical eyes examining the product. These eyes need to look behind the hype being generated around ISO 14001. This book has argued that the ISO 14000 series may well be of use to different stakeholders at different times and in different contexts. However, ISO 14001 set out to answer a profound question about how to achieve sustainable industrial development and it failed to do this. The question the ISO asked in 1992 remains a sound one. It still needs to be addressed. This book has presented a 'gap analysis' between sustainable industrial development, environmental management and the non-performance based ISO 14001 management system. In doing so, it hopes to refocus global corporate attention on the key issues that need to be addressed in the coming years to achieve a healthy relationship between economic, environmental and social development.

Developing Country Organizations Contacted

Argentina
Comision PanAmericana de Normas
  Técnicas (COPANT)
Instituto Argentino de Racionalización
  de Materiales (IRAM)

Brazil
General Coordinator: Grupo de Apoio
  a Normalizacão Ambiental (GANA)

Chile
Instituto Nacional de Normalizacion
  (INN)

Colombia
Instituto Colombiano de Normas
  Tecnias (ICONTEC)
Ministerio del Medio Ambiente

Ecuador
Instituto Ecuatoriano de Normalización
  (INEN)

India
Bureau of Indian Standards (BIS)

Indonesia
Standardization Council of Indonesia
  (DSN)
Environmental Impact Agency
  (BAPEDAL)

Israel
Standards Institution of Israel

Jamaica
Bureau of Standards (JBS)
Natural Resource Conservation
  Authority (NRCA)

Malaysia
Environment Department (ED)

Standards and Industrial Research
  Institute of Malaysia (SIRIM)

Mexico
Dirección General de Normas (DGN)
SC 32 Administration (medio)
  Ambiental
Instituto Mejicano de Normalización y
  Certificación

The Philippines
Bureau of Product Standards (BPS)

Singapore
Productivity and Standards Board (PSB)
Regional Institute of Environmental
  Technology (RIET)

South Africa
South African Bureau of Standards
  (SABS)
Specialists in Environmental
  Management and Audits (SEAs)

South Korea
Korean National Institute of
  Technology and Quality (KNITQ)

Thailand
Thai Industrial Standards (TISI)

Uruguay
Instituto Uruguayo de Normas Técnicas
  (UNIT)

Vietnam
Directorate for Standards and Quality
  (TCVN)

Zimbabwe
Standards Association Zimbabwe

The ISO 14000 Series

ORGANIZATION EVALUATION STANDARDS

ISO 14001	Environmental Management Systems – Specification with Guidance for Use
ISO 14004	Environmental Management Systems – General Guidelines on Principles, Systems and Supporting Techniques
ISO 14010	Guidelines for Environmental Auditing – General Principles on EA
ISO 14011/1	Guidelines for Environmental Auditing – Audit Procedures Part 1: Auditing of Environmental Management Systems
ISO 14012	Guidelines for Environmental Auditing – Qualifications Criteria for Environmental Auditors
ISO 14013	Management for Environmental Audit Programs (deleted from TC 207 agenda – no further work scheduled)
ISO 14014	Initial Reviews (deleted from TC 207 agenda)
ISO 14015	Environmental Site Assessments
ISO 14031	Evaluation of the Environmental Performance of the Management System and its Relationship to the Environment.
ISO 1403x	Evaluation of the Environmental Performance of the Operational System and its Relationship to the Environment

PRODUCT EVALUATION STANDARDS

ISO 14020	Goals and Principles of All Environmental Labelling
ISO 14021	Environmental Labels and Declarations (ELD) Self-Declaration Environmental Claims – Terms and Definitions
ISO 14022	ELD – Self-Declaration Environmental Claims; Symbols
ISO 14023	ELD – Self-Declaration Environmental Claims; Testing and Verification
ISO 14024	ELD – Environmental Labeling Type I; Guiding Principles and Procedures
ISO 1402X	ELD – Environmental Labelling Type III
ISO 14040	Life-Cycle Assessment – Principles and Practices
ISO 14041	Life-Cycle Assessment – Life-Cycle Inventory Analysis
ISO 14042	Life-Cycle Assessment – Impact Assessment
ISO 14043	Life-Cycle Assessment – Interpretation

ISO 14050   Terms and Definitions – Guide on the Principles for ISO/TC
            207/SC6 Terminology
ISO 14060   Guide for the Inclusion of Environmental Aspects in Product
            Standards (renamed to ISO Guide 64 – no longer a standard)

Composition of TC 207:
Voting and Participation by Developing Countries

Technical committees have participating and observing members. In 1995, TC 207 drew its members from some 57 countries (42 P-members, 15 O-members). By the Rio Earth Summit meeting in June 1996 when the ISO 14001 standard was voted an international standard, the membership of the technical committee had grown to 51 P- and 17 O-members, with several new participants and some observing members becoming participating members (new members denoted with a *).

FULL MEMBERS OF ISO WHO ARE PARTICIPATING MEMBERS IN TC 207

Argentina (IRAM)
Instituto Argentino de Normalización

Australia (SAA)
Standards Australia

Austria (ON)*
Österreichisches Normungsinstitut

Belgium (IBN)
Institut belge de normalisation

Brazil (ABNT)
Associação Brasileira de Normas Técnicas

Canada (SCC)
Standards Council of Canada

Chile (INN)
Instituto Nacional de Normalización

China (CSBTS)
China State Bureau of Technical Supervision

Colombia (ICONTEC)
Instituto Colombiano de Normas Técnicas y Certificación

Cuba (NC)
Oficina Nacional de Normalización

Czech Republic (COSMT)
Czech Office for Standards, Metrology and Testing

Denmark (DS)
Dansk Standard

Ecuador (INEN)*
Instituto Ecuatoriano de Normalización

Finland (SFS)
Finnish Standards Association

France (AFNOR)
Association française de normalisation

Germany (DIN)
Deutsches Institut für Normung

India (BIS)
Bureau of Indian Standards

Indonesia (DSN)
Dewan Standardisasi Nasional – DSN (Standardization Council of Indonesia)

Ireland (NSAI)
National Standards Authority of Ireland

Israel (SII)
Standards Institution of Israel

Italy (UNI)
Ente Nazionale Italiano di Unificazione

Jamaica (JBS)
Jamaica Bureau of Standards

Japan (JISC)
Japanese Industrial Standards
Committee
c/o Standards Department
Ministry of International Trade and
Industry

Kenya (KBS)*
Kenya Bureau of Standards

Korea, Republic of (KNITQ)
Korean National Institute of
Technology and Quality

Malaysia (SIRIM)
Standards and Industrial Research
Institute of Malaysia

Mauritius (MSB)*
Mauritius Standards Bureau

Mexico (DGN)*
Dirección General de Normas

Mongolia (MNISM)*
Mongolian National Centre for
Standardization and Metrology

The Netherlands (NNI)
Nederlands Normalisatie-instituut

New Zealand (SNZ)
Standards New Zealand

Norway (NSF)
Norges Standardiseringsforbund

The Philippines (BPS)
Bureau of Product Standards
Department of Trade and Industry

Portugal (IPQ)
Instituto Português da Qualidade

Romania (IRS)*
Institutul Român de Standardizare

Russian Federation (GOST R)
State Committee of the Russian
Federation for Standardization,
Metrology and Certification

Singapore (PSB)
Singapore Productivity and Standards
Board (PSB)

South Africa (SABS)
South African Bureau of Standards

Spain (AENOR)
Asociación Española de Normalización
y Certificación

Sweden (SIS)
Standardiseringen i Sverige

Switzerland (SNV)
Swiss Association for Standardization

Syrian Arab Republic (SASMO)
Syrian Arab Organization for
Standardization and Metrology

Tanzania, United Republic of (TBS)
Tanzania Bureau of Standards

Thailand (TISI)
Thai Industrial Standards Institute
Ministry of Industry

Trinidad and Tobago (TTBS)
Trinidad and Tobago Bureau of
Standards

Turkey (TSE)
Türk Standardlari Enstitüsü

Ukraine (DSTU)
State Committee of Ukraine for
Standardization, Metrology and
Certification

United Kingdom (BSI)
British Standards Institution

United States of America (ANSI)
American National Standards Institute

Uruguay (UNIT)
Instituto Uruguayo de Normas Técnicas

Venezuela (COVENIN)
Comisiión Venezolana de Normas
Industriales

Zimbabwe (SAZ)
Standards Association of Zimbabwe

FULL MEMBERS OF ISO WHO ARE OBSERVING MEMBERS IN TC 207

Algeria (INAPI)
Institut algérien de normalisation et de
propriété industrielle

Costa Rica (INTECO)*
Instituto de Normas Técnicas de Costa
Rica

Croatia (DZNM)*
State Office for Standardization and
Metrology

Egypt (EOS)
Egyptian Organization for
Standardization and Quality Control

Iceland (STRI)
Icelandic Council for Standardization

Libyan Arab Jamahiriya (LNCSM)
Libyan National Centre for
Standardization and Metrology

Poland (PKN)
Polish Committee for Standardization

Slovakia (UNMS)
Slovak Office of Standards, Metrology
and Testing

Slovenia (SMIS)
Standards and Metrology Institute
Ministry of Science and Technology

Sri Lanka (SLSI)
Sri Lanka Standards Institution

Viet Nam (TCVN)
Directorate for Standards and Quality

Yugoslavia (SZS)
Savezni zavod za standardizaciju

CORRESPONDENT MEMBERS OF ISO WHO ARE OBSERVING MEMBERS IN TC 207

Barbados (BNSI)
Barbados National Standards Institution

Estonia (EVS)*
National Standards Board of Estonia

Hong Kong
Industry Department

Lithuania (LST)
Lithuanian Standards Board

Taiwan*
(Member name and membership category not listed in ISO membership list)

Participation in ISO 14001 formulation, by Developing Countries

	ISO Oslo MEM	ISO Oslo MEM F,C,S	TC 207 Rio MEM	TC 207 P or O	Attended	Delegation Size	Rio Attended	Del Size
Developing Countries	61		40		24	77		
Africa: UN=46	12		6		4	5		
North Africa: UN=6	5		3		2	0		
Algeria	1	–	1	O	1	?		
Egypt	1	–	1	O	0			
Libyan A J	1	–	1	O	1	?		
Morocco	1	–	0	–				
Tunisia	1	–	0	–				
Other Africa: UN=40	7		3		2	5		
Ethiopia	1	–	0	–				
Ghana	1	–	0	–				
Kenya	1	–	0	–				
Mauritius	1	F	1	P	1	3		
Nigeria	1	–	0	–				
UR Tanzania	1	F	1	P	0			
Zimbabwe	1	F	1	P	1	2		
Latin America and Caribbean: UN=38	14		12		6	34		
South America: UN=12	7		7		3	29		
Argentina	1	F	1	P	0	0		
Brazil	1	F	1	P	1	23		
Chile	1	F	1	P	1	4		
Colombia	1	F	1	P	1	2		
Ecuador	1	F	1	P	0	0		
Uruguay	1	F	1	P	0	0		
Venezuela	1	F	1	P	0	0		
Other Latin America: UN=26	7		5		3	5		
Barbados	1	–	1	O	0	0		
Costa Rica	1	–	0	–				
Cuba	1	F	1	P	0	0		
Jamaica	1	F	1	P	1	2		
Mexico	1	F	1	P	1	1		
Panama	1	–	0	–				
Trinidad & Tobago	1	F	1	P	1	2		

Asia: UN=22	0		14		10	33
West Asia: UN=13	5		1		1	1
Cyprus	1		0			
Iran, Islamic Rep. of	1	–	0	–		
Saudi Arabia	1	–	0	–		
Syrian Arab Republic	1	–	0	–		
Turkey	1	F	1	P	1	1
Central Asia: UN=2	2	0	0	0		
Kazakhstan	1	–	0	–		
Uzbekistan	1	–	0	–		
Eastern & Southern Asia: UN=23	15		13		9	32
Bangladesh	1	–	0	–		
China	1	F	1	P	1	7
Hong Kong	1	–	1	O	1	?
India	1	F	1	P	1	2
Indonesia	1	F	1	P	1	3
DPR. Korea	1	F	1	P	1	
Korea, Republic of	1	F	1	P		
Laos, People's Dem Republic	???					
Malaysia	1	F	1	P	1	13
Mongolia	1	F	1	P	0	0
Pakistan	1	–	0	–		
Philippines	1	F	1	P	0	0
Singapore	1	F	1	P	1	2
Sri Lanka	1	–	1	O	0	0
Thailand	1	F	1	P	1	3
Viet Nam	1	F	1	P	1	2
The Pacific: UN=7	0		0		0	0
Developing Europe: UN=3	1		1		0	0
Slovenia	1	–	0	–		

Legend:

ISO Members:	F: Full Member	C: Corresponding Member
	S: Subscribing Member	–: Unknown
TC 207 Members	P: Participating Member	O: Observing Member
	–: Unknown	

Source: *International Environmental Systems Update* and the ISO

Agenda 21
Principles for Multinational Corporations

In the area of global corporate environmental management:
1   introduce policies and commitments to adopt equivalent or not less stringent standards of operation as in the country of origin [Chapter 19.53(d) and 20.30];
2   recognize environmental management as among the highest corporate priorities and as a key determinant to sustainable development [30.3];
3   be encouraged to establish worldwide corporate policies on sustainable development [30.22];
4   ensure responsible and ethical management of processes from the point of view of health, safety and environmental aspects [30.26];
5   establish environmental management systems, including environmental auditing of production or distribution sites [20.13(i)];
6   strengthen partnerships to implement the principles and criteria for sustainable development [30.7];
7   have a special role and interest in promoting cooperation in technology transfer and in building a trained human resource pool and infrastructure in host countries [34.27];
8   share their environmental management experiences with the local authorities, national governments, and international organizations [30.22];
9   report annually on their environmental record as well as on their use of energy and natural resources [30.10(a)].

In the area of environmentally sound production and consumption patterns:
10   play a major role in reducing impacts on resource use and the environment through more efficient production processes, preventive strategies, cleaner production technologies and procedures throughout the product life cycle [Chapter 30.2 and 30.4];
11   integrate cleaner production approaches into the design of products and management practices [20.18(c)];
12   arrange for environmentally sound technologies to be available to affiliates in developing countries [30.22];
13   increase research and development of environmentally sound technologies and environmental management systems in collaboration with academia, scientific/engineering establishments, and indigenous people [30.25];
14   establish cleaner production demonstration projects/ networks by sector and by country [20.19(b)];

15 integrate cleaner production principles and case studies into training programmes and organize environmental training programmes for the private sector and other groups in developing countries [8.38(c) and 20.19(b)];

16 consider establishing environmental partnership schemes with small- and medium-sized enterprises [30.23].

In the area of risk and hazard minimization:

17 undertake research into the phase-out of those processes that pose the greatest environmental risk based on the hazardous wastes generated [Chapter 20.18(b)];

18 encourage affiliates to modify procedures in order to reflect local ecological conditions [30.22];

19 provide data for substances produced that are needed specifically for the assessment of potential risks to human health and the environment [19.16];

20 develop emergency response procedures and on-site and off-site emergency response plans [19.50(h)];

21 apply a 'responsible care' approach to chemical products, taking into account the total life cycle of such products [19.51(b) and 20.18(d)];

22 be transparent in their operations and provide relevant information to the community that might be affected by the generation and management of hazardous waste [20.14(f)];

23 adopt, on a voluntary basis, community right-to-know programmes based on international guidelines, including sharing information on the causes of accidental releases or potential releases and the means to prevent them [19.51(c)];

24 make available to governments the information necessary to maintain inventories of hazardous wastes, treatment/disposal sites, contaminated sites that require rehabilitation, and information on exposure and risks [20.23(a)];

25 report annually on routine emissions of toxic chemicals to the environment even in the absence of host country requirements [19.51(c)];

26 phase out, where appropriate, and dispose of any banned chemicals that are still in stock or in use, in an environmentally sound manner [19.53(j)].

In the area of full-cost environmental accounting:

27 be invited to participate at the international level in assessing the practical implementation of moving towards greater reliance on pricing systems that internalize environmental costs [Chapter 8.37];

28 cooperate in developing methodologies for the valuation of non-marketed natural resources and the standardization of data collection [8.50];

29 work towards the development and implementation of concepts and methodologies for the internalization of environmental costs into accounting and pricing mechanisms [30.9];

30 work with governments to identify and implement an appropriate mix of economic instruments and normative measures such as laws, legislation, and standards [30.8].

In the area of international environmental support activities:

31 develop an internationally agreed-upon code of principles for the management
    of trade in chemicals [Chapter 19.51(a)];

32 be full participants in the implementation and evaluation of activities related to
    Agenda 21 [30.1].

Source: 'Follow-up to the United Nations Conference on Environment and Development as
related to Transnational Corporations: Report of the Secretary General to the Commission
on Transnational Corporations', April 1993, E/C.10/1993/14

Selected Corporate Statements Supporting Global Environmental Management

INDUSTRY ASSOCIATIONS

Banks: Statement by Banks on Environment and Sustainable Development, UNEP

We will, in our domestic and international operations, endeavour to apply the same standards of environmental risk assessment (Statement 2.4). We expect, as part of our normal business practices, that our customers comply with all applicable, local national and international environmental regulations (Statement 2.2).

CERES: Coalition for Environmentally Responsible Economies, US

We intend to make consistent, measurable progress in implementing these principles and to apply them to all aspects of our operations throughout the world (CERES, Introduction). We will conduct and make public an annual self-evaluation of our progress in implementing these principles and in complying with applicable laws and regulations throughout our worldwide operations (CERES Principle # 10).

ICC: International Chamber of Commerce, France

To continue to improve corporate policies, programmes and environmental performance, taking into account technical developments, scientific understanding, consumer needs and community expectations, with legal regulations as a starting point; and to apply the same criteria internationally (Business Charter for Sustainable Development, Principle # 3).

Keidanren: Japanese Federation of Economic Organizations, Japan

Even though ... problems [of data availability and collection] may exist, formulation of a complete policy for the protection of the environment of the host country is a responsibility of good corporate citizenship on the part of the expanding corporation and it is hoped that each corporation will establish specific policies with this point in mind (Preamble) ...a corporation should strive to obtain full understanding about the importance of environmental protection to its affiliates in the host country (Keidanren Principle # 1).

Keizai Doyukai: Japan Association of Corporate Executives, Japan

Japan should take the initiative in promoting an international framework to tackle the preservation of the global environment, and this should be a major pillar of Japan's international contribution. To do this, Japan should make its basic concept and policies clear both at home and abroad. It must be able to respond flexibly to harmonize economic development and environmental preservation and take into consideration the importance, urgency and the respective situation of countries requiring aid (Keizai Doyukai Report, 1993 p 6).

COMPANIES

Ciba-Geigy: Switzerland, 1993

We apply the same objectives for safety and environmental protection in all countries where we operate (Principles, p 5). We strive to achieve sustainable growth by balancing our economic, social, and environmental responsibilities (*Annual Environmental Report 1993*, p 1).

General Motors: US, 1994

GM's environmental strategy consists of three key objectives, one of which is: worldwide implementation of environmental policy and strategy through leveraged resources (*GM Environmental Report 1995* p 28).

ICI: UK, 1994

This policy applies throughout ICI and our subsidiaries worldwide (Preamble). ICI pledges to 'encourage, through positive interaction within the industry, the worldwide development and implementation of the principles of ... the International Chamber of Commerce's Business Charter for Sustainable Development (Policy).

Mobil: US, 1994

In 1991 we also established a corporate policy on employee and facility safety. Its aim is to ensure that our operating divisions and subsidiaries conduct their activities worldwide with full concern for the safety of their facilities in order to protect the safety and health of employees, communities adjacent to our operations and general public (Protecting the Environment, 1991, p 2–3) ... Our policy goes beyond compliance and states that Mobil and its affiliates will continue to conduct their worldwide activities with full concern for safeguarding public health and protecting the environment in the absence of local laws and regulations (*Protecting the Environment*, 1993, p 30).

Monsanto: US, 1995

Our commitment is to achieve sustainable development for those aspects of the environment where we have an impact. Our commitment is to achieve sustainable development for the good of all people in both developed and less-developed nations (Monsanto Pledge announcement).

Showa Denko: Japan, 1993

Participate eagerly in various activities for the protection of the global environment and contribute to the good of society by helping restructuring of the economic and social systems into a more harmonious one with the global environment to strive for a global issue of environmental preservation (Report titled: *HFC 134a*, p 2).

Notes

PREFACE

1   George Gallup Memorial Survey, *The Health of the Planet Survey: A Preliminary Report on Attitudes Toward the Environmental and Economic Growth Measured by Citizens in 22 Nations to Date*, New Jersey, June 1992, p ii, pp 16–17. Subsequent surveys have confirmed this trend in public opinion. See UNCTAD (1996) *Self-Regulation of Environmental Management: An Analysis of Guidelines Set by World Industry Associations for their Member Firms* United Nations, Environment Series No 5, UNCTAD/DTCI/29, New York and Geneva

2   UN Environment Programme (1997) *Global Environmental Outlook* Oxford University Press, 1997, pp 2–5

3   Status of the standards and copies are available from the ISO Secretariat, Case Postale 56, CH-1211 Geneva 10, Switzerland, tel: +41/22/ 749-0111; fax: +41/22/733-3430; http://www.iso.ch; or from national standard-setting bodies

4   Examples of these assertions can be found in: Dr Phillipe Bergeron, managing director, Regional Institute of Environmental Technology (RIET), Singapore, 'The ISO 14000 Series and their Implications to Trade and Competitiveness' paper presented to *The Asia Conference on Trade and the Environment*, 27 and 28 June, 1996; publicity material for ISO 14001 Draft International Standard Registration, incorporating the 'Green Dove Award' from SGS International Certification Services Inc, the largest international certifier of ISO 14001 sites with 60 per cent of the market (May 1997); Roxann Stec and Glenn Rabac (1995) *ISO 14001: Executive Overview.* Perry Johnson, Inc, Burlington, Massachussets, pp 1–2

5   Shelton, C (ed) (1997) *ISO 14001 and Beyond.* Greenleaf Publishing, Sheffield

INTRODUCTION

1   ISO 14001 (1996) E, 'Introduction', p v

2   UNCTAD (1996) *Self-Regulation of Environmental Management* p 6

3   Michael McCloskey, chairman of the US-based Sierra Club, 'Exploring the Uses and Potential Benefits of ISO 14000' presentation to the US Environmental Protection Agency ISO 14000 Roundtable, 26 April 1996, Wharton School, University of Philadelphia, US

4   Among developing-country officers surveyed for this book, a number commented that they could not enforce their existing environmental legislation

5   Definitions are from *The American Heritage Dictionary of the English Language* (1970) American Heritage Publishing Co and Houghton Mifflin Company, New York, pp 1256–1257

6   European Union, Council Regulation (EEC) No 183 6/93 of 29 June 1993 allowing voluntary participation by companies in the industrial sector in a community eco-management and audit scheme

7   Spencer Cooke, A/SustainAbility, (1996) *From EMAS to SMAS: Charting the Course from Environmental Management and Auditing to Sustainability Management. The EPE Workbook for*

Implementing Sustainability in Europe, Version 1.1, European Partners for the Environment, Westmalle, Belgium.

8   Spencer-Cooke, A/SustainAbility Ltd (ed) (1996) *From EMAS to SMAS* The Global Environmental Management Initiative (GEMI), a group of mainly US-based international firms, predicted that EMAS would result in public reporting on the lines of the Toxic Release Inventory in the US, which requires reporting on a set number of toxic chemical releases over certain thresholds. See GEMI (1994), *Environmental Reporting in a Total Quality Management Framework: A Primer* GEMI, Washington DC

9   Lai, H (1996) ISO 9000 *Quality Management Systems: guidelines for enterprises in developing countries* 2nd edition, International Trade Centre, UNCTAD/WTO and ISO, UN, Geneva; and Arora, S C (1996) *Applying ISO Quality Management Systems*. International Trade Centre UNCTAD/WTO, Geneva

10 ISO 8402 (1994) *Quality Management and Quality Assurance – Vocabulary* ISO, Geneva

11 ISO 9000–1:1994 (E) 4.3 'Distinguishing between quality system requirements and product requirements' and 4.5 'Facets of quality'; and ISO 9001: 1994(E), 4 'Quality system requirements'

12 ISO 9001:1994(E) 4.6 'Purchasing; ISO 9004–1:1994(E) 'Quality management and quality system elements – Part 1: Guidelines'; 5 'Quality system elements'

13 ISO (1996) *ISO 14001, Environmental Management Systems – specification with guidance for use* 1st edition, para 4.2 Environmental Policy, p 2

14 'ISO 14001: A Critical View' in *Environmental Manager*, May 1996, John Wiley & Sons, New York, vol 7(3), p 13–15

15 ISO 14001, para 4.3 'Planning', p 3

16 ISO 14001, para 4.4.2 'Training, awareness and competence', p 3

17 ISO 14001, para 4.4.3 'Communication'; 4.4.4 'Environmental management system documentation'; 4.4.5 'Document control'; 4.4.6 'Operational control'; 4.4.7 'Emergency awareness and response'; 4.5 'Checking and corrective action'; 4.5.1 'Monitoring and measurement'; 4.5.2 'Non-conformance and corrective and preventive action'; 4.5.3 'Records', pp 4–5

18 ISO 14001, para.1: 'Scope', p 1

19 ISO 14004, approved June 1996

20 'ISO 14001 Specification Expected by Mid-September' *International Environmental Systems Update*, CEEM Information Services, Fairfax, Virginia, vol 3(7) pp 8–9 (referred to hereafter as IESU)

21 ISO 14001, para 3.6

22 *Guidelines for Environmental Auditing* contains these four standards: ISO 14010 General Principles on Environmental Auditing; ISO 14011/1 Audit Procedures – Auditing of Environmental Management Systems; ISO 14012 Qualifications Criteria for Environmental Auditors; ISO 14014 Guidelines for Initial/Preparatory Environmental Reviews

23 'SC2 Eliminates Two Work Items; Keeps Site Assessment Work' in *IESU* vol 3(7), July 1996, p 10

24 ISO 14001, para 3.8

25 ISO 14031: 'Evaluation of Environmental Performance'. After approval at an autumn 1996 meeting in Stockholm, the first committee draft of the EPE standard was sent to

member bodies in December 1996. Comments were due by 15 March, 1997, with the revised draft sent out 1 April for a mid April 1997 meeting in Kyoto

26 'EPE Standards Remains Working Draft' *IESU*, vol 3(7), July 1996, pp 11–13

27 Numbered ISO 14040, 14041, 14042, and 14043 respectively. For a full list of the ISO 14000 series of standards, see Annex B

28 ISO 14001

29 ISO 14020

30 'Standards: bridging document addressing differences between ISO, EMAS almost completed' in *International Environmental Reporter* 29 May, 1996, pp 430–431. 'International Accreditation Forum Accepts Provisional Criteria', June 5 1997, reported on http://www.iso14001.net, viewed January 1998

31 'Marketplace', National Public Radio, 13 May 1996. Transcript printed under the title 'ISO 14000 Hits the Air with Skepticism' *IESU* vol 3(7), p 27

32 Manuela Palomares-Soler and Peter Thimme, 'Environmental Standards: EMAS and ISO 14001 Compared' *European Environmental Law Review*, vol 5 No 8/9, August/September 1996, pp 247–249, Kluwer Law International, London

33 Tage Andersen of the Danish Environmental Protection Agency in a letter dated 13 March 1996 to the Secretary General of the European Environmental Bureau, Brussels

34 Pernilla Knuttson, Deputy Assistant Under-Secretary, Ministry of the Environment, Sweden, letter to Raymond Van Ermen, European Environmental Bureau, 5 March 1996. Letter on file with the EEB and with Benchmark Environmental Consulting

35 CEN CR 12969 (1997) 'Bridging Document Between Regulation 93/1836/EEC (Eco-Management and Audit Scheme) and EN ISO 14001, EN ISO 14010, EN ISO 14011 and EN ISO 14012', August; and Gelber, Matthias (1998) 'Will Revision Help EMAS Hold Its Own Against ISO 14001?' *Business and the Environment's ISO 14000 Update*, vol iv, no 2, February

36 The UNCTAD Ad Hoc Working Group on Trade, Environment and Development reviewed issues at their third session in November 1995. See, for example, TD/B/WG.6/9 and 10. UNCTAD has also published a series of environmental reports. The UNEP Industry & Environment Office, in collaboration with the International Chamber of Commerce and the International Federation of Consulting Engineers, has published *Environmental Management Standards and Implications for Exporters to Developed Markets*, New York, 1996. The UNIDO Industrial Sectors and Environmental Division organized an Expert Group Meeting to Discuss the Potential Effects of ISO 9000 and ISO 14000 Series and Environmental-Labelling on the Trade and Developing Countries in October 1995 and presented the results of a survey in UNIDO Doc ISED 9 (Spec), 12 February 1996

37 UNDP (1996) *ISO 14000 Environmental Management Standards and Implications for Exporters to Developed Markets* UNDP Private Sector Development Programme, New York

38 ISO (June 1996) *Raising Standards for the World: ISO's long-range strategies 1996–1998*, from the ISO worldwide web page on the internet (http://www.iso.ch/press/strategy), items 3.3 and 4.3

39 By December 1995, Mobil Oil Company, which surveys the use of ISO 9000, reported that over 125,000 ISO 9000 certificates had been issued: a 33.3 per cent increase over the previous year. Reported in ISO, *ISO Annual Report 1996* Geneva

CHAPTER 1

1   Clements, R (1996) *Complete Guide to ISO 14000* Prentice Hall, New Jersey

2   This is the basis of many of his presentations, including: 'ISO 14000' at the conference *International Business Forum on Agenda 21*, CDS International, New York, 16–18 June 1997

3   ISO (March 1997) *The ISO 14000 Environment*, front page, photograph and caption, ISO, Geneva

4   NEC Advertisement, *The Smithsonian*, April 1997, p83. NEC is a $41 billion company with 102 subsidiaries and affiliates in 31 countries. They have an environmental policy committed to 'coexistence with nature' since 1991

5   'SAGE Strategic Plan', ISO/IEC Doc. SAGE 75 (long)

6   'SAGE Strategic Plan', ISO/IEC Doc. SAGE 75 (long)

7   See the review article 'Sustainable Development: Is It Industry's Business?' *Business and the Environment*, Cutter Information Corp, Massachusetts, February 1997, pp 2–5

8   Gleckman, H (1995) 'Transnational Corporations' Strategic Responses to Sustainable Development' in Bergensen, H and Parmann, G (eds) *Green Globe Yearbook 1995* Oxford University Press, Oxford, pp 93–106

9   UNCTAD (1996) *Self-Regulation of Environmental Management* UNCTAD, Geneva

10 The concept of technology transfer is not popularly accepted among the industry association guidelines except by the Japanese associations

11 UNCTAD (1996) *Self-Regulation of Environmental Management* UNCTAD, Geneva

12 In addition to the reference to sustainable development that was removed, there was a reference among the policy commitments to pollution prevention that was altered to 'the prevention of pollution'. See European Environmental Bureau *ISO 14001: An Uncommon Perspective* Benchmark Environmental Consulting, Maine

13 UNCTAD (1993) *Environmental Management in Transnational Corporations: report on the Benchmark Corporate Environmental Survey* UN, New York (ST/CTC/149)

14 Amoco Corporation (1995) *Amoco Compliance Program* Chicago, Illinois

15 NEC (1995) *Ecology and Technology: Environmental Management Activities Report* NEC, Tokyo, Japan

16 NEC (1995) *Ecology and Technology*, pp 18–19

17 Proctor & Gamble (1995) *1995 Environmental Progress Report, Proctor & Gamble Company* Cincinnati, Ohio

18 Dow Chemical Company (1996) *1996 Progress Report on Environment, Health and Safety: Continuing the Responsible Care Journey. Steps Towards Sustainability* The Dow Chemical Company, Midland, Michigan

19 Toyota (1996) 'Preventing Global Warming' in *Toyota: Environmental Programs and Activities*, Toyota City, Japan, p 20; Volkswagen AG Research, Environment and Transportation, *The Volkswagen Environmental Report* Wolfsburg, Germany (no date, circa 1996)

20 Baram, M (1994) 'Multinational Corporations, Private Codes, and Technology Transfer for Sustainable Development' *Environmental Law*, vol 24:33, pp 32–65; Roht-Arriaza, N (1996) 'Private Voluntary Standard-Setting, the International Organization for Standardization, and International Environmental Lawmaking' *Yearbook of International Environmental Law*, pp 105–161

21   The World Bank (1996) *Pollution Prevention and Abatement Handbook, Part II: Environmental Management Systems and ISO 14000* The World Bank, Washington, DC

22   Roht-Arriaza (1996) op cit p 123

23   I. Orhan Türköz, Chairman of Environmental Standards, Turkish Standards Institute, Ankara, letter to Riva Krut, 31 December 1996, on file with authors

24   UNEP/SustainAbility (1994) *Corporate Environmental Reporting: a measure of the progress of business and industry towards sustainable development* UNEP-IEO, Technical Report No 24, Paris

25   Gleckman, H (1995) in Bergensen, H, and Parmann, G (eds) *Green Globe Yearbook 1995* Oxford University Press, Oxford, p 239

26   IBM (1995) *Progress Report 1995* IBM Corporation, Armonk, New York, p 16

27   UNCTAD (1996) *Self-Regulation of Environmental Management*; and Baram, M (1994) pp 53–54

28   Irwin, F (1997) 'Charting a Sustainable Course for the Industrial Sector: Initiatives in the European Union' World Wildlife Fund, Washington, DC

29   See Roht-Arriaza, N (1996) op cit pp 120–124; *International Environmental Reporter*, 1 November, 1995, p 823

30   *Asia Respondent # 7*

31   'Follow-up to the UN Conference on Environment and Development as Related to Transnational Corporations' Report of the Secretary General to the Commission on Transnational Corporations, April 1993, United Nations, New York, E/C10/1993/14

32   Letter of 1 December 1996 to Dr Riva Krut from I Orhan Türköz, Chairman of Environmental Standards and the TSI in Ankara, on file with the authors

33   A discussion of the meaning of a 'commitment to compliance' is in Chapter 4

34   Bell, C (1997) 'The ISO 14001 Environmental Management Systems Standard: One American's View' in Sheldon (ed) *ISO 14001 and Beyond* Greenleaf Publishing, Sheffield, pp 61–92; p 82

35   'Rules and Standards' in *The Framework Convention on Climate Change*, May 1992; in *Green Globe 1995*, pp 117–119

36   FAO International Code of Conduct on the Distribution and Use of Pesticides, in *Green Globe 1995* pp 136–137; Vienna Convention for the Protection of the Ozone Layer, including the Montreal Protocol, on Substances that Deplete the Ozone Layer, Vienna 1985, in *Green Globe 1995*, p 122

CHAPTER 2

1   Liew Min Leong (January 1997) ISO president, 'Continuing ISO's Growth Momentum', editorial in *ISO Bulletin* ISO, Geneva, p 2

2   Newham, M (1996) 'Kenyan Industry Found to Lack Information on Upcoming ISO 14001 Environmental Series' *BNA International Environmental Reporter*, Washington, DC, 12 June

3   Cameron, J (1996) 'ISO 14000: Globalization and the trading system', keynote paper at the 2 July conference organized by the Australian Centre for Environmental Law, *ISO 14000: Regulation, Trade and the Environment* Canberra, Australia

4   International Environmental NGO Statement to Fifth Meeting of the OECD Environmental Policy Committee at Ministerial Level; OECD Doc ENV/EPOC/MIN(96)13, 19 February 1996, para 31

5   Electronics Industry Alliance, website at http://www.eia.org, May 1997

6   Also see 'Developing Nations See Obstacles to ISO 14001 Use' in *IESU*, July 1995, p 15

7   'Organisational Structure of ISO/TC207 : Environmental Management and US Participation', Global Environmental Management Initiative (GEMI), Management Standards Work Group, Washington, DC, 1995

8   In 1995, DEVCO funded participation in TC 207 meetings for two officials, each from Brazil, Colombia, India, Indonesia, Jamaica, Malaysia, Mauritius, Thailand, Trinidad and Tobago, Vietnam and Zimbabwe. In 1996, participation was increased to include Argentina, Cuba and Mexico

9   Statistics from the attendance list; see Annex D

10 WTO, G/TBT/5, para 19

11 It had 111 members in March 1995, a mid-point in the TC 207 negotiations

12 The European Union is a regional member of the ISO.

13 Numbers are based on the membership list published on the ISO worldwide web page (<http://www.iso.ch>)

14 ISO/IEC directives, 1995, article 1.15

15 The ISO Committee on Consumer Policy has published the *COPOLCO Directory* in 1996 'to practical assistance to consumers and their representatives on how they can influence standardization'

16 Personal communication with Arthur Weissman, chair of the ISO working group on guiding principles on environmental labelling programmes

17 ISO Rules of Procedure, 5.4

18 The ISO General Assembly has four policy development committees, two of which deal with special constituents: consumers (COPOLCO) and developing countries (DEVCO)

19 ISO statutes, article 8; and rules of procedure, clause 4.2

20 ISO/IEC directive, article 1.52

21 Orhan Türköz, I, Chairman of Environmental Standards, Turkish Standards Institute, letter to Dr Riva Krut, 31 December 1996; on file with Dr Krut at Benchmark Environmental Consulting and with Dr John Cuddy at UNCTAD, Geneva

22 ISO/IEC directive, article 1.5.7

23 Proposal for a new field of technical activity (ISO/IEC SAGE 75); also referred to as ISO/TS/P – 179, annex 1, part 3

24 ISO/IEC SAGE strategic plan; (ISO/IEC SAGE 75, Rev 4) p 1

25 ISO/IEC directive, article 1.5.10

26 The October 1992 recommendation from the head of ISO to the technical management board did not include the exclusion of work on environmental performance. The exclusion for work in this area by ISO was, however, incorporated into the final agenda item of the technical management board on 25 January 1993

27 The International Electrotechnical Commission undertakes standard setting for products and services in the electronic industry. Its procedures parallel those of the ISO

28 The nominated project leader 'will have access to appropriate resources for carrying out the development work' (ISO/IEC directives, article 2.1.7)

29 ISO/IEC directives, article 1.10.1

30 ISO/IEC directives, article 1.8.2, 'Responsibilities'

31 'Organizational Structure of ISO/TC207: Environmental Management and US Participation', Global Environmental Management Initiative (GEMI), Management Standards Work Group, Washington, DC, 1995

32 ISO/IEC directives, articles 2.5.1 and 2.5.9

33 The final international standard is available in English, French and Russian. Russian translation and interpretation is provided by the Russian national standard-setting body. Since national standard-setting bodies implement the ISO standard, they are likely to translate it for practitioners in their national languages

34 ISO/IEC Guide 2: 1991, cited in Directives, part 1, p 23

35 ISO/IEC directives, para 2.5.6

36 July 1997, 'ISO 14001 Specification Expected by Mid-September' *IESU*, vol 3(7)

37 ISO/IEC directives, para. 2.5.6

38 ISO/IEC directives, article 2.9

39 ISO/IEC directives, article 2.9.3

40 Discussions have started between ISO technical committees dealing with ISO 9000 and ISO 14001 and at the International Forum on Accreditation to develop some joint approaches to the issue of mutual recognition

41 ANSI–RAB National Accreditation Program. Criteria for Bodies Operating Registration of Environmental Management Systems, E3.03B, provisionally adopted by the NAP EMS Council; still subject to public review and comment. Revision date: 09/20/96

42 Cameron, J (1996) op cit

43 ISO (1995) 'ISO and international standardization', standard text reproduced in ISO *1995 Annual Report* and *1996 Annual Report*, Geneva

CHAPTER 3

1 The GATT Annex on Sanitary and Phytosanitary (SPS) Measures urges parties to harmonize measures to protect commercial plants and animals and to harmonize regulatory standards to protect human health from contaminants in the food supply. The pre-1994 and 1994 GATT defines international standards, guidelines and recommendations for food safety as those set by the Codex Alimentarius Commission; for animal health as those set by the International Office of Epizootics; and for plant health as those developed under the auspices of the Secretariat of the International Plant Protection Convention. The long-standing SPS annex shares a number of implementation features with the new TBT annex

2 Conformity assessment systems for food quality are generally developed under Codex Alimentarius, an international commission supported by the World Health Organization and the Food and Agricultural Organization

3 In 1996 the ISO briefed the TBT 'on the relevance to trade of the ISO 9000 series on quality management standards, and on the upcoming ISO 14000 series of environmental

management standards' ISO, *1995 Annual Report*, Geneva, p 4

4   GATT (177) *The Results of the Uruguay Round of Multilateral Trade Negotiations – The Legal Texts*, vol 27, GATT, Geneva

5   TBT, p 1

6   The ISO 14000 series on ecolabelling, if and when adopted, would be a relevant international standard for judging the trade appropriateness of environmental labels.

7   TBT, p 1

8   There are several important procedural and semantic differences in these two international agreements. The first, as noted above, is the term standard, which under ISO refers to mandatory and voluntary standards and under the TBT agreement is limited to voluntary standards. These GATT definitions are based on ISO/IEC formal definitions, except that standards as defined by ISO/IEC Guide 2 may be mandatory or voluntary (GATT TBT, annex 1)

9   TBT, Article 2.4

10 Dispute-Settlement Understanding, article 13.2 and appendix 4; TBT Article 14.2

11 TBT, article 2.2

12 TBT, article 2.4

13 TBT, article 2.5

14 WTO: GT/TBT/5 paragraph 17 and 23 states: 'The [TBT] Committee noted the rights and obligations... regarding the use of relevant international standards... as the basis for technical regulations, standards and conformity assessment procedures. The Committee stressed the importance of compliance with these provisions... [the Committee] noted the importance of avoiding the promulgation of national technical regulations where they were not necessary, limiting them to their specific requirements, and, in accordance with the relevant provisions of the Agreement, aligning them with international standards.'

15 TBT, article 4

16 TBT, annex 3B

17 TBT, annex 3C

18 The report of the first triennial review of the TBT reiterated this view, calling for 'closer cooperation between the WTO and relevant international standardizing bodies, as well as among officials and experts in non-governmental standardizing bodies at the national level' (WTO, G/TBT/5 paragraph 21)

19 Kean argues that the new TBT agreement made illegal the use of those process and production methods that were not consistent with international standards. In this situation, the pressures to get special market preference for one's own country have begun to create a new form of market barriers. In Kean's view, ISO systems are not covered by the term process and production methods and as such are not banned by the 1994 GATT; Bruce R Kean ' ISO 14000 Regulation, Trade and Environment', proceedings of the Australian Centre for Environmental Law Conference, 2 July 1996

20 G/TBT/W/41, 25 April 1997, Note from the Government of Canada

21 TBT, annex 3.D

22 TBT, article 2.6

23 TBT, article 12.4

24 TBT, article 12.8

25 TBT, article 11.2

26 ISO (1995) *ISO Programme for Developing Countries, 1995–1997*, ISO, Geneva, 1995

27 TBT, article 10.9

CHAPTER 4

1   Environment and Energy Study Institute Task Force on International Development and Environmental Security (1991) *Partnership for Sustainable Development: A New US Agenda for International Development and Environmental Security* EESI, Washington, DC, p 3. Also see Sun Lin and Sally Bullen (1995) 'Trade Provisions in Multilateral Environmental Agreements' in Sun Lin (ed) *UNEP's New Way Forward: Environmental Law and Sustainable Development* UNEP, Nairobi, pp 35–50; p 35

2   UNCTAD (1995) *Environment, international competitiveness and development: lessons from empirical studies*, Report by the UNCTAD Secretariat to the Ad Hoc Working Group on Trade, Environment and Development, TB/B/WG.6/10, para 45

3   UNCTAD (1997) *Report of the Expert Meeting on Possible Trade and Investment Impacts of Environmental Management Standards, Particularly the ISO 14000 Series, on Developing Countries, and Opportunities and Needs in this Context* 29–31 October, Geneva; TD/B/COM.1/10, 10 November

4   'ISO 14000 in Asia: an ASER Survey' in *Asia Environmental Report* London, April 1997, pp 9–11

5   Chairman, Environmental Standards, Turkish Standards Institute, letter of 31 December 1996 to the authors, op cit

6   Krut, R (1997) 'ISO 14001: Strategic Issues for Corporate Environmental Leaders' *Corporate Environmental Strategies*, spring, vol 4 no 3, pp 61–66

7   UNCTAD (1997) *Report of the Expert Meeting on Possible Trade and Investment Impacts* para 5

8   *Asian Respondent # 7*

9   UNCTAD (1995) *Newly emerging environmental policies with possible trade impact: A preliminary discussion*, Report by the UNCTAD Secretariat to the UNCTAD Ad Hoc Working Group on Trade, Environment and Development, TD/B/WG.6/9, para 100

10 'Pilots, Workshops, Seminars, Mandates: Asia is rife with ISO 14000 interest' *IESU*, vol 3(4), 1996, p 20

11 *African Respondent # 1* and *Asian Respondent # 7*

12 The substantial human and financial resources needed to comply with the ISO 9000 requirements were intimidating to entrepreneurs; this was recognized in a recent international conference on the trade effects of the ISO 9000 series on developing countries. UNIDO, *Expert Group Meeting on the Potential Effects of ISO 9000 and ISO 14000 Series and Environmental Labelling on the Trade of Developing Countries* Vienna

13 See Gleckman (1996) 'Promising Much But Delivering Little' *Business and the Environment: ISO 14000 Update* Cutter Information Corp, Arlington, MA, US. A standard sales pitch for a training conference lists advantages of certifying to ISO 14001. It includes elements such as the following: 'For those businesses providing goods and services to the international marketplace, lack of conformance with ISO 14000 may represent a barrier to trade in those countries in which conformance is required. As with ISO 9000, conformance

with ISO 14001 may become a supplier prerequisite in certain industries or market sectors.' See Environmental Business Association of New York State, Inc: Two Day Conference on Understanding and Implementing ISO 14000, 27 and 28 March 1996, New York; Roxann Stec and Glenn Rabac (1995) *ISO 14001: The Groundwork for Environmental Management* Perry Johnson, Inc, Burlington, Massachusetts; *ISO 14001 Registration: Now There's Living Proof* SGS International Certification Systems Inc, publicity catalogue (undated; circa 1995)

14 UNCTAD (1995) op cit, para 105

15 UNCTAD (1995) op cit, para 98

16 Roht-Arriaza (1995) 'Private Voluntary Standard-Setting' *Ecology Law Quarterly*, vol 22, no 3, p 125

17 Gil Hedstrom, A D Little, presentation to the panel, 'The Drivers, Benefits and Concerns of ISO 14000' at the conference, ANSI/GETF/EPA ISO 14000: A National Dialogue. One in a Series of National Conferences and Roundtables Designed to Facilitate a Dialogue on Issues Surrounding ISO 14000 and its Implementation, MIT, Massachusetts, 9 to 10 October, 1996

18 Chris Wilson, Digital Equipment Corporation, presentation on the panel 'Strategic Considerations and ISO 14000' at the conference ANSI/GETF/EPA ISO 14000: A National Dialogue, MIT, Massachusetts 9 to 10 October, 1996

19 'ISO 14000 in Asia: an ASER Survey' *Asia Environmental Report* London, April 1997, pp 9–11

20 Riva Krut and Carol Drummond (1997) *Global Environmental Management: Candid Views of Fortune 500 Companies,* Report of the US AID Asia Environmental Partnership, Washington, DC

21 Riva Krut and Carol Drummond (1997) ibid

22 Amy Zuckerman, author on ISO international standards and Massachusetts-based marketing executive; personal communication with Riva Krut, September 1996

23 Neil Gunningham (1996) 'From Adversarialism to Partnership? ISO 14000 and Regulation', paper presented to the conference of the Australian Centre for Environmental Law, ISO 14000: Regulation, Trade and Environment, 2 July 1996, Canberra, Australia

24 Volkswagen (no date; circa 1996) *The Volkswagen Environmental Report,* Wolfsburg, Germany, p 66

25 Businesses for Social Responsibility (1997) 'Greening the Supply Chain: Benchmarking Leadership Company Efforts to Improve Environmental Performance in the Supply Chain' BSR Education Fund, Washington, DC

26 Computer Industry Environmental Council (CIQC) Standard 0014, developed in October 1996. See June Andersen, Environmental Programmes Manager, IBM, and Hsia Chung, Procurement Programmes Manager, Hewlett Packard (1997) 'The Development of an Industry Standard Supply-Base Environmental Practices Questionnaire' speech at the International IEEE/ISEE Conference. The questionnaire is posted at http://www.sw.sun.com/CIQC/docs/environmental.html.

27 Wilson and McClean (1996) 'Is ISO Implementation/ Certification for You? 10 Propositions to Consider' *IESU*, Vol. 3(3), pp 25–26

28 Riva Krut and Carol Drummond (1997) op cit

29 *Latin American Respondent # 10*

30 Aidan Davy (TK) 'Environmental Management Systems; ISO 14001 Issues for Developing Countries' in Sheldon Davis (ed) *Beyond 14001*, Greenleaf Publishing, Sheffield, pp 169–182; p 181

31 *African Respondent # 2*

32 UNCTAD (1995) para 100

33 Riva Krut and Carol Drummond (1997) op cit

34 'In our country, they are especially worried about economic impacts on SMEs. These enterprises will be the main group to be affected adversely. The big companies are involved – they will take it in their stride.' *Asian Respondent # 3*

35 'Mexican Industry Views ISO 14001...' *IESU* vol 2(12), 1995, p 25; the same applies for example to China, as stated in *RIET in Focus*, vol 1(4), 1996, Singapore, p 7

36 UNCTAD (19955) op cit para 55–61

37 *South American Respondent # 5*

38 'Standards: Cost of ISO 14000 Could Be Burdensome for Small, Medium Firms, US Official Says' *International Environment Reporter (INER)*, 14 June, 1995, p 454–5. In highly concentrated markets, this will mean that transnational corporations can, at their choice, add an ISO 14001 certification to their purchase requirements and so eliminate from the bid process many smaller and medium-sized firms.

39 The environmental ministry is highly involved and is conducting an analysis on the consequences of implementing ISO 14000 on small- and medium-sized enterprises. They have started a pilot programme already involving 18 companies: they consider the cost and the technical viability. *South American Respondent # 6*

40 *Agenda 21*, Chapter 30.23 and 20.19(b)

41 The US consultant day rate was $1800; the NSF was $1200. This spread is used to calculate the difference between a Malaysian professional from the Standards Setting Institute ($430 per day) and a private sector consultant ($645)

42 UNDP (1996) *ISO 14000: Environmental Management Standards and Implications for Exporters to Developed Markets* United Nations Development Programme, New York, Annex 3. Polly Strife gives a figure of $100,000 to $ 200,000 in her article referring to the cost of 'revamping existing environmental management systems to meet ISO standards'. Polly Strife (1996) 'Questioning ISO's Benefits for Leaders' *Environmental Forum*, Environmental Law Institute, Washington, DC, January/February, p 9

43 *South American Respondent # 3*

44 The Malaysian estimate has a $216 registration fee. UNDP estimates a $650 fee for the final report and a $550 fee for registration, plus a $1800 to $3600, plus expenses, fee for a 'surveillance audit' (one to three days, depending on size of firm)

45 See Chapter 2.

46 Clive Mason, Deputy Director of RIET, in a speech held at the China–Europe International Conference on Environmental Technology, Beijing, 14 September, 1995

47 *African Respondents # 2* and *# 3*

48 *South American Respondent # 3*

49 *South American Respondent # 1*

50   UNIDO (1996) 'Trade implications of international standards for quality and environ-
     mental management systems (ISO 9000/ISO 14000 Series): Survey Results' UN
     Industrial Development Organization, Industrial Sectors and Environment Division,
     ISED.9(SPEC.)

51   'RAB sinks $1 Million Into ISO 14001 Accreditation Plan' *IESU*, vol 2(12), 1995, p 15

52   Singapore Launching Program to Help SMEs Understand Requirements of ISO 14000
     Series, BNA-INER, 13 November 1996, p 1013

53   'Mutual Recognition MOU signed by European accreditation bodies' *IESU*, vol 3(2)
     1996, p 1

54   'European Certification Group Approves New Guidelines for Accreditation Bodies'
     INER, September 1996

55   *Agenda 21*, Chapter 30.22

56   *South American Respondent # 5* and *South American Respondent #6*

57   Similar benefits ideally stemming from a good environmental management system were
     recorded in a study of the *Harvard Business Review*, where it was stated that: 'Ultimately
     enhanced resource productivity makes companies more competitive' in *RIET in Focus*,
     vol 1(2), Singapore, April 1996, p 7

58   W Althammer (1995) 'Handelsliberalisierung und Umweltpolitik – ein Konflikt?'
     Zeitschrift für Umweltpolitik und Umweltrecht, April, p 444

59   'The very competitiveness of the Asians will bring about an environmental impact, as
     soon as they realize that better environmental performance brings about economic
     advantages (waste avoidance as main example).' *Asian Respondent # 7*

60   *Asian Respondent # 10*

61   UNIDO (1996) op cit

62   For example, adhering to ecological product standards (limit values, etc, in this case) for a
     single blue dye would require investments of US $13 million in the case of some leading
     firms in India (caused by needs for upgrading technology and establishing second-grade
     treatment plants); stated in: UNCTAD (1995) *Environmental policies, trade and competitiveness:
     conceptual and empirical issues; Ad Hoc Working Group on Trade, Environment and Development,
     Second Session*, Geneva, 6 June, TD/B/WG6/6, 29 March 1995

63   For detailed data see: UNCTAD (1994) *Ecolabelling and market opportunities for environmental-
     ly friendly products; Ad Hoc Working Group on Trade, Environment and Development, First Session*,
     Geneva, TD/B/WG 2/5, 6 October 1994; UNCTAD (1995) *Trade, Environment and
     Development Aspects of Establishing and Operating Ecolabelling Programmes; Ad Hoc Working
     Group on Trade, Environment and Development, Second Session*, Geneva, TD/B/WG 6/5, 28
     March 1995

64   *South American Respondent # 6*. Also see K Dawkins (1995) 'Eco-labelling: information for
     consumer action or restrictive business practice?' Institute for Agriculture and Trade
     Policy, Minneapolis, Minesota, USA

65   'REIT member ready to ride environmental management system wave' *REIT in Focus*, vol
     2(1), January 1996

66   ESCAP (1996) 'Trade-environment linkages in ESCAP: seeking harmony', draft report
     for ESCAP International Trade and Economic Cooperation Division, p 82

CHAPTER 5

1 Joe Cascio, keynote presentation 'ISO 14000 Environmental Management Standards – A Primer' to the conference ANSI/GETF/EPA, ISO 14000: A National Dialogue, MIT, 9 to 10 October, 1996. The incident is retold in Riva Krut (1997) 'ISO 14001 – Some Strategic Issues for Corporate Environmental Leaders' *Journal of Corporate Environmental Strategy*, spring

2 Harris Gleckman 'Transnational Corporations' p 100

3 Many national and international consulting firms and publishers are circulating materials and reports maintaining that ISO 14001 certification will bring regulatory relief. One argument is that companies adopt an environmental management system for a range of reasons, including 'desire to benefit from regulatory incentives that reward companies showing environmental leadership through certified compliance with an environmental management system'. Caroline Hemenway (ed) (1995) *What Is ISO 14001: Questions and Answers*, second edition, CEEM Publications Services with the ASQC Quality Press, p 5. Another example: 'Although ISO 14000 is intended to be voluntary, some government agencies (including the US Department of Energy) are going one step further, making registration to the new standard a *requirement*, just as some governments and suppliers did when ISO 9000 was released.' Roxann Stec & Glenn Rabac (1995) *ISO 14000: The Groundwork for Environmental Management – an Executive Overview* Perry Johnson Inc, Massachusetts, p 1–2

4 North American Council on Environmental Cooperation (1997) Council Resolution #97-05, 'Future Cooperation Regarding Environmental Management Systems and Compliance' Pittsburgh, June 12

5 Aidan Davy (1997) 'Environmental Management Systems: ISO 14001 Issues for Developing Countries' in Christopher Sheldon (ed) *ISO 14001 and Beyond: Environmental Management Systems in the Real World* Greenleaf Publishing, Sheffield, pp 169–182

6 Details of this case are taken from: Canada, Province of Alberta, 'Proceedings taken in the Provincial Court of Alberta, Court House, Fort Saskatchewan, Alberta, 25 January 1996, Prospec Chemicals Ltd' Docket 51141166 P10101-02; and Susan McRory, Crown Counsel, 'Crown Statement of Facts' Provincial Court of Alberta, Judicial District of Fort Saskatchewan, between Her Majesty the Queen and Prospec Chemicals. Also see 'Canada court orders certification for firm, in unusual ruling: judgement portends due diligence benchmarking.' *IESU*, April 1996, p 9–10

7 Ellen Pekilis, Project Manager of Environmental Programmes, Standards Division, Canadian Standards Association, correspondence with Dr Riva Krut, 6 February 1997; correspondence on file with Dr Krut and UNCTAD

8 Assistant US Attorney-General Lois Schiffer, as quoted in 'DOJ expresses ISO 14001 skepticism; Questions Enforcement Role' IESU, March 1996, p 1 and 3. Because of the absence of a compliance commitment, an American attorney argues that ISO 14001 standards will not be proof of due diligence in the context of environmental prosecution. Although some environmental management systems do insist on compliance, ISO 14001 does not, goes the argument, and therefore 14001 may not be enough to demonstrate that reasonable care was taken. See 'The ISO Standard may not Necessarily Protect Companies in Cases of Environmental Prosecutions' *CA Magazine*, November 1996, reproduced in 'ISO 14001: News Briefs' *ISO 14000 – News and Views*, March 1997, from The Law Offices of S Wayne Rosenbaum, Carlsbad, California

9   The concept of ISO Plus was presented by Riva Krut at a panel on 'ISO 14000, Drivers, Benefits and Concerns' at the ANSI/GETF/EPA Conference ISO 14000 – A National Dialogue, and gained currency in debate in the sessions afterward. The counterargument was made by Bob Ferrone, an ISO 14001 consultant at that time with Ferrone and Knight, a consulting group in Massachusetts, and a member of the US TAG to TC 207

10 Eric Schaeffer, Director, EPA Office of Enforcement and Compliance, EPA, Washington, DC, speech to the *Annual Conference of the National Council of State Legislatures*, St Louis, Missouri, July 27 1996

11 United States Environmental Protection Agency (1996) Communications, Education and Public Affairs (1703), 'Note to Correspondents' 19 January 1996; 'Incentives for Self-Policing: EPA Fact Sheet' circa January 1996

12 California EPA, Multi-State Working Group (1997) 'Guidance on the Evaluation of Pilot Projects Evaluating the Environmental, Economic and Compliance Performance of Organizations Implementing ISO 14001 Environmental Management System'; the MSWG is under the stewardship of the California EPA and Robert Stephens

13 'States, US EPA Unsure how ISO 14001 Factors into Reform: public data called key' *BNA International Environmental Reporter*, 30 October 1996, Washington, DC

14 UNDP (1996) *ISO 14000 – Environmental management standards and implications for exporters to developed markets* UNDP, New York

15 Paul Hofhuis (1996) Environmental Counsel, Dutch Ministry, Washington, DC, presentation to the *Annual Conference of the National Council of State Legislatures*, St Louis, Missouri

16 Ministry of Housing, Spacial Planning and the Environment, Department for Information and International Relations (1993) *Environment and Companies: a guide for governmental authorities and companies; Company environmental management as a basis for a different relationship between companies and governmental authorities*, VROM 9567/b/1-96, The Hague, pp 3–4

17 *ISO 14001*, 3.1: 'Definitions: Continual Improvement' and paragraphs 4.2: 'Environmental Policy' pp 1 and 2

18 *ISO 14001*, para 4.2c: 'Environmental Policy', p 2

19 Naomi Roht-Arriaza 'Private Voluntary Standard-Setting' pp 120–124

20 *African Respondent # 1*

21 Letter of Ahmad Husseini of the Canadian Standards Association and Convener of ISO/TC 207/SC3/WG2 to John Henry, Secretary ISO/TC 207/SC3, 1 December 1995

22 Joe Cascio, presentation on ISO 14000 to the MIT Working Group on Business and the Environment, MIT, 25 June 1995. See also 'International Environmental Management Standards: ISO 9000s Less Tractable Siblings' *ASTM Standardization News*, April 1994

23 Benchmark (1996) *ISO 14001: An Uncommon Perspective*, pp 15–17

24 *African Respondent # 2*

25 *Asian Respondent # 3*

26 United Nations (1997) 'Major Groups and Rio + 5: Report of the Secretary-General' for consideration by the Commission on Sustainable Development and the UN General Assembly, extract: Chapter 30: 'The Role of Business and Industry' para 81, United Nations

27 UNCTAD (1996) *Self-Regulation of Environmental Management* pp 38–39

28 Shelton Davis (1996) 'Public Involvement in Environmental Decision-Making: Some Reflections on the Western European Experience' unpublished paper, The World Bank, Washington, DC

29 See EPA (1997) 'Proposal for Using Voluntary Environmental Management Systems in State Water Systems' Federal Register Document, *Federal Register*, 21 January, vol 62, no 13, pp 3036–308; Kim Wilhelm (1997) Department of Toxic Substances Control, Cal/EPA Focus: ISO 14000, 'Establishing Voluntary International Environmental Standards for Worldwide Uniformity' *California/EPA Report*, vol 5 no 12, cited in *ISO 14000 – News and Views*, March 1997

30 United Nations Economic Commission for Europe (1995) p 21; cited in Shelton Davis (1996), p 2

31 For a report on the background of this statement by James Connaughton, see 'ISO 14001 should not be required by law or regulation, attorney says' *INER*, 21 February 1996. See also Harris Gleckman (1996) 'Promising much but delivering little' *Business and the Environment, ISO 14000 Update*, Cutter Information Corporation, Arlington, MA

32 Renato Navarette, Chairman of ISO Developing Countries, in *RIET in Focus*, vol 1, no 3, Singapore, 1996, p 13

33 'Irish national standard gains stature after recognition by commission under EMAS' *INER*, 6 March, 1996. See also story dated 20 March, 1996 and 17 April, 1996

34 Carl Lankowski, American Institute for Contemporary German Studies, Washington, DC, August 1996, personal communication

35 Letter from Tage Andersen of the Danish Environmental Protection Agency to Raymond Van Ermen, Secretary-General of the European Environmental Bureau, dated 13 March 1996; on file with authors

36 Letter from Tage Andersen, 13 March 1996, ibid

37 Letter from Tage Andersen, 13 March 1996, ibid

38 'In Indonesia, the government would like to see the environmental audit done for the public and not leave this information solely to the company and the consultants, as this information is seen to be crucial to local communities and authorities.' *Asian Respondent # 4*

39 *African respondent # 3*

40 These issues are of particular concern in the US. See Catherine Cowan, Assistant Commissioner of the Department of Environmental Protection, New Jersey US, presentation to the Annual Conference of the National Council of State Legislatures, St Louis, Missouri, 28 July 1996. For example for good environmental performers, New Jersey may waive the old-style single-media permitting applications in favour of multi-media permitting, simplifying the permitting application process for firms and regulators and reducing the cost for both. It also allows for better assessment of environmental quality and limit values

41 'States, US EPA Unsure How ISO 14001 Factors into Reform: Public Data Called Key' *INER*, 30 October 1996

42 Eric Schaeffer, US EPA, panelist at the session on ISO 14001 at the 1996 US National Conference of State Legislators, June 1996, St Louis, Missouri

43 State of Michigan, Department of Environmental Quality: Air Quality Division (1997) *Air Pollution Control; Proposed Rules: ORR 96-056EQ* (submitted to the Legislative Service Bureau on 12/13/96), Part 14: Clean Corporate Citizen Program

44 Kim Wilhelm, Department of Toxic Substances and Control, and Ravi Ramalingam, ARP (1997) 'Establishing Voluntary International Standards for Worldwide Uniformity' in Cal/EPA Report vol 5 no 12, reproduced in *ISO 14000 – News and Views*, 3 March 1997, Law Offices of Wayne Rosenbaum, Carlsbad, California

45 Council of the South African Bureau of Standards (1993) *South African Standard Code of Practice, Environmental Management Systems*, pamphlet, SABS 0251:1993, Gr9, Pretoria

46 SABS local subcommittee members of ISO/TC 207 (circa 1995 or 1996) *Environmental Management System News*, no 2, newsletter, Pretoria

47 *Environment Taiwan Newsletter*, March 1996, Energy and Resources Laboratories, Hsinchu, Taiwan, ROC

48 *Asian Respondent # 4*

49 *Asian Respondent # 1*

50 *Asian Respondent # 4*

51 *Asian Respondent # 7*

52 *Asian Respondent # 4*

53 *Asian Respondent # 7*

54 *African Respondent # 1*

55 Resources for the Future (1997) *Industry Incentives for Environmental Improvement: Evaluation of US Federal Incentives*, GEMI, Washington, DC, winter

CHAPTER 6

1 The first review in November 1997 'considered that adjustments to the rights and obligations… were not necessary', WTO (1997) G/TBT/5, November 19, para 4

2 'The experts… recognized the importance of enhancing the representation and effective participation of developing countries in ISO's work in general, including in the build-up to the revision of the ISO's EMS standards in 1999. This requires financial and technical assistance, as well as better coordination at the national level between standardization bodies, the government, and other stakeholders.' UNCTAD (1997) *Report of the Expert Meeting on Possible Trade and Investment Impacts of Environmental Management Standards, Particularly the ISO 14000 Series, on Developing Countries, and Opportunities and Needs in this Context* Geneva, October; TD/B/COM.1/10, 10 November

Index

Other Earthscan Titles

Regulatory Realities
The Implementation and Impact of Industrial Environmental Regulation

Andrew Gouldson and Joseph Murphy

This book describes how enhanced industrial environmental regulation can lead to improved industrial environmental performance at reduced cost. It examines the implementation and impact of different approaches and compares mandatory and voluntary regulations in the UK and Europe.

The authors outline the influence of different regulatory structures and styles on the nature of policy as practice, and highlight the importance of a clear and comprehensive framework of standards, targets and performance measures. They show that profitable innovation which protects the environment is at the heart of successful regulation and put forward proposals for government and industry in order to improve the relationship between environmental protection and industrial competitiveness.

Regulatory Realities combines descriptive policy analysis with prescriptive policy advocacy to show how enhanced regulation can lead to greater environmental and economic efficiency. It provides clear, reliable information for decision makers and students in all areas related to industrial environmental performance and environmental policy.

CONTENTS: Environment, Economy and Policy Reform • Environment, Innovation and Technical Change • Mandatory Regulation and the EU's Integrated Pollution Prevention and Control Directive • Voluntary Regulation and the EU Eco-Management and Audit Scheme • The Implementation and Impact of Industrial Environmental Regulation in the UK • The Implementation and Impact of Industrial Environmental Regulation in the Netherlands • Synthesis and Summary: Reshaping Regulatory Realities

Paperback £15.95 1 85383 458 0 1998

Clean and Competitive?
Motivating Environmental Performance in Industry

Rupert Howes, Jim Skea and Bob Whelan

'This fascinating and illuminating book is replete with sophisticated analysis of the business–environment interface. It is objective and pragmatic, but never takes its eye off the fundamental challenge to business and society posed by the imperative of sustainable development. A state-of-the-art account of this complex area.' Paul Ekins, Director, Forum for the Future

Clean and Competitive? explores the challenge of motivating industry to address environmental issues. The authors explore in detail industrial responses to prominent environmental issues, including: climate change; air quality; water pollution; waste minimisation; and product recycling. They assess various approaches to environmental problems, such as: traditional regulation; partnership; Voluntary agreements; and market-based instruments. Finally, they recommend practical ways forward for addressing an ever more complex environmental agenda.

CONTENTS: The Business–Environment Debate • Managing the Environment • Global Environmental Issues: Ozone Depletion and Climate Change • National Environmental Issues:

Acid Rain; Air Quality and Road transport; and Volatile Organic Compounds • Regional and Local Environmental Issues: Water Quality and Contaminated Land • Integrated Pollution Control • Waste Minimisation: a Route to Profit and Cleaner Production • Voluntary Approaches to Environmental Management: End-of-Life Electrical and Electronic Equipment Recycling • Economic Instruments • Next Steps

Paperback £14.95 1 85383 490 4 1998

Corporate Environmental Management 1
Systems and Strategies
Second Edition

Edited by Richard Welford

'A readable work which deserves a place in every corporate library' *The European*

'covers everything you could possibly want to know about corporate environmental management ... if you only afford one book, this is worth serious consideration' *Supply Management*

This second edition focuses upon EMAS and ISO 14001, while the auditing approach within the ISO 14000 series is also examined. The examination of strategy now places more emphasis on cost reduction and differentiation as a means to achieving a competitive advantage through environmental management, while many areas such as that on life cycle assessment, have been updated.

Corporate Environmental Management 1 is the first in a series of three books providing basic tools needed by business people and management courses.

CONTENTS: Part 1 The Context of Corporate Environmental Management • Part 2 The Tools of Corporate Environmental Management • Part 3 Wider Applications of the Systems Based Approach

Paperback £15.95 1 85383 559 5 September 1998

Corporate Environmental Management 2
Culture and Organisations

Edited by Richard Welford

The first book to address the fundamental role of a company's culture and organisation in determining its environmental performance. **Part 1** provides an introduction to organisation theory and organisational behaviour. **Part 2** demonstrates the linkage between environmental problems and organisational issues. Problems, challenge, contradictions and complexities are tackled in **Part 3**, which looks at pragmatic and practical approaches and examines ways in which proactive cultures can be introduced into business. The role of values and leadership and an overarching agenda for human resource management are also considered.

Paperback £15.95 1 85383 412 2 1997

The third volume in the series **Corporate Environmental Management 3: Towards Sustainable Development***, is forthcoming in 1999.*